T0305839

Harry S. Truman

THE ECONOMICS OF
A POPULIST PRESIDENT

THE ECONOMICS OF
A POPULIST PRESIDENT

E. Ray Canterbery

Florida State University, USA

 **World Scientific**

NEW JERSEY · LONDON · SINGAPORE · BEIJING · SHANGHAI · HONG KONG · TAIPEI · CHENNAI

Published by

World Scientific Publishing Co. Pte. Ltd.

5 Toh Tuck Link, Singapore 596224

USA office: 27 Warren Street, Suite 401-402, Hackensack, NJ 07601

UK office: 57 Shelton Street, Covent Garden, London WC2H 9HE

Library of Congress Cataloging-in-Publication Data
Canterbery, E. Ray.
 Harry S. Truman: the economics of a populist president / E. Ray Canterbery.
 pages cm
 ISBN 978-9814541831 (hardcover : alk. paper)
 1. Truman, Harry S., 1884–1972. 2. Presidents--United States--Biography.
3. United States--Politics and government--1945–1953. 4. United States--Economic
policy--1945–1960. I. Title.
 E814.C365 2013
 973.918092--dc23
 [B]
                                                    2013025747

British Library Cataloguing-in-Publication Data
A catalogue record for this book is available from the British Library.

Cover image: President Harry S. Truman at his desk at the White House signing a proclamation declaring a national emergency, 16 December 1950; US National Archives and Records Administration image (National Archives Identifier: 541951).

Back cover image: President Harry S. Truman delivering a radio speech, 3 January 1946; Harry S. Truman Library (73-2135).

In-house Editor: Chye Shu Wen

Typeset by Stallion Press
Email: enquiries@stallionpress.com

Printed in Singapore

To Conrad, Ethan, Kendall, Sydney, and Zachary

About the Author

A former Professor of Economics at Florida State University (Tallahassee), **E. Ray Canterbery** is one of the most respected economists of his generation. In 2003 John Kenneth Galbraith, who knew both Michal Kalecki and John Maynard Keynes, called Canterbery, "the best." In 2004 he was a Truman Scholar and conducted research at the Harry S. Truman Library. Canterbery is the author of many acclaimed and widely-cited books and articles, including the classic *The Making of Economics* (4th edition), the popular *A Brief History of Economics* (2nd edition), as well as the tour de force *Wall Street Capitalism, Alan Greenspan: The Oracle Behind the Curtain, The Literate Economist, F. Scott Fitzgerald: Under the Influence* (with Thomas D. Birch), the satirical novel, *Black Box, Inc.*, and, most recently, *The Global Great Recession*. His books are available in several languages. He served as President of the Eastern Economics Association in 1986–1987 and President of the International Trade and Finance Association in 1998–1999.

In January 1996, Prentice-Hall, Inc. selected Canterbery for their Hall of Fame Economist Baseball Cards for "significant contributions to the economics discipline", including "developing one of the first complete mathematical theories of foreign exchange; a new theory of the labor market and of personal incomes (vita theory), which later was integrated into international trade theory; independently of Pasinetti, developing a production model of the total value added required in both labor and profits, proving also that profit margins equal price markups; providing several ideas that have become real world economic policies."

The International Biography Centre in Cambridge, England includes Canterbery among 500 persons worldwide in its *Living Legends* (2002), 2,000 scholars worldwide in their *Outstanding Scholars of the 21st Century* (2002), and the select *1000 Great Americans* (2002). The American Biographical Institute also includes him in its *Great Minds of the 21st Century* (2002). He is also listed in *Marquis Who's Who in the World* and *Who's Who in America,* as well as other biographical sources.

Contents

Introduction

Many years ago I had my first encounter with Harry S. Truman. It was the summer of 1964. I was writing my Master's thesis in economics, which covered the President's Council of Economic Advisers (CEA) under President Truman, as well as under other Presidents. On a whim, I decided to visit the Truman Library and Museum. At the time, I did not know that Truman spent much of his post-Presidential years at the Library. The stacks in the Library were open for researchers to browse. While browsing, Mr Truman came racing through the stacks, stopped and asked what I was looking for. He was 80 years old, but had the energy and speed of a much younger person. Later, I would read about his apparent tirelessness and quickness. It was legendary. When I mentioned the CEA, he began to pull books and documents off the shelves. They seemed to fly off the shelves. But what impressed me the most was the kindness and humbleness of the man.

In 2004 I returned to the Truman Library as a Truman Scholar. The stacks were now closed and Harry Truman was deceased, so the researchers had to rely on the help of the staff of the Library. They were very patient and helpful. They told stories about another researcher, David McCullough, who would appear in an old beat-up car from time to time. This was the McCullough who wrote the Pulitzer-prize winning *Truman*; it was published in 1992 and is a valuable source for Truman scholars. My enterprise was more narrowly focused on Truman's economics. As it turns out, there is very little about economics in any of the Truman biographies. This is a gap I hope to fill. *Truman* is a monumental work, filled with detail, and it covers every year of Truman's life. Despite this, or because of the detail, the Library staff said that numerous citations in the book were incorrect. Perhaps this is inescapable because the same can be said of all the Truman biographies. Nonetheless, one must pay attention to the extensive interviews McCullough conducted with Truman's own family, friends, and Washington colleagues.

More recently, Robert Dallek, an admirer of McCullough, wrote a much shorter book, *Harry S. Truman*. It was published in 2008 in the American Presidents series edited by Arthur M. Schlesinger, Jr. and Sean Wilentz. It is a remarkable book on a much smaller scale, being succinct and still covering the major highs and lows of Truman, as President. Dallek cites Alonzo L. Hamby's *Beyond the New Deal: Harry S. Truman and American Liberalism* (1973), among many books, which is also cited by McCullough. Hamby followed up with his *Man of the People: A Life of Harry S. Truman* (1995), which was not printed in time for McCullough. In his economics Truman waged a war with some Liberals while living up to the "Man of the People" label. Hamby's books are useful sources on the early years of Truman.

The US Constitution calls for a tripartite governing institution. From the beginning with George Washington, however, the Executive Branch has been the source of many of the actions of government. Uniquely, the President can issue executive orders and thus override the Congress, if not the Supreme Court. Fiscal policy, the use of government taxes and revenue to stabilize a free-enterprise economy, is initiated by the President, with the advice of the President's Council of Economic Advisers (CEA). The CEA did not exist prior to the Employment Act of 1946 which was promoted and signed into law by President Truman. This Act, partly a product of the Great Depression, the CEA as well as the Joint Economic Committee, are sufficiently important to warrant a separate chapter in this book.

Again, the Employment Act of 1946, the CEA, and the Joint Economic Committee of Congress barely receive much more than a mention in the Truman biographies. Truman himself set the stage. In Volume 1 of his *Memoirs*, he devotes five pages to the Employment Act of 1946 and two pages to the CEA. In brief fashion, Truman discusses anti-inflation measures and the shift from a military to a civilian economy. To be fair, some comments about the economy come under the heading of finances, US government, and labor disputes. The volume covers only the first year of Truman's presidency, but is 596 pages long. Volume 2 of Truman's *Memoirs* again gives the CEA about two pages and the Employment

Act, five pages, though the volume covers all the remaining years of his presidency at only 594 pages. In the index, under the heading "Economy, US," the reader is directed to the Fair Deal program, full-employment program, New Deal program, reconversion, stabilization, Agriculture, and etc. So, part of the apparent short shift to "economics" is found in the labeling. Being first and foremost a politician, Harry S. Truman thought in terms of political programs. For example, the Fair Deal program gets 13 pages and its components such as fair employment practices a few more pages.

But aren't the Marshall Plan and the Truman Doctrine about economics? Yes, partly, and no, partly. In Volume 2, Truman devotes more pages to the Marshall Plan than to the domestic economy *per se*, but he assigns many more pages to General George C. Marshall. Likewise, World War II is relegated to theaters of war, but he devotes many pages to Dwight D. Eisenhower and General Douglas MacArthur. Clearly, personalities were important to Truman and he often thought in terms of "great men." We should nonetheless note that he fired Great Man General MacArthur for insubordination! When Eisenhower was elected President, Eisenhower would have nothing to do with Truman. The greater the man, the harder the fall and the more there is to tell. Truman's treatment of both men is better than their treatment of him.

In the instances of the Truman Doctrine and the Marshall Plan it is difficult to separate the economics from foreign policy issues. In the case of war, including the Korean War, the protection of lives dominated the President's thoughts. In Truman's case, the matter of treaties and negotiations played major roles. Then all this too is complicated by personalities such as those of Marshall, Eisenhower, and MacArthur. For many years Truman looked up to and admired all three. Perhaps, then, it is just as well that economic theories have little to no play in the biographies or in Truman's *Memoirs*. All the better for me to fill the large gap. Truman does mention Lord John Maynard Keynes, though the reference is to Keynes' role in obtaining a loan for Great Britain. After all, Harry S. Truman was a pragmatic populist. As we shall see, it is a theme that resonates with particular strains of economic thought and we will see this at work in my separate chapters on the Truman Doctrine and the Marshall Plan.

We can further simplify while going further out on a limb. President Truman was a progressive populist. Populist — but what exactly do we mean by that term? Progressive populists believe that people are more important then corporations, and the government should be of the people, by the people and for the people. The latter sounds a lot like Abraham Lincoln, who was a radical in his day. Today, though one cannot be absolutely certain about it, being a progressive populist is ironically not popular in the United States Congress. This does not relieve us of contradictions. Truman was a liberal who was often at war with "liberals." Being a populist supersedes liberalism.

As to Presidential timber, Truman was not the first progressive populist. William Jennings Bryan (March 19, 1860–July 26, 1925) was a dominant force in the populist wing of the Democratic Party, standing three times as its candidate for President of the United States (1896, 1900, and 1908). Bryan was a devout, many would say zealous, Christian, a supporter of popular democracy (direct vote), and a vigorous enemy of the gold standard as well as banks and railroads. During his time, private banks and railroads were tightly controlled and powerful. He was a leader of the silverite (silver to be used as money instead of gold) movement in the 1890s, a peace advocate, a prohibitionist, and an opponent of Darwinism on religious (Christian) grounds. With a deep and commanding voice, he was one of the best known orators and lecturers of his era. He was called "The Great Commoner" because of his faith in the wisdom of the common people. Many of these traits would impress a youthful Truman.

Bryan was defeated by William McKinley in the intensely fought Presidential campaigns of 1896 and 1900. Bryan nonetheless retained control of the Democratic Party. He gave over 500 speeches on the road in 1896 while the other candidates stayed on their front porches. In his three Presidential bids, he promoted free silver in 1896, anti-imperialism in 1900, and trust-busting in 1908, while calling on Democrats to fight the trusts (big corporations) and big banks, and embrace anti-elitist ideals of "republicanism." But we must remember him as being of the Progressive wing of republicanism. President Woodrow Wilson appointed him Secretary of State in 1913, but Wilson's strong demands on Germany, after the *RMS Lusitania* was torpedoed in 1915, led Bryan to resign in protest. After all, he had been the peace candidate (as was Wilson).

Striding on different grounds around these times was Theodore Roosevelt (October 27, 1858–January 6, 1919), who turned up as the 26th President of the US (1901–1909). He was not elected to his first term: He was Vice President when President William McKinley was assassinated. Elected at 42, he remains the youngest President. Roosevelt attempted to move the Republican Party (GOP) leftward toward Progressivism, including trust busting of corporations and increased regulation of banks. Elected to a full term on his own in 1904, being at the time the only person to do so. Much later, he was emulated by Harry S. Truman. Roosevelt won by the largest percentage of the popular vote since the uncontested election of 1820. He coined the phrase "Square Deal" to describe his domestic agenda, emphasizing that the average citizen would get a fair share under his policies. A second Roosevelt would later follow with his "New Deal," followed by Truman's "Fair Deal," all deals in the same spirit.

"Teddy" Roosevelt's foreign policy was summed in his slogan: "Speak softly and carry a big stick." He was the force behind the completion of the Panama Canal; sent the Great White Fleet on a world tour to demonstrate American power, and negotiated an end to the Russo-Japanese War, for which he was awarded the Nobel Peace Prize. Though as a former President, he supported his friend William Howard Taft for his successful 1908 Republican nomination. On his return from a tour of Africa and Europe in 1910, he broke bitterly with then President Taft on issues related to Progressivism and personalities. In 1912 he tried and failed to block Taft's renomination, but launched the Progressive Bull Moose Party that called for far-reaching populist reforms. He lost to Democrat Woodrow Wilson. As to politics, the rift between Taft and Roosevelt led to the conservative wing of the Republican Party being led by Taft and the Progressive wing led by Roosevelt. The Progressives were more sympathetic toward labor unions and laboring folks in general and were also in favor of popular election of Federal and state judges and opposed to having judges appointed by the President or state governors. The conservatives favored high tariffs on imported goods to encourage consumers to buy American-made products (as did most progressives), favored corporate leaders over labor unions, and were generally opposed to the popular election of judges. Conservative President Taft, for example, abandoned Roosevelt's anti-trust policy.

Teddy Roosevelt died at the relatively young age of 60, after contracting diseases in his Amazon jungles expeditions. In a way Roosevelt embodied the fading American Frontier. He was a "Rough Rider" to the very end.

The 1912 Democratic National Convention eventually nominated T. Woodrow Wilson (December 28, 1856–February 3, 1924) as its candidate for President, but only after many close fights. Champ Clark of Missouri, the Speaker of the House of Representatives, was the initial frontrunner. His chances were hurt when Tammany Hall, the powerful but corrupt Democratic political machine in New York City, threw its support behind Clark. Instead of helping him, this led William Jennings Bryan, the great orator, three-time Democratic

Presidential candidate and still leader of the party's liberals, to turn against Clark as the candidate of "Wall Street." Bryan then threw his support to New Jersey Governor Woodrow Wilson, the moderate reformer. Not all liberals were Progressives, nor all Progressives were liberals, but they had shared values that would be enduring.

In his first term as President, Wilson persuaded an already solid Democratic Congress to pass major progressive reforms. In his first term, Wilson pushed a legislative agenda that few Presidents have equaled, and remained unmatched until the New Deal.[1] This agenda included the establishment of the Federal Reserve System by the Federal Reserve Act of 1913, about which more later. The agenda further included the Federal Trade Commission Act, The Clayton Anti-trust Act, the Federal Farm Loan Act and a progressive income tax. He also had Congress pass the Adamson Act, which imposed an 8-hour workday for railroad workers. Wilson, at first unsympathetic, became a major advocate for women's suffrage after public pressure convinced him that to oppose woman's suffrage was politically unwise. Although Wilson promised African Americans "fair dealing... in advancing the interest of their race in the United States" the Wilson Administration implemented a policy of racial segregation for Federal employees, setting an unfair standard for the country. Though a liberal, he was not a perfect one. This aspect of liberalism would be left for Franklin Roosevelt and Truman to unravel.

In foreign policy, Wilson spent much of 1914 through the beginning of 1917 trying to keep America out of the war in Europe. While he offered to be a mediator, neither the Allies nor the Central Powers took his requests seriously. Carrying his big stick, Teddy Roosevelt strongly criticized Wilson's refusal to build up the US Army in anticipation of the threat of war. Wilson thought that an army buildup would provoke war. Secretary of State William Jennings Bryan, that other progressive whose pacifist recommendations were ignored by Wilson, resigned in 1915. By December 18, 1916 it was clear that common ground did not exist for negotiations. The Central Powers saw victory as certain, and the Allies required the dismemberment of their enemies' empires. Still, Wilson stayed out of the war even as German submarines were killing sailors and civilian passengers. Renominated in 1915, Wilson used as a major campaign slogan: "He kept us out of of war."

---

[1] John Milton Cooper, *Woodrow Wilson, A Biography* (New York: Knopf, 2009), p. 201.

Still, he warned Germany that unrestricted submarine warfare would not be tolerated. Following the attempt to enlist Mexico as an ally against the US, Wilson took America into World War I (WWI) to make "the world safe for democracy." While not signing a formal alliance with the United Kingdom or France but cooperating as an "associated" power, the US raised a massive army through conscription, with command handed over to General John J. Pershing, allowing Pershing a free hand as to tactics, strategy and even diplomacy. Finally, Wilson decided that the war had become a real threat to all humanity and without US intervention western civilization could be destroyed. In his declaration of war on April 2, 1917, he announced "a war to end war". This provided the basis of Wilson's Fourteen Points, which included a proposed League of Nations. All this brought the US into an alliance that would have worldwide consequences. With 50 Representatives and six Senators in opposition, the declaration of war against Germany was passed by the Congress on April 4, 1917 and approved by the President on April 6, 1917. As it was the custom, and continued to be the custom, the Executive branch of government initiated war.

It was a terrible war. But Wilson, WWI, and his proposed League of Nations (forerunner of the United Nations) served to bring the United States onto the world stage. After the Great War there understandably was a great desire for peace and normalcy. What we got, after a brief, sharp economic recession was the narcissistic consumption mania of the Jazz Age (as named by F. Scott Fitzgerald and chronicled in *The Great Gatsby*) that ended with the Great Crash of 1929 and the beginning of the Great Depression. Isolationism dominated the 1920s and 1930s as much as expansionism characterized the Wilson Administration. This era ended with the bombing of Pearl Harbor and the start of World War II. A second Roosevelt would reign until his death brought Harry Truman on stage. Isolationism would end and the Marshall Plan and the United Nations would become realities under Truman.

Despite his accomplishments and breadth as the only PhD President, Wilson was blind-sighted by a war that ended with the Peace Treaty framed by the Fourteen Points of an ailing Wilson. The Great War brought death and destruction not only to Europe's peoples, but also to Europe's colonial empires and traditions. At war's end, President Woodrow Wilson and Comrade Lenin (also known as Vladimir Ilich Ulyanov) faced each other at opposite ends of a devastated continent and began to shape the next 70 years of world history. Wilson would dominate the peace conference in Paris, and his Fourteen Points would be the foundation of the Versailles Treaty and the seeds of World War II (WWII). Lenin would lead the Bolshevik revolution in Russia and then die, leaving Stalin to set the stage for the Cold War.

In 1919, John Maynard Keynes went to Paris as the senior Treasury official on the British delegation to the Peace Conference at Versailles and the official representative of the British Empire on the Supreme Economic Council. Still, while he had a wonderful view, he had no power to interfere with the course of the game. He watched in great frustration as President Woodrow Wilson was outfoxed by Clemenceau of France.

Keynes resigned in anguish in June 1919, disillusioned and disheartened by the terms of the treaty that officially ended the Great War. The Versailles Treaty created, he said, a "Carthaginian peace"; the sums that Germany and its alliance (Austria-Hungary, Bulgaria and the Ottoman Empire) were forced to concede in reparations to the Allies (France, Russia, the United Kingdom, Italy, and later the United States) were both excessive and impossible to collect. Versailles would bring nothing but trouble. Keynes retreated to Vanessa Bell's residence and hurriedly wrote a polemic attacking the treaty. *The Economic Consequences of the Peace* (1919), which combined the skill of a novelist with unsparing insight of the Bloomsbury critic. The instant success of his devastating, brilliant book thrust Keynes before the public eye and established his reputation as a pundit. It remains a literary classic and is a bold book.

In it, Keynes attacked his contemporaries, the conference's Great Men. Of Clemenceau he wrote "he felt of France what Pericles felt of Athens — unique value in her, nothing else mattering; but his theory of politics was Bismarck's." Clemenceau, said Keynes, "had one illusion — France, and one disillusion — mankind, including Frenchmen, and his colleagues not least."[2] Of Woodrow Wilson he wrote, "... like Odysseus, he looked wiser when seated."[3] Worse, in Chapter III of *The Economic Consequences of the Peace*, Keynes adds, "He not only had no proposals in detail, but he was in many respects, perhaps inevitably, ill-informed as to European conditions. And not only was he ill-informed — that was true of Mr Lloyd George also — but his mind was slow and unadaptable....There can seldom have been a statesman of the first rank more incompetent than the President in the agilities of the council chamber." France succeeded in imposing the harshest possible reparations on Germany (and her allies). Wilson's

---

[2] John Maynard Keynes, *The Economic Consequences of the Peace* (London: Macmillan & Co., 1919), p. 32.
[3] *Ibid.*, p. 40.

Fourteen Points were, to a large extent, sacrificed, but his main objectives, the creation of states based on the principle of national self-determination and the formation of the League of Nations, were embodied in the treaty. However, the US Senate refused to ratify the treaty (because Wilson would not compromise), and the United States merely declared the war with Germany at an end in 1921. Though Keynes sparred no one, Wilson was damaged the most, in part because he was such a large target. The polemic elevated Keynes even as it diminished Wilson.[4]

Still, Wilson was awarded the 1919 Nobel Peace Prize. The Treaty came close to passage in mid-November 1919 when Henry Cabot Lodge and his Republicans with the pro-Treaty Democrats, were close to a two-thirds majority for a Treaty (and the League of Nations) with reservations. Wilson rejected the compromise and enough Democrats followed his lead to permanently end the changes for ratification.

All of which brings us to the issue of Presidential greatness. More importantly, it raises the question of whether a Progressive President or a Progressive Populist can be ranked as "great" or "near great."

What makes a President great or "near great," as Dallek, one of Truman's main biographers, characterized Truman? Is the President in charge or is he (not yet being a she) controlled by events? These are questions that all biographers wrestle with, usually with no definitive answers. It was Truman who ultimately confronted the Pendergast machine of Kansas City, decided to drop atomic bombs on Japan, confronted Stalin at Potsdam, sent troops to Korea, led the legendary Whistle-Stop Campaign of 1948, and fired another great or perhaps ingrate, General Douglas MacArthur. By the same token, Truman was a by-product of Kansas City politics. He did not start WWII or the Korean War, did not invent the atomic bomb (though authorized reluctantly the development of the Hydrogen bomb), and did not birth MacArthur. Sometimes the President rises to the occasion and he is the "great man;" other times events go out of control. Neither Truman nor MacArthur could control the Chinese during the course of the Korean War. Moreover, the Marshall Plan would have failed without the help of the Europeans.

With respect to greatness, polls cannot be totally ignored, nor completely believed. Truman was ranked number five among the great Presidents by a panel

---

[4] The above several paragraphs are based on E. Ray Canterbery, *A Brief History of Economics,* 2nd Edition (Singapore, New Jersey, London: World Scientific, 2011), pp.185–186.

of historians and political scientists. However, in most of the public polls, such as the Gallup Poll, he is consistently ranked number seven or at least eighth, or among the near great. The exception is the Harris Interactive Poll of January 16–23, 2012, where he ranks sixth among "Presidents since WWII," but 10th among "best overall in US history." The outcome in the polls depend very much on how the question is posed, who is answering it, and when it is asked. George Washington, Abraham Lincoln, and Franklin D. Roosevelt are consistently ranked at the top of the lists. Often ranked just below those three are Presidents Thomas Jefferson and Theodore Roosevelt. The remaining places in the top ten are often rounded out by Truman, Woodrow Wilson, Dwight Eisenhower, and Andrew Jackson. John F. Kennedy made it to the bottom of the top ten in two surveys (out of six). Harry S. Truman is certainly in good company. Washington was first in the hearts of his countrymen, Lincoln freed the slaves and conducted the Civil War, and Franklin Roosevelt's terms were marked by his pragmatic fight against the Great Depression and by most of WWII. Roosevelt met the aforementioned John Maynard Keynes and was not impressed, though Roosevelt's New Deal economic policies were "Keynesian" when they worked to stabilize the economy. Truman was much more "Keynesian," though blended with populism. All of which requires more explanation to come.

We would be remiss if we did not mention those Presidents at or near the bottom. The bottom ten often include Warren G. Harding, James Buchanan, Andrew Johnson, Franklin Pierce, William Henry Harrison, Ulysses S. Grant, Millard Fillmore, John Tyler, Zachary Taylor, and Richard M. Nixon. Harrison and James A. Garfield died shortly after entering office, and therefore are sometimes excluded from the rankings. None of these were progressive populists.

Never mind Keynes, what about monetary policy? To the biographers and to Truman of his *Memoirs*, the Federal Reserve, which has been around and conducting money policy since 1914, might as well not have existed. Neither "monetary policy" nor "Federal Reserve System" appear in the indexes. Even the personalities are not mentioned. As we will learn, there were special reasons for this related to war and to Truman's populism. Ironically, Keynesian economics and progressive populism go a long way in filling these gaps. Thus, despite or because of the Federal Reserve System being a by-product of the progressive populism of an earlier age, and the single most progressive legislation of Woodrow Wilson.[5]

Already we have identified what it means to be a progressive populist. When, we may ask, did Harry Truman become one? Asked differently, what were the progressive and populist influences on Truman, not to ignore liberalism? We find elements of Truman's youth to be influential. We should not be surprised to find young Truman encountering William Jennings Bryan, Teddy Roosevelt, and Woodrow Wilson along the way. His early reactions are matters of record, to which we next turn.

---

[5] For much more history and insight into the Federal Reserve, see E. Ray Canterbery, *Alan Greenspan: The Oracle Behind the Curtain* (Singapore: World Scientific, 2006).

Chapter 1

The Early Years

arry S. Truman was a product of a frontier city with deep roots in an agrarian culture. To be exact, he came out of what was also then the frontier of the United States. Both had a lot to do with growing up to be a populist. Soon, Harry would encounter three presidential hopefuls who happened to be progressive populists, or at least, populists. First, we will consider the ground upon which the early Trumans would grow their crops.

On the Old Frontier with the Early Trumans

In 1841 the westernmost part of Missouri was the "extreme frontier" of the United States. In a migration that had begun twenty years earlier, a great many people came to Missouri from Kentucky. In the summer of 1846 Anderson Truman came in from that state. His people were English and Scotch-Irish and farmers as far back as anyone knew. Anderson was slight, gentle, soft-spoken, 30 years old, and without prospects. Still, Mary Jane Holmes had seen enough in him to defy her mother and marry him. Mother Holmes thought Mary Jane had married beneath *her* station because the Trumans owned no slaves.

Here began the overland trails to Santa Fe, California, and Oregon. Jackson County was the threshold, the jumping-off point to the dry grasslands reaching all the way to the Rockies. Independence was the queen city of the trails and the country's first western boom-town. Truman and others were to go on to found nearby Kansas City. In the 1840s the permanent population of Independence was about 700, but on any given spring day two or three thousand would be milling about at Jackson Square. The Kentuckians came mostly for the land, the high, rolling fertile open country of Jackson, with its clear springs and two rivers, the Little Blue and the Blue, both flowing out of Kansas Territory. Here the Prairie grass was high and green. Wildflowers, wild herbs — meadow rose, turtlehead, snakeroot, wolfberry, thimbleweed — grew in fragrant abundance on the prairie.

Six to eight yoke of oxen could plow through the sod, something horses could not do. But beneath the hard crust, the dark prairie loam could be two to six feet deep. In places along the river bottoms, it was 20 feet deep. The rich and beautiful upland in the vicinity of Independence was often called the "garden spot" of the Far West.

The climate was one of extremes. Temperatures could rise or fall 50 degrees in a matter of hours. Summers were either too dry or too wet and either way were nearly always broiling hot. In winter came the awful cold, often too cold to work. On this frontier, few expected things to go easily, least of all a farmer.

Across the line in Kansas, the old issue of slavery was building to a terrible climax that was to affect the lives and outlook of nearly everyone in Jackson. To many in western Missouri the Civil War began not in 1851 with the attack on Fort Sumter in South Carolina, but in 1854, when Congress passed the Kansas-Nebraska Act, leaving to the residents of the territories of Kansas and Nebraska the decision of whether to allow slavery. Following the Missouri Compromise of 1820–1821, Missouri had come into the Union as a slave state. Some 50,000 slaves were held along Missouri's western border. In Jackson County alone there were more than 3,000, and their owners dreaded the prospect of a free territory so close, to which a slave might escape. For the owner, his slave was very often his most valuable possession. For years before the Civil War began in the East, the terrible Border War — civil war in every sense — raged all up and down the Missouri-Kansas line and continued until the surrender at Appomattox. The wounds of some nine years of war in Missouri were a long time healing.

For Martha Ellen Young — Matt or Mattie, as she was known — life had picked up again three years after the war. Kansas City was growing rapidly and the transcontinental railroad was completed. By 1872 there were seven railroad lines in and out of Kansas City. This marked the end of the steamboat and wagon train era. The social occasions Mattie Young loved best were the dances at home in the front parlors, or at neighboring farms. She was a spirited dancer. One night she met John Truman, son of Anderson Truman, who, since the end of the war, had returned with his family to Jackson Country and taken up farming nearby. At 5 foot 4, John was two inches shorter than Mattie. In any case, they seemed to have known each other for some time before announcing their plans to marry in 1881, by which time Mattie was 29.

Born an Agrarian, Raised to be Fair

Their first child was still-born. John and Mattie's second child, a boy, was born on May 8, 1884. The baby's first name was Harry, after his Uncle Harrison. In a quandary over a middle name, Mattie and John were undecided whether to honor her father or his, in the end they compromised with the letter 'S'. So, Harry S. Truman he would be.

Harry Truman often said in later years that he had the happiest childhood imaginable. His grandfather would take him riding over the countryside in a high-wheeled cart behind a strawberry roan trotting horse. Every day for a week, one summer, they drove six miles to the Belton Fair and sat together in the judges' stand watching the races and eating striped candy. Harry would also remember a swing under an old elm close to the house and another swing indoors in the front hall used for rainy days. The long porch on the north side of the house made a perfect race track for their red express wagon. The farm was a wonderful place where they went hunting for bird nests and gathered wild strawberries in the prairie grass as tall as they. Also there were herds of cattle, saddle horses, draft horses, mules, sheep, hogs, chickens, ducks and geese. Harry's father gave him a black Shetland pony and a new saddle. He would let the boy ride beside him as he made his rounds on the farm.

It was a time of security and plenty. Most memorable for Harry was the abundance of food — dried apples, peaches, candy and nuts of all kinds, wonderful cookies, pies, corn pudding, roasting ears in summer. There also was peach butter, apple butter, grape butter, jellies, and preserves. From his Aunt Ada, the boy learned to play euchre. Uncle Harry told amusing stories and taught him a card game called cooncan, a form of gin rummy then more popular than poker. According to Uncle Harry's recollection, the child liked everybody.

His mother understood him best. She was brighter than anyone and cared most about his well-being. That is what he thought. She taught him to read before he was five. And she took him off to Kansas City for expensive eyeglasses. Small boys with eyeglasses were almost unknown in rural Missouri. In the summer of 1890, the summer his mother bought him his eyeglasses, the family left the farm and moved to Independence, so that Harry could have proper schooling.

When eight-year old Harry S. Truman started school in 1892, he could already read.[1] Harry appears to have liked school from the beginning. He began first grade at the old Noland School. In his *Memoirs*, the former President wrote, "My first year in school was a happy one. My teacher was Miss Myra Ewing, with whom I became a favorite, as I eventually did with all my teachers." Second grade was a bad time for him. He developed diphtheria and dropped out of school because the illness left his arms, legs, and throat paralyzed for some months. As a second grader in the classroom of Minnie L. Ward, the records show that he was an excellent student. His first term grades included a 95 in spelling, a 95 in reading, a 92 in writing, a 99 in language, a 99 in numbers and a 95 in deportment.[2] He liked Miss Minnie Ward, his second-grade teacher. Harry attended summer school with Miss Jennie Clements to "catch up." In the fall, when the original Columbian School opened, he skipped third grade and went directly to Miss Mamie Dunn's fourth grade class.[3] By his later account — "I do not remember a bad teacher in all my experience."[4] Part of this had to do with Harry. He knew how to make them like him. By getting along with people, he found that he could nearly always get what he wanted.

He was an exceptionally alert, good little boy of sunny disposition, who, with glasses that magnified his blue eyes, made him look as bright and interested as could be. By the fourth grade he was reading "everything I could get my hands on — histories and encyclopedias and everything else."[5] For his tenth birthday, Harry's mother gave him a set of four volumes titled *Great Men and Famous Women*. He counted the moment as one of life's turning points. He especially liked the volume on *Soldiers and Sailors*, and dreamed of becoming a

---

[1] Roberta Page, "Truman's School Years," p. 1, Harry S. Truman Library. This also appeared in the *Independence Examiner, Truman Centennial Edition,* May 1984. Roberta Page is the Publications Coordinator, Independence School District.

[2] See *ibid.* As we will come to note, his second grade spelling score did not hold up well.

[3] See *ibid.*

[4] Harry S. Truman, *Memoirs, Volume 1: Year of Decisions* (New York: Doubleday, 1955), p. 118.

[5] Quoted by David McCullough, *Truman* (New York: Simon & Schuster, 1992), p. 43.

great general. Andrew Jackson and Robert E. Lee were his favorite American heroes.

Harry lived in a house full of books. He read the Bible twice through by the time he was 12, three times by 14. He pored over *Plutarch's Lives*, and read a set of Shakespeare. Nearby was the Missouri Pacific depot, and Harry was fascinated by trains. At night he would listen for the Kansas-Nebraska Limited, which did not stop in Independence.

He kept to himself more than most boys his age and was often lonely as a child. Caroline Simpson, a black cook and cleaning lady hired by the family, taught Harry to cook. This and other characteristics set him apart from the other boys. He was abnormally neat and clean. Never a fighter, he was not popular like other boys. He was teased because of his glasses. His boyhood friends remembered him as different and serious, not exactly a sissy. With girls of his own age he was so shy he could barely speak. This, despite meeting a blond-haired, blue-eyed little girl named Elizabeth Wallace in the Presbyterian Sunday School class.

Harry was surrounded by women. There were his mother, Caroline Simpson, his teachers, and Grandma Young, who came often to visit. He got along with them well, kidding and telling stories. Though he was "his mother's son," Harry and his father had much in common. Small and compact, like a jockey, John, the father, had a weathered, sunburned face and crow's feet that gave a hint of a smile around his eyes. He was touchy about his size; he would explode at the least affront, and fight like a buzz saw. Still, he was good-natured ordinarily. Like many other men of the times, John had a strong, sentimental veneration of women. Considered a liberal in religion, he raised his children to have faith in themselves and their potentialities.

A piano in the parlor had become part of the good life in America, a sign of prosperity. Though piano lessons were for the young women of the household, Harry took to it wholeheartedly, made progress and gained approval of his parents. He had regular lessons with Florence Burrus, who lived next door. Harry remembered these years like those on the farm, as nothing but wonderful times.

Besides the women, national holidays and politics provided what little excitement there was from one year to the next. A memorable day for young Harry Truman came with Grover Cleveland's second victory, in 1892. He was eight years old. It would be 20 years before Democrats could celebrate another presidential victory, that of Woodrow Wilson.

Formal High School Education in the Shadows of the "Old South"

As he started high school, friendships took on a new importance. He still had no best pal among the boys. His only really close friends were his girl cousins Ethel and Nellie Noland, who were as good-natured and well read as he, interested in everything, not at all vain, and devoted to him. The Noland sisters knew how much Harry secretly cared for Elizabeth Wallace, who was in his class. If he succeeded in carrying her books to school and back home for her, it was a big day. She stood out in class, always dressed in the latest thing, and was a natural all-round athlete. Elizabeth was popular and was his ideal.

Harry attended superb schools in a small city of many schools. In addition to Woodland College for Women, there was Presbyterian College also for women, and St. Mary's Academy for girls. Independence was a town of culture that supported two bookstores. Moreover, it was only a ten-mile ride by trolley to Kansas City. Yet the pervading atmosphere was southern — antebellum Old South. Handkerchiefs were waved whenever the band played "Dixie," and the United Daughters of the Confederacy thrived. There were formal parties in which Jesse James's brother Frank often appeared, causing great excitement. In high school, one of Harry's favorite teachers, Ardelia G. Hardin (later, Mrs Palmer), who taught Latin, would describe how her father had been hit three times during Pickett's Charge at Gettysburg and left for dead. The summer of 1901, the year Harry finished Independence High School, the newspaper declared on its editorial page how the community need not be surprised if there was a Negro lynching in Independence.

Knowledge gathering was not confined to school. From Sunday School and his own reading of the Bible, Harry knew many passages by heart. At home he was taught to say what you mean, mean what you say, and keep your word. Never forget a friend. Never get too big for your britches.

And there was part-time work. At age 14, while still in high school, Harry went to work at J. H. Clinton's drugstore. Harry's first paying job was to come in each weekday morning at 5:30 to open up the place, sweep the sidewalk, mop the floor, wipe the counters, and do as much overall dusting and cleaning as possible before 7:00 am when Mr Clinton came down and it was time for Harry to leave for school. Early in the morning the good church members and Anti-Saloon Leaguers would come for their morning drink behind the prescription case at ten cents an ounce. They were hypocrites. Far better, Harry thought, were the tough old birds around town who bought a proper drink in a real saloon whenever they wished, regardless of appearances.

Harry grew dutifully, conspicuously studious, spending long afternoons in the town library. He and Charlie Ross vowed to read all of the books there, encyclopedias included. According to Mrs Palmer, "I believe he even read the Encyclopedia Britannica."[6] Harry liked Mark Twain and Franklin's *Autobiography*. He also read Sir Walter Scott because Scott was Elizabeth Wallace's favorite author. Ethel Noland remembered, "I don't know anybody in the world that ever read as much or as constantly as he did. He was what you call a book worm."[7]

History became a passion. He read through a shelf of standard works on ancient Egypt, Greece, and Rome. He seemed to have a real feel for history. His list of heroes lengthened to include Hannibal, Cincinnatus, Scipio, Cyrus the Great, and Gustavus Adolphus, the seventeenth-century Swedish king.[8] While other boys at the time venerated Andrew Carnegie and Thomas Edison, he considered the great men to be great generals. Truman had a long-standing interest in biography and military and political history. He saw that it takes men to make history or else there would be no history. History did not make the man, he now was quite certain.[9]

Harry was among the few boys who went to high school. Like piano lessons, high school was mostly for girls. He was good in Latin, very good in math, poor in spelling, and greatly influenced by his teachers who were all women except for Professor W. L. C. Palmer, the principal, who taught science, the one subject Harry didn't care for. They were "the salt of the earth." They taught the old values — loyalty, love of home, unquestioning patriotism — no less than Latin, history, or Shakespeare. Harry later said, the influence of his teachers on his life was second only to that of his mother. Harry liked his history teacher, Margaret Phelps, best. Matilda D. Brown, the English teacher, also was impressive: Two of Harry's composition books done under her guidance survived, one from 1899, the other dated 1900–1901. When writing of the corrupting influences of money and what he

---

[6] Page, *op. cit.*, p. 2.
[7] Noland, Oral History, Harry S. Truman Library.
[8] In history there is a long line of Scipio's. Since Truman liked Roman generals, the Scipio he had in mind must been Scipio Africanus Major (236–183 B.C.), a Roman general who conquered Hannibal in the 2nd Punic War.
[9] This summarizes Truman's recollection of his boyhood interest in history. See Harry S. Truman, *Memoirs of Harry S. Truman, Volume 1: Year of Decisions* (New York: Doubleday,1955), pp. 119–120.

called "the passions," the boy seemed wise beyond his years. His grades remain unknown, since the school's records were destroyed in a fire.

He continued to excel at the piano. He had twice weekly lessons with Mrs E. C. White, a gifted teacher, in Kansas City. He had studied under Fannie Bloomfield Zeisler, one of the leading American pianists of the era, and with Theodore Leschetizky, who had been a teacher of Paderewski. Zeisler opened a new world for him, and he began practicing two hours a day. He thought he had the makings of a concert pianist, and apparently Mrs White agreed. He would play the piano the balance of his life.

He loved music. He adored the great classical works. He was drilled by Mrs White in Bach, Beethoven, and Mendelssohn's *Songs Without Words*. The rest of his life he could play Paderewski's *Minuet in G* and several Chopin waltzes by heart. He was moved by Beethoven's *Sonata Pathetique* and Chopin's *Funeral March*. He loved Mozart most of all and eventually mastered the difficult Ninth Sonata.

Many of the concert greats of the day came to Kansas City. In 1898, the year he worked in the drug store, he heard Fannie Bloomfield Zeisler perform. She played Scarlatti's *Pastorale* and *Capriccio,* and Beethoven's *Sonata, Opus 111*. In 1900, Paderewski came on tour and Mrs White arranged a meeting backstage with the maestro, who treated Harry to a private demonstration of how to play his *Minuet in G*. He was a boy brimming with musical aspirations, his head filled with Shakespeare and noble Romans. He liked Independence, Missouri, its proximity to Kansas City, its people, and he liked being Harry Truman.

By now, he had thinned out, stretched out, to perhaps 5 foot 7, which was nearly as tall as he would get. Neat, clean, cheerful, he had still the gift for getting along with almost anyone. There was one thing he did not do well. He had no knack for trade. As he would later explain to "Bessie" Wallace, "When I buy a cow for $30 and then sell her to someone for $50 it always seems to me that I am really robbing that person of $20." This was an antecedent of the populist — the dislike of profiteers.

Harry and his Father: The "Bryan Men"

Harry and his father found common ground in the sociability and excitement of politics. The big Democratic picnics every August would be among the fondest of

Harry's boyhood memories. In the summer of 1900 Harry went with his father to Kansas City to attend the Democratic National Convention. It was the convention that renominated the Great Commoner, William Jennings Bryan, to run a second time against William McKinley. Bryan's nominating speech touched off a demonstration that lasted half an hour. Thereafter, Harry and his father declared themselves "Bryan Men," and though Bryan and his running mate, Adlai Ewing Stevenson I of Illinois, went down in defeat in November to McKinley and Theodore Roosevelt, Bryan remained an idol for Harry, as the voice of the common man.[10] It was Harry's first direct exposure to populism. The Democrats made imperialism the losing issue in the election of 1900, but McKinley's "prosperity" carried the country, with the Republicans playing the theme of the "Full Dinner Pail."

Nearing graduation, Harry decided to try for West Point. He prepared for the examinations by taking extra hours in history with Miss Phelps. The bookish Harry, who fenced with the girls, had never been in a fight in his life and admittedly was afraid of guns. Still, he thought he might make a general, if not a concert pianist. The night of graduation was May 30, 1901, Memorial Day, and Harry was 17. West Point was to turn him down because of his poor eyesight.[11]

John Truman made and lost a fortune in wheat futures. At age 51 in 1901, he was broke. He sold the family home and moved to a modest neighborhood in Kansas City, where he took a job for wages, something no Truman had done before. Of this catastrophe, Harry would only say in later years, "He got the notion he could get rich. Instead he lost everything at one fell swoop and went completely broke."[12]

What with the family fortunes so bleak, college was out of the question. He took an accounting course at little Spaulding's Commercial College in downtown Kansas City, but that had to be abandoned as too costly. To help the family finances, he went to work in the mail-room at the *Kansas City Star*. Then, he went to work on the Santa Fe Railroad, which was doubling its tracks into Kansas City. He worked ten-hour days, six days a week for $30 a month, plus board, which meant living with the labor gangs in their tent camps along the river. The talk

---

[10] Thus began a long line of Stevenson politicians. Stevenson I's son was Adlai Ewing Stevenson II, Governor of Illinois, presidential candidate in 1952 and 1956, and UN Ambassador (1961–1965). Stevenson II's son, Adlai Ewing Stevenson III, was a Senator from Illinois (1970–1981).

[11] As we shall see, a somewhat latter eye exam for the military would reveal the poorness of Harry's uncorrected vision.

[12] Quoted by Jonathan Daniels, *The Man of Independence* (Philadelphia: Lippincott, 1950), p. 59.

included profanity which Harry later mastered. The longer he was with the men, the more he liked them. It was a very down-to-earth education.

In April 1903, he was hired as a clerk at the National Bank of Commerce, starting at $20 a month, which was about what his father was making at his night watchman's job. He stayed for two years. He was considered bright, of excellent character and of good habits. In time he was earning $40 a month.

Harry spent little. He paid $10 for piano lessons with Mrs White, which he soon could not afford. His one indulgence was the theater, which he loved, and sometimes cost as much as $2. He went to the Orpheum and saw the Four Cohans and Sarah Bernhardt. He went to concerts and the opera at Convention Hall.

With a population of 200,000, Kansas City was growing by leaps and bounds. It had all the energy and confidence that characterized the country at the turn of the century. Things were happening there. Once, Harry rushed out of the bank and down Tenth Street to hear President Theodore Roosevelt speak from the back of a railroad car. Though it came from a Republican, he thought Roosevelt gave a good speech.[13]

In May of 1905, the month Harry turned 21 years old, he signed up with a National Guard unit. While not exactly West Point, Harry began drilling with Missouri's Light Artillery, Battery B, First Brigade. By now, Kansas City was a wide-open town; it had more sporting houses and saloons than churches. It was a city redolent of sex and temptation, the home of the *Twelfth Street Rag*. But Harry appears to have had little or no experience with such joyous low life. Still he would reflect that had things gone differently he might have wound up playing the piano in a whorehouse, but there is no evidence he ever set foot in such a place.

Refused another raise at the Bank of Commerce, Harry quit and went to work for the Union National Bank. The pay was better at $75 a month and it was a pleasanter place to work. As an assistant teller, he was soon making $100 a month, Harry thought, a magnificent salary. With a new job, bigger paycheck, new friends, his drill sessions with the National Guard, Harry was as busy and happy as he had ever been. He bought a Panama hat, had his photograph taken, and saw Sir Henry Irving and Ellen Terry in the *The Merchant of Venice* at the new Willis Wood Hall.

In October 1905, Harry left Kansas City and went to the farm at Blue Ridge. The family needed him. Harry's friends were sure he would not last as a farmer.

---

[13] As noted earlier, Teddy Roosevelt led the progressive wing of the Republican Party.

Harry S. Truman, ca. 1908.
Source: Harry S. Truman Library (79-21).

And the change *was* dramatic. For five years, until he rediscovered Bessie Wallace, his preoccupations were to be almost exclusively those decided by crops, seasons, weeds, insects, rain and sunshine, livestock, farm machinery, bank loans, and the dictates of an energetic, opinionated father who was determined to succeed at last. Everything revolved around the farm.

The farm, at 600 acres, was among the largest in the county, more than four times the size of the average Missouri farm. Every day was work and Harry did everything there was to do — hoeing corn and potatoes in the burning heat of summer, haying, doctoring horses, repairing equipment, sharpening hoes and scythes, mending fences. They raised registered short-horn cows and bulls, sheep, mules, thoroughbred horses, and Hampshire hogs, and Harry became highly knowledgeable about livestock. He also kept the books on the crops sold and bought. It is said that once on a farm, a person can detect the distinct scent of manure, even political manure.

The land was rich. Moreover, the Truman's began rotating crops in advance of other farmers in the area. To hold back erosion, Harry dumped bales of soiled straw into gullies, then sowed timothy seed. No one around those parts had tried that before. The down-to-earth Harry developed two new traits: He could make a batch of biscuits as good as any woman and he could admit a mistake.

Harry enlarged his social circle by joining the Masons. He soon was a Master Mason. He also was becoming much stronger physically. Working together through all seasons, John Truman and his son became closer. Being a good farmer in Missouri was tops for any man. Writing in October 1911, Harry summed up generations of bedrock faith in the old Jeffersonian dream of a nation of farmers. Farming was part of what ultimately would make Harry Truman a populist. Farmers were more independent and made better citizens, thought Harry.

From the farm to North Delaware Street where Bessie Wallace presided was four or more hours round trip by horse and buggy. Harry would go there for Sunday dinner and play the piano for them afterward. Bessie also accepted his invitations to concerts and the theater in Kansas City. She also went with him to meet his piano teacher, Mrs White. But it was through hundreds of letters that Harry poured himself out to Bessie. He discovered much satisfaction from writing. The letters were cheerful, often funny, consistently interesting, and straightforward, much like the writer. For her part, Bessie's vitality and good humor made her popular in her own circles. Among other things, they exchanged views on writers. Harry thought that Mark Twain was the patron saint of literature. He owned a 25-volume set of Twain's works. At the urging of Bessie, he read and enjoyed Dickens' *David Copperfield*. He was enthralled with Mr Micawber and said he knew a half dozen like him, always calculating to the penny. In June 1911 he proposed.

What Harry liked became clear. Bessie also learned what he didn't like: dentists, guns, snobs, hypocrisy in any form, prizefighters, divorce, the *Kansas City Star* (for its Republican bias), lawyers, and Richard Wagner, who he thought must have been in cahoots with Pluto, the ruler of the underworld in classical mythology.

He wanted to live up to his own expectations, but he did not know what to do with his life. Like David Copperfield, he wanted to know if he would turn out to be the hero of his own story. He had dropped out of the National Guard and said he was like Mark Twain. "He says that if fame is to be obtained only by marching to the cannon's mouth, he's perfectly willing to go there provided the cannon is empty...."[14]

He had been offered a job running a small bank. He had little heart for it, having seen bankers up close. Banking, he thought required that you take advantage of adverse conditions and sell good men out. In farming, you did not have to do that. He thought also of Cincinnatus and politics. But he had good reason to be upbeat about farming. The years Truman spent on the farm were to be known as the golden age of American agriculture, with farm prices climbing steadily. It was the right time to be a farmer. Wheat was up to 90 cents a bushel in 1912, which meant for Harry and his father continuously harder, longer days of work. They worked, even in the dark.

John was appointed road overseer for the southern half of Washington Township. The improved quality of work on the roads under John Truman's supervision was soon apparent. By now, Harry knew he wanted money but knew it to be a less than satisfactory measure of success, let alone personal value. He also saw the seductions and pitfalls of politics. He knew it to be a dirty business and he scorned the kind of posturing it produced in some men. Yet he was fascinated by it. In a remarkable letter to Bess, as he now called her, he wrote,

> Politics sure is the ruination of many a good man. Between hot air and graft he usually loses not only his head but his money and friends as well. Still, if I were real rich I'd just as soon spend my money buying votes and offices as yachts and autos .... To succeed politically he must be an egoist or a fool or a ward boss tool.[15]

On a Sunday in November 1913, Bess said that if ever she married anyone it would be him. Later, she wrote a letter confirming the promise. Harry and Bess agreed; they were secretly engaged. On a date in Kansas City, he took her to see Julia Sanderson and Donald Brian in a new show, *The Girl from Utah*, and held her hand as the leading man sang a song by Jerome Kern, "They'll Never Believe Me." In one letter to Bess, he referred to himself as "a common everyday man." Yet, upon the engagement, Harry thought there were no bounds now to his hori-

---

[14] Letter from Harry S. Truman to Bessie Wallace, May 17, 1911, Harry S. Truman Library.
[15] Letter from Harry S. Truman to Bess, postmark illegible, Harry S. Truman Library.

zons. He was a clodhopper who had ambitions to be the Chief Executive of the US. To Bess's mother nonetheless the prospect for a debt-ridden, farm-boy suitor was extremely remote, no matter how persistent or well mannered he might be. She did not think any man was good enough for Bess.

War versus the Farm and Bess

Soon his mother would give him money to buy a car. Though he was to love automobiles all his life, this would be *the* automobile of his life. Harry bought a big, black, five-passenger 1911-model Stafford, hand-built by Terry Strafford of Kansas City. Only 300 of these cars were ever made. It was a rich man's car that sold for $2,350. Harry paid $650. He would come and go as he pleased now; mostly he was going to see Bess in Independence. Harry and his car became the center of attention. Uncle Harrison, Harry's namesake, enjoyed a spin in the car with the top down. In three months he drove 5,000 miles. Not since his first pair of eyeglasses had anything so changed his life.

Two events in midsummer 1914 occupied Harry. The Great War began in Europe[16] and John Truman became very ill. John, at the age of 63, had to have an operation for a severe hernia. Harry's father died the morning of Monday, November 2, 1914, with Harry at his side. This meant that running the farm fell on the shoulders of Harry. He was to give the farm everything he had. As he worried about the weather and about his debts, he kept on as road overseer for another six months. From February to August he also served as postmaster in Grandview, though in name only, since he left the work to a widow, who he thought needed the money more than he did. He was 30 years old.

The farm was doing well; they were sitting on a fortune. The price of wheat in 1916 hit a new high of $1.65 a bushel. Moreover, good land in Jackson country was selling for $200 an acre. The farm was worth at least $100,000. Later Harry would remember the years on the farm as the best time he ever had in his life. He never lost the farm habits of early rising and hard work. His mother would say that he got his common sense on the farm.

---

[16] "The Great War" was soon named World War I (WWI), only latter to be called "The War to End All Wars" by President Woodrow Wilson. It was a global military conflict that took place mostly in Europe between 1914 and 1918. It was total warfare which left millions dead and did much to shape the modern world.

Harry could have stayed out of the war. At the age of 33 in the spring of 1917, he was two years beyond the age limit set by the new Selective Service Act. He had been out of the National Guard for nearly six years. His eyes were far below the standard requirements for any of the armed services.[17] Finally, he was the sole supporter of his mother and sister. As a farmer, he was supposed to remain on the farm, as a patriotic duty. So he went. He left the responsibility for the farm and care of his mother to his sister Mary Jane. Bess Wallace's response to his decision was to say they should be married at once. But he said no. He thought she must not tie herself to a man who could come home a cripple or not at all.

Though he still disliked guns and had never been in a fight, he was stirred by the war messages of Woodrow Wilson. Besides, he saw this as a noble crusade across the sea, "over there" in old Europe. He began playing it now on the piano, along with other rousing and sentimental songs such as "Good-by Broadway, Hello France" and "Keep the Home Fires Burning."

It was a murderous war. The old battlefield heroics were undone by new weaponry — the machine gun, automatic rifles, massed artillery, poison gas, flamethrowers, the airplane, and the tank. In 1915 there had been two million casualties on the Western Front. At the Battle of the Somme, between July and October, the Germans alone lost more men than were killed in all four years of the American Civil War. It would be costly to "make the world safe for democracy," as Wilson put it.

Harry rejoined the National Guard. His unit became the 129th Field Artillery of the 59th Brigade attached to the 35th Division. He formally accepted a Commission as a 1st Lieutenant on September 14, 1917, "as of date June 22, 1917."[18] As noted in his physical exam, he was now 5 feet 8 inches tall and weighed 151 pounds. "Over there," the first units of the American Expeditionary Forces were in France, under the command of General John J. Pershing. As for Harry, he went to Doniphan, a huge new tent encampment adjacent to Fort Sill

---

[17] In a physical examination, August 9, 1917, uncorrected vision in his right eye was 20/50, in his left, 20/400. The written note by the examining doctor just to the right of the left eye reading says either "blind" or "blurred." The corrected vision in the right with eyeglasses was 20/30 and the left eye, 20/40. His hearing is 20/20; pulse rate, normal; weight, 151 lbs. and; height, 68 inches. His chest expands by 3½ inches upon "expiration." Everything else is described as "normal" or "good." For these and other details, see Report of Physical Examination of Harry S. Truman, August 9, 1917 from his "Military Personnel File," Harry S. Truman Library.

[18] Acceptance of Commission, First Lieutenant by Harry S. Truman, September 14, 1917. Military Personnel File of Harry S. Truman, Harry S. Truman Library.

in Oklahoma. His duties included instruction in the handling of horses. He acquired an ability to curse like Captain Kidd. In addition to his regular duties, Harry was assigned to run the regimental canteen. The canteen was soon paying dividends. Among his pals in service was James M. Pendergast, the nephew of the Kansas City politician T. J. Pendergast.

The night of March 19, 1918, he moved out by troop train. Then, he sailed the night of March 29, 1918 on the *George Washington*. It sailed into the crowded harbor of Brest on April 13. By this time the American Expeditionary Forces in France numbered nearly a million men. 400 miles away from the docks at Brest, one of the most savage battles in history was raging. For Harry and his troops good food, wine, and cognac were all plentiful. If ever he had to give up being a Missourian, Harry said, he would be a citizen of France. At the end of April he was assigned to an elite artillery school near Chaumont, in Lorraine, where Pershing had his headquarters. Sometime in May he was ordered to rejoin his old regiment, stationed at Angers. By now he was Captain Truman — in command of four artillery guns and 194 men.

About this time, Harry wrote one of his many long letters to Bess, this one he wrote from his bed. He writes,

....We go to work tomorrow and I have been seeing the town which is quite wonderful to me. It isn't Paris but if Paris is as much livelier as it is bigger, Paris is some town. Wine and beer are sold here and most of the 35th Division have been in Okla[homa] so long that they are trying to drink all there is here. They can't as the supply seems to be inexhaustible. Prices are worked strictly on the American plan in French money and they skin us alive. Our dinners costs us 10 franks a piece about $1.80. So you see things are not so cheap. One fellow bought him a Sam Brown belt for 40 franks (I don't know why I spelt that with a k) and gave the man a ten dollar bill. He got 60 francs in change and the belt so he made a belt and three francs by the deal and didn't know it until someone told him that ten dollars was 57 francs.

This is a beautiful place. I wish I could tell you where it is (call Boxley up). The room I have at the Hotel des Voygers is furnished in mahogany with double lace curtains at its windows. It has a picture of Henry IV and his children on one side and Henry VIII of England at some state function on the other. There is a fire place (no fire) with a white marble mantelpiece, which has a Dutch clock under a glass case. (The clock doesn't run probably on account of its age). It is a beautiful gold affair with a couple of 17th century pikeman on top of it. It is flanked by two exquisitely beautiful lamps and there is a large mirror over the whole thing about four feet square. The chairs are upholstered in red plush. It looks more like some count's bedroom than a hotel room.

I went to a picture show and saw Pearl White in one of the sections of a spasm that has been running a year or so over in USA. The name and explanations were in French and I've forgotten its name but was a good old mellerdramer and I hadn't seen this episode. There was a comedy and another complete film that was good and a dancer named Miss Theer. We got tired and left before the show was over or I guess we could have been there yet. It began at 2:30 and we left at 5:30 all for 1 franc 34 centimes about 35 cents.

We had a most pleasant voyage and found a well founded rumor that we were sunk when we got to port. The navy has the army beaten forty wags for wild stories.

I've got to quit because its ten p.m. And lights go out a[t] 9 o'clock and I'm liable to get arrested.

Write me as below. Yours always[19]

The letter is rather stiffly signed "Harry S. Truman," followed by his military address. His letters reveal a concern with details, among other things. He was always a keen observer.

Besides being a loyal letter-writer, Harry was a model officer and extremely popular with the men of Battery D. His warmth and liking of people carried the day. He was a disciplinarian but he was very fair. Working the men hard, insisting on strict behavior, making them walk the chalk, and driving himself no less, gave him satisfaction and pride. Whatever dislike or fear of guns appears to have vanished. It was a big responsibility to take 194 men to the front. Soon they were in Alsace, at the extreme eastern end of the front.

Taking up a position close to the German lines, Harry was ordered to fire a gas barrage. Thus, his first action would be to shell the enemy with poison gas. Battery D became part of the first big American push, half a million men on their way to Saint-Mihiel, south of Verdun. Soon the 129th was en route to the Argonne Forest. The Supreme Command had decided on a colossal, all-out offensive to end the war. The attack would extend along the entire Western Front from Verdun to the sea. The Meuse-Argonne offensive, as it would be known, was

---

[19] Letter from Harry S. Truman to Bess Wallace, April 14, 1918, Truman Papers, Harry S. Truman Library. This is typical of the letters he wrote. They are complete with misspellings and some misplaced punctuation. It nonetheless reflects Truman's self-schooling as well as the informality of his style. It is also part of the charm of the young soldier; this, despite the formal salutation.

the largest action in American military history until then. After a 100 miles advance, the 129th Regiment's designated position was near a crossroads village called Neuvilly. In the distance, across an open no man's land was the German stronghold of Boureuilles.

The bombardment began on Thursday, September 25, 1918. In three hours more ammunition was expended than during the entire Civil War. The Germans, though greatly outnumbered, were solidly dug in on high ground. The 129th Field Artillery was ordered forward. In mid-October, the regiment took up new positions on the bleak heights east of Verdun, above the Meuse River Valley. On the morning of November 14, Battery D was firing again when at about 8:30am, Captain Truman was notified that at 11:00am the Germans would sign an armistice agreement. The Great War was over and to the victors it seemed a triumph for civilization. It was left to the statesmen to make a lasting peace, or so it was thought.

Two weeks and two days after the Armistice, Captain Harry Truman was on leave in Paris and dining at Maxim's. After dinner he and several other officers went to the Folies Bergère. They went on to see Notre Dame and Napoleon's Tomb. He was photographed at the Arc de Triomphe, and rode a taxi the length of the Champs-Elysees, up the Rue Royale, down the Madeleine, back up the Rue de Rivoli, over the Seine by the ornate Alexander III Bridge. He also visited the Luxembourg Palace, the Tuileries Gardens, the Louvre, and strolled the Boulevard de l'Opera.

From Paris he took a train to Nice, with the blue Mediterranean on one side and the foothills of the Alps on the other. It made him think of Von Weber's *Polacca Brillante*, which was composed there. From Nice he went on to Monte Carlo. He and Major Gates went to the opera, to a performance of *Thais*. He returned to a division encampment near Verdun notable only, he said, for its copious mud.

He was thinking only of home and what was ahead for him there. While he wrote in his letters of returning to the farm, he mentioned also the possibility of running for political office — for eastern judge in Jackson county, possibly even for Congress. He wanted to serve on the House Military Affairs Committee. Most of all, he longed to get back to the green pastures of Missouri and to Bess.

Harry had one more chance to see Paris. There, he saw Woodrow Wilson ride by. In a shop on the Rue de la Pais, he bought a wedding ring. Then on April 9, 1919 he sailed for New York on the former German liner *Zeppelin*.

At heart, Harry Truman was a nineteenth century man. Chester A. Arthur was President when he was born and the most pressing issue was whether the nation should continue building a wooden Navy. Now he was 33 years old at a time when the Great War marked the end of the old century and the beginning of something new. It was a great dividing line and much that came after 1918 never appealed to Harry Truman. Until he met George C. Marshall, he wondered if "modern times" were capable of producing a great man.

It was the age of the Roaring Twenties and Harry was unfit for it. He disliked cigarettes, gin, and fad diets. Moreover, he disapproved of women smoking or drinking, even of men taking a drink if women were present. He disliked the very sound of the Jazz Age, including what became known as Kansas City jazz. Life as depicted in the novels of F. Scott Fitzgerald was entirely foreign to his experience. He never learned to dance (never mind the Charleston) or to play golf. Poker was his game, not bridge. F. Scott Fitzgerald had said, "It was characteristic of the Jazz Age that it had no interest in politics at all." But Harry discovered politics to be his life work during the Twenties.[20]

The war was a watershed for Harry. He had come from the farm but could not go back to it. A hit song of 1919 was "How you gonna' keep 'em down on the farm after they've seen Paree?" He was not the same man. He had new confidence in himself. He had led men and he liked that better than anything he had ever done before. He had courage and was no longer the boy who ran from fights, and he could inspire courage in others. Most of all, he had been a big success as a soldier.

Bess, for one, liked what she saw. The signing of the Peace Treaty at Versailles and Harry and Bess's wedding took place on the same day. Harry was 35; Bess was 34. And it was during the war that he met and befriended Eddie Jacobson and Jim Pendergast, who, along with Bess, were to have much to do with his new and different life. A month before the wedding, Harry and Eddie Jacobson took a lease on a store in downtown Kansas City. They opened a men's furnishing store, a haberdashery.

Truman & Jacobson was on the ground floor of the Glennon Hotel, catty-cornered from the larger Muehleback Hotel, a choice location. Harry would keep the books; Eddie would do the buying. They would take turns with

---

[20] For much more on the Jazz Age and Fitzgerald, see E. Ray Canterbery and Thomas D. Birch, *F. Scott Fitzgerald: Under the Influence* (St. Paul, MN: Paragon House, 2006).

the customers. It was a first-class operation that specialized in famous brands. They would sell no suits or coats, but rather a full line of "gents furnishings" — shirts, socks, ties, belts, underwear, hats. Times were prosperous and 12th Street of *Twelfth Street Rag* fame was jumping. Conventioneers poured in and out of the Muchlebach. Silk underwear and silk shirts for men were the rage. By year's end they had sold $70,000 worth of goods, which meant a high return.

In 1920 the handsome Republican Presidential candidate, Senator Warren G. Harding of Ohio, called for a return to "normalcy." Normalcy seemed indeed to be what the country wanted, as Harding and his running mate, Calvin Coolidge, defeated the Democratic ticket of James Cox and Franklin Roosevelt with a bigger majority than in any previous election. Truman and Jacobson, restocking their shelves in Kansas City, seemed in perfect step with the times. The one looming worry; farmers were hurting as the price of wheat tumbled. Overall, farm prices fell 40 percent and the farmers' plight began to spread. By mid-year 1921 Harry and Eddie's flourishing business had evaporated. The country was in a full-scale post-war depression. Truman & Jacobson failed in 1922. Harry would end up being strapped for money for the next 20 years. Harry, perhaps rightly, blamed the Republicans in Washington. But it was the Wilson administration that had suddenly cut government spending and raised taxes in 1920, only to be followed by the tight money policy of Secretary of the Treasury Andrew Mellon. It was an event that Harry Truman would recall just after World War II.

Harry described Jimmy Pendergast as a nice boy and as smart as the old man he's named for. The original James Pendergast was the legendary Alderman Jim, the first Pendergast in Kansas City politics and founding father of what became a famous, or infamous, depending on your point of view, Kansas City dynasty. He was a Democrat and his real love was politics. He remained on the city council for 18 years, never losing an election.

It was the Pendergast organization that was his legacy, as leadership passed to his brother Tom. Like his brother, Tom was a saloon-keeper who abhorred drunkenness. He drank only an occasional glass of beer. He acquired more saloons and expanded into the wholesale liquor business. He went on to establish the Ready-Mixed Concrete Company, one of the first companies to mix concrete in a plant, then deliver it by truck to the construction site. He became known as a builder.

Jim Pendergast met with Harry Truman at his haberdashery, which was already in trouble. The Pendergasts wanted Harry to run for eastern judge of

Jackson County, a courthouse job in Independence. Harry accepted their offer with no hesitation. His record was plain; he was a Baptist and a Mason who could talk farming with farmers as no big-city Irish politician ever could. He had a fine war record and had been an honest road overseer. Unrecorded were the opinions of Bess, her mother, and Mamma Truman.

Truman's "early years" end with the beginning of his political life. We will pick up this story with Harry's first political office, and we will have much more to say about what is generally meant by "populism." History, which served Harry Truman so well during his time, will be our aid as well.

Chapter 2

The Political Making of a Populist

[Tight money] reflects a reversion to the idea that the tree can be fertilized at the top instead of the bottom — the old trickle-down theory.

Harry S. Truman, 1947

The danger to democracy comes not from the masses but from the concentration of wealth in the hands of a few — and the income tax is the best remedy for that.

Harry S. Truman, 1961

We have arrived at the edge of Harry S. Truman, politician. But he was no ordinary politician. Already, we have inferred how populism was in the background. In the Introduction, we briefly defined what we mean by Progressive Populism. There nonetheless is a gap to be filled. We need to understand the history of "populism" to be sure that our definition is suitable. Thus, we will momentarily detour from the story of Harry the politician, to say more about what we mean by "populism." Still, it helps to know what we have already discovered: Truman grew up during the heyday of American populism.

It is possible to trace the Truman heritage in populism all the way back to the Founding Fathers, which makes it uniquely American. Thomas Jefferson and Andrew Jackson represent an influential line of this American thought. Their view stresses the importance of wide and roughly equal distribution of property ownership, the central form in which wealth was then held. While suspicious of government, this thinking is also focused on the concentration of private economic wealth and power. There was an emphasis on the importance of democratic input to constrain government power, but also an understanding of society in terms of class conflict. Advocates upheld a market-based economy composed of farmers and artisans who controlled both property and their labor. The growth of private concentrations of wealth, embodied in early corporations, justified strong state regulatory intervention. By the turn of the twentieth century, the growth in the importance of money shifted the focus of wealth distribution from real property to wealth held in financial instruments.

Not only was Harry Truman growing up during the rise of American populism, he believed in it. So did his father, John. American populism grew out of the complaints of farmers like the Trumans. The arrows of complaints were aimed at two main targets: the railways and commercial banks. The targets were sufficiently big; they were easy to hit. In the three decades prior to 1897 — what Mark Twain called the Gilded Age[1] — transportation charges for grains did fall, but so did the wholesale prices of corn and wheat, more or less equally. Farm income also was growing but not as fast or as reliably as income in manufacturing. As to bankers, they were making money on money by charging interest. The Internal Revenue Service (IRS) justifiably names interest, "unearned income." The hardworking sod-busters were paying idle fat cats enjoying bankers' hours for the privilege of working hard from daylight to sundown. Worse, the national banks, created by federal power, were not allowed to accept farm mortgages as loan collateral. The farmers considered this to be discrimination, and they were right. Further farmer discontent was fueled by the great instability of income in farming, often related to weather cycles.

A Brief History of US Populism

The great discontent of the farmers is not absent irony. The extraordinary agricultural development of post-bellum America ended in social and economic conflict. The Populists, Grangers, and their allies declared a new war — a war on the

---

[1] In the United States, the Gilded Age is the era spanning 1870 to 1910 during which unbridled free-market capitalism led to the accumulation of wealth and capital in a few hands through cutthroat competition, resulting in abusive monopoly power, including the formation of trusts. For much more on the Gilded Age, see E. Ray Canterbery, *A Brief History of Economics: Artful Approaches to the Dismal Science*, Second Edition (Singapore: World Scientific, 2011), pp. 11, 146, 402, 412, and 471.

excesses of the Gilded Age. By the end of the New Deal, their main demands had been realized. (During this Age, populists gained the capital 'P'.) The Populists had gained universal public education, women's suffrage, secret ballots, direct election of senators, federal land banks, the Commodity Credit Corporation, the Federal Reserve note (paper money), the Export-Import Bank, and many other reforms created since 1892 by the Federal government. Much had gone the way of stiff petticoats and Prince Edward smoking jackets. The populist reform movement did not really end until the Jimmy Carter Administration, reaching its Democrat Party nadir with Bill Clinton, ironically a self-proclaimed "Populist." But true populism is a contact sport, and Harry Truman was an "extremist" in that regard. As noted, he was preceded by the tenacious William Jennings Bryan and the rough and ready Teddy Roosevelt.

The Populists believed themselves to be the losers in late nineteenth century America. They were the underdogs. They took their case to the federal level where the greatest political power rested. They became the majority opinion and they understood the power of the ballot, the power of direct democracy at the federal level. Consistent with this view of power was their demand for a secret ballot to override the corrupt practices of the urban political machines, and their demand for women's suffrage to gain the vote of the other half of the adult population. Sympathy in the Populist platforms for labor served a similar purpose. Improved public education would serve the dual purpose of providing a ladder to success and providing a better-informed electorate at a time when the share of people graduating from high school was only 7 percent (in 1900). Ignorance could only serve the purposes of the wealthy.

The broader and more direct economic demand was an obvious attempt to use the Federal government for income and wealth redistribution. They understood that redistribution in the other direction had already been accomplished — for industry, by tariffs; for railroads, by subsidies; for corporations, by the courts and legislatures. While the beneficiaries had claimed their outcomes to be from the workings of the free market, the Populists knew them to be the largesse of government intervention on behalf of the wealthy.

What do we make of "free markets" in the world of Populism? Oddly, in the conventional world of the economist (who first appeared in the guise of Adam Smith), all markets are alike and ultimately free. This is the face that Populists have always slapped. The central focus of the economist is the price mechanism. The basic idea emerged with the French physiocrats around mid-eighteenth century.

Their idea was that free exchange and the market leads to a harmonious society. The harmony, as Adam Smith was to show, comes with reconciling individual self-interest with the public's interest. Individuals acting out of self interest in the marketplace harmonize the interest of their society. This happens automatically with an "invisible hand" but only under some carefully crafted conditions.

Need we say it, some Populist demands have never been met. The free market ideology sometimes comes out on top. Still, there are the demands. At the top was the abolition of the national banking system. The Populists never liked banks or bankers, but the national banks were particularly objects of scorn. These banks, chartered by a Federal government, characteristically discriminated against agriculture by refusing to make mortgage loans on farm real estate. Meanwhile, state bank note issues were taxed out of existence to guarantee the success of the national bank issues. Farmers, even before the IRS, have long viewed interest as unearned income, a kind of income monopolized by the bankers and rich families.

The Populists also wanted railroads and the telegraph system nationalized. Here the farmers eventually got at least half a loaf. Federal government power had created and enforced rights of way, eminent domain, special franchise monopolies for rail routes, and subsidies of various kinds. While these enterprises were regulated by the government, they benefited from the regulation. Agricultural interests thought railroad rates for their commodities were too high. Over the three decades before 1897, freight rates declined but so did the prices of cotton, corn and wheat, about equally. Thus, the relative cost of freight was little changed during the Gilded Age and the relative condition of the farmers failed to improve.

Real freight rates did decline after 1906, but only because the farmers succeeded politically. The Interstate Commerce Commission (ICC) acquired rate-setting power and the commissioners, under political pressure from agriculture, refused to raise rates as commodity prices soared. In 1917 the government took over the railroads. Meanwhile, the farmers had enjoyed a decade of falling freight rates.

The Populists wanted to end subsidies to corporations. The US Supreme Court's 1886 decision that corporations were individual persons ended any hope that this demand would be met. As it turned out, entire industries were created out of government subsidization. The Commodity Credit Corporation paved the way. The aircraft, space and defense industries depended upon federal assistance. The first computer was built by the government. (Eventually, coming up to date with the Barack Obama Administration, even the auto industry — as in General Motors and Chrysler Corporations — was bailed out.) On these matters, the Populists have mixed feelings because giant industry hires a multitude of union workers.

The Populists also wanted to prohibit foreign or corporate ownership of land and other natural resources. Land, they believed, should be reserved only for farming and conservation. Many early conservation measures were based on these concerns. By 1868 California had set aside Yosemite from private ownership; the Federal government did the same for Yellowstone Park in 1872. Teddy Roosevelt played the central role in the conservation movement leading to public ownership of parks.

Populism's heyday was near the turn of the twentieth century. At the Democratic convention of 1896, William Jennings Bryan spoke eloquently about democracy, workers, taxation, and monetary policy. His noteworthy speech attacked private bankers and the gold standard. The nation, he said, was in need of someone to stand against organized wealth. He concluded that the right to coin and issue money and the policy of money was a function of government. Bryan criticized efforts to exclude the humbler members of society from the benefits of growth and government. His democratic vision is that the masses should prosper and this wealth will find its way up to the higher classes which depend on the larger public.

The Progressive Era was to follow with its emphasis on progressive income and estate taxes. Corporate campaign contributions are banned, women receive the vote, and the seventeenth amendment provides for the direct election of the Senate. In this era, government's role is enlarged as it acts both to promote business and also to stabilize the economy from the negative consequences of "free-market" capitalism. Anti-trust legislation and policy against giant corporations is pursued.

In reaction to conservative monetary policy and economic instability, farmers formed the Farmers' Alliance to educate and organize Americans. Efforts were undertaken to create a farmer-labor coalition to push for Populist and democratic political-economic reform. Specific demands were ultimately enunciated in the Omaha Platform of 1892. Populist planks called for agricultural assistance, labor and industrial reforms, political reform, and government regulation or ownership of the transportation and communication industries. Financial reform was centered on a federally administered national banking system, currency expansion, and a flexible currency system, all of which had been denied by the gold standard, in which the money supply depended upon uncertain gold production.

Still, the most lasting effect of Populist concerns has been with the income distribution. This, they presumed, required the reform of money. The Populists correctly sensed a connection between the rate of growth in the paper money supply and the interest rates they hated. They were right to complain that the national banks failed to increase the money supply as fast as real output, imitating the gold standard. As a result, agricultural prices declined dramatically between 1864 and 1896. The other kinds of currency were "commodity money." The 1878 Silver Purchase Act had been insufficient in the creation of new money backed by silver. The Populist view on silver and gold led to their support of William Jennings Bryan four times for the American presidency. (We recall how Bryan had impressed both Harry Truman and his father, John.) Gold production was rising too slowly to provide sufficient commodity money from that source. Besides, gold-backed money was supported by Eastern moneyed interests who saw it as the source of higher interest rates and commodity price declines. To counter these forces, the Populists advanced an innovative "sub-Treasury scheme," which would utilize agricultural output to increase the supply of money.

The "sub-Treasury scheme" was based on the idea that the money supply should grow as rapidly as agricultural output. This made economic sense at a time when agriculture remained the dominant American industry. At harvest time farmers could either sell their crops to regional Treasury offices or use them as collateral for government loans. The US Treasury would print new money to be used for these transactions. With the money supply growing apace with agricultural output, commodity prices would no longer be depressed at harvest time, and farmers' income also would not be depressed. It took a long time but in 1933, the Commodity Credit Corporation essentially did this job for the farmers, using Federal Reserve notes. With the rise of manufacturing, the "sub-Treasury scheme" was applied to manufacturing output.

There remained the problem of loans for agricultural mortgages. This problem was finally eased in 1916 when the Farm Loan Act established the Federal Land Banks to make loans on farm mortgages, the first of many subsequent federal efforts. In this, as well as so many of the Populist efforts, they were attempting to maintain total demand in the economy.

The New Deal proceeded in the same spirit. But there was an added element, the many doctrines of John Maynard Keynes, as interpreted by Franklin Roosevelt's advisers, some of whom were Keynesian before Keynes. This was what John Kenneth Galbraith and I have called "primal Keynesian." Though Keynes's writings are confusing, his original ideas also were Populist in tone and intent, including an underlying tenet of restrained income and wealth inequalities, this despite Keynes' elitist origins. The aristocratic Franklin Roosevelt, in the same vein, was a pragmatic Keynesian, thanks to his advisers. The New Deal accomplished several things. It ended the Gold Standard. Income inequalities were moderated through progressive taxes, social programs, and support for the labor movement. At the same time aggregate demand though Keynesian policies was promoted. The disruptive effects of financial speculation were tempered by enhancement of the political stature of business and labor relative to finance.

Truman: A Populist Candidate

Pushing Populism to the background but not out of sight, we return to Truman's political life. The decision to run for eastern judge of Jackson County was Truman's first major political foray. He had the endorsement of county Democratic party leader, T. J. Pendergast. Candidate Truman opened his campaign two months short of his 38th birthday, March 8, 1922. Harry spoke in every township and precinct. The main event of the political summer took place at a picnic at Oak Grove attended by 4,000 people. To gain added attention Harry arrived by plane. With a rousing speech, for many who were listening, the primary election for eastern judge was over, and Harry Truman had won. The deciding factor was Harry Truman. People liked him, largely because he so obviously liked them. The fall election was a mere formality.

To the victor belong the spoils, Andrew Jackson's old adage, was gospel again in Jackson County, Missouri. A county debt of more than a million dollars was cut in half. The county's credit rating improved. As did county services, and most notably, the quality of work on the roads. Truman made himself familiar with every road and bridge in the county. Still, Harry felt restless for more to do. In 1923–1925 he attended the Kansas City School of Law.

Meantime, life at home with Bess was sweet. Bess was pregnant. The baby, soon to be named Margaret, arrived on February 17, 1924. Harry was nearing 40.

With the exception of his wedding day, this was the biggest event of Harry Truman's life thus far. It was a bright moment in what otherwise was to be a bad year for him. Little Margaret was the center of attention for great-grandmother, grandmother, four Wallace aunts and uncles in the adjoining houses to the rear who remained childless. The arrival changed the atmosphere of the family.

On the political front, everywhere was a dismal time for the Democrats. The national convention had picked an unknown candidate for President, John W. Davis, who was destined to lose. William Jennings Bryan was rudely shouted down, when he tried to speak. A single ray of hope was provided by Franklin Roosevelt, who, though crippled with polio, made the nominating speech for Al Smith, who nonetheless lost the nomination. (Al Smith successfully won the nomination in 1928 as the crippled Roosevelt "walked" to the podium to nominate him once again.) These and other speeches by Roosevelt led Tom Pendergast to say that Roosevelt "has the most magnetic personality of any individual I have ever met."[2]

The Republicans nominated the unremarkable Calvin Coolidge. Coolidge, who sat out the campaign in the White House, won by a popular margin of nearly two to one. As for Harry Truman, he faced a tough re-election campaign for his judgeship. Truman had the support of the Kansas City *Star* and the Independence *Sentinel*. They called him the very model of the public man. Despite being opposed by the notorious Klu Klux Klan, Harry Truman was defeated for reelection by Henry Rummel, an Independence harness-maker who, years before, had made a harness for Truman as a child. Harry liked and respected the old man and was kind to him during the campaign. It was the only election Truman ever lost. He was out of a job again.

In the intervening time, Harry became something of a man of affairs in Kansas City. He began selling memberships in the Kansas City Automobile Club, working on commission during 1925–1926. He was never idle. He got involved in the ill-fated Citizens Security in Englewood, adjacent to Independence. He soon discovered that he had been lied to about the bank's assets. He and his partners got out as quickly as possible and broke even. This was followed by another misadventure with the Community Savings and Loan Association of Independence. Harry was misled by a Spencer Salisbury. Harry later got even when he used his influence in Washington to put federal investigators on to Salisbury's subsequent business activities in Independence, with Salisbury

---

[2] Quoted in Arthur M. Schlesinger, Jr., *The Crisis of the Old Order* (Boston: Houghton Mifflin, 1957), pp. 276–277.

spending 15 months in Leavenworth prison. It was a populist victory, again with a capital 'P'.

Harry also kept in close touch with Jim and Mike Pendergast in 1925 and 1926. They decided that he would run for presiding judge. Harry ran in the primary unopposed, and in November was swept into office. The term of office was four years, and he served two consecutive terms, from January 1927 to January 1934. Nearly everyone — civic leaders, business people (Republicans included), fellow politicians, the press, students of government (then and later), and the electorate — considered his performance outstanding. When he ran the second time for presiding judge in 1930, his margin of victory was substantial.

Harry, the emerging Populist, had learned not to trust banks. As noted, this distrust came out of, in part, painful personal experience. As judge, instead of borrowing country funds from Kansas City banks at 6 percent interest, as had been the practice for years, he went to Chicago and St. Louis and negotiated loans at 4 percent, then 2.5 percent. Admonished by the Kansas City banks, he said he thought the taxpayers of the county had some rights in the matter, too. So, he had a Populist victory, going up against the big banks, Bryan-style.

Good roads remained Harry's priority. He needed to raise $6.5 million in a bond issue; it had never been done before. Deep skepticism was expressed by the *Kansas City Star* and by Tom Pendergast. Truman went off on a speaking tour during the mud season, so no one needed reminding of the condition the roads were in. The voters were shown a map of where the improvements would come. The bond issue was enlarged to include a new courthouse and jail for Kansas City, a new country hospital, and a home for retarded children. The courthouse, jail, and children's home were voted down. The roads and hospital carried, with the vote taking place on Harry's 44th birthday in 1928. It was a stunning victory. The roads were not only built, but built well. Trees were planted along the sides, as Harry remembered from France and Paris's tree-lined boulevards.

Eventually, and with a new bond issue, Harry would have a new courthouse. He selected the Art Deco design. He also decided that there would be an equestrian bronze of Andrew Jackson for the front of the courthouse. He commissioned the sculpturor of a prior statue of Jackson, Charles L. Keck of New York, for the job. He had a real man on a real horse.

On contracts Harry refused to engage in favoritism. This greatly annoyed Tom Pendergast who had made so many promises to so many contractors. Harry insisted that contracts go to the lowest bidders. Pendergast finally gave up trying to influence Harry and told him to run things the way he wanted to. He never again asked Harry to do anything dishonest.

By his own account, Harry did not always do the right and honest thing:

> I wonder if I did the right thing to put a lot of no account sons of bitches on the payroll and pay other sons of bitches more money for supplies than they were worth in order to satisfy the political powers and save $3,500,000. I believe I did do right. Anyway I'm not a partner of any of them and I'll go out poorer in every way than I came into office.[3]

Harry estimated that he could have pocketed $1.5 million, had he so chosen. As it was, he had less than $150.

During the Great Depression, years in which Adolf Hitler was rising to power and Japan invaded Manchuria, Harry was playing poker in a back room over the Farmer & Merchants Bank. He had a regular Monday night game with some old friends, several of them Army pals. The game had a 10-cent limit, a little beer or bourbon, Prohibition notwithstanding. Often the conversation turned to politics.

As early as 1931 there was talk of Harry Truman for governor, a prospect that pleased him. In fact Harry wanted nothing so much as the governorship. But Tom Pendergast had another candidate in mind. There was much anguish over his future. He was told that he could become a Congressman. By now Tom Pendergast was perhaps the most powerful political boss in the country.

With Franklin Roosevelt and the New Deal taking over Washington, Pendergast's power seemed unlimited. This despite the ruling spirit behind gambling, prostitution, bootlegging, the sale of narcotics, and racketeering in Kansas City being Tom Pendergast. Kansas City was wide open, with forty dance halls and more than a hundred nightclubs, offering floor shows, dancers, comedians, and some of the best blues and jazz to heard anywhere in America — the Bennie Moten Orchestra at the Reno, Count Basie and his Kansas City Seven doing "The One o'clock Jump," trumpeter Hot Lips Page at the Subway, blues singer Julia Lee at the Yellow Front Saloon.

In the fall of 1933, the Roosevelt administration appointed a Republican as director of the federal reemployment service in Missouri. Tom Pendergast complained to Washington, with the immediate result that the Republican was fired

---

[3] Quoted by David McCullough, *Truman* (New York: Simon & Schuster, 1992), p. 187.

and the job was given to Judge Truman. Harry agreed to serve without pay. Harry found himself reporting to Harry Hopkins, Roosevelt's public works official, and traveling to Washington on government business for the first time. About this time, Truman had made up his mind to run for Congress. Soon the Pendergast machine would ask him to run for the United States Senate. His candidacy was announced on May 14, 1934. For the first time, his opponents would point to the Pendergast machine as his greatest liability.

Declaring the Great Depression as the main issue, Harry praised the New Deal. He spoke of the capitalistic domination of government in bygone Republican times, praised the decision of FDR to end the "rule of the rich" and give the average American a chance. He noted how 90 percent of the wealth of the country was in the hands of 4 percent of the population. Hence Roosevelt was the man of the hour; chasing the moneychangers from the temple so that the common people could have a chance at the good things of life. The party of Jefferson, Jackson, and Franklin D. Roosevelt was the party favoring the everyday man. Harry won the primary election by 40,000 votes, many from Jackson County and the farmers there. In the general election in the fall, Harry won easily, and took the oath of office on January 3, 1935.

Once again, we need to be reminded that Populism, like Harry Truman, had agrarian roots. Truman's growing distrust of private banks found its voice in William Jennings Bryan. Harry learned from first-hand experience as a judge the importance of low interest rates. Not surprisingly, it was the farm vote and debtors that put Harry Truman in the Senate. Harry's affection for New Deal policies came from his Populist tendencies. As we will come to know, his Populism soon was to infect his economic policies as President.

Chapter 3

Mr Truman Goes to Washington

Mr Truman went to Washington in the midst of the Great Depression. In May 1934 he filed as a Democratic candidate for the Senate. On August 7 he defeated incumbent Republican Roscoe C. Patterson. On January 3, 1935 Truman was sworn in as a US Senator along with 12 other Democrats. By the mid-1930s Washington DC was being transformed from a sleepy small southern city into a large metropolitan area of great diversity. It was being transformed by the activist Roosevelt administration.

The seeds of the Great Depression had been planted earlier. During the economic boom of the Roaring Twenties, the traditional values of rural America were challenged by the Jazz Age, symbolized by women smoking, drinking, and wearing short skirts. F. Scott Fitzgerald named the Age even as he and wife Zelda defined it by their crazy booze-driven behavior.[1] The average American was busy buying automobiles and household appliances, and speculating in a wild stock market, where big money could be be made. These appliances and common stock however were bought on credit. Although businesses had made huge gains from the mechanization of manufacturing, the average workers' wages had only increased 8 percent. The imbalance between the rich and the poor, with 0.3 percent of society earning the same total income as 42 percent, combined with production of more and more goods and rising personal debt, could not be sustained. On Black Tuesday, October 29, 1929, the stock market crashed,

---

[1] For much more on the Fitzgeralds and the Jazz Age, see E. Ray Canterbery and Thomas D. Birch, *F. Scott Fitzgerald: Under the Influence* (St. Paul: Paragon House, 2006).

triggering the Great Depression, the worst economic collapse in the history of the modern industrial world. Zelda Fitzgerald crashed shortly thereafter. The depression spread from the United States to the rest of the world, lasting from the end of 1929 until the early 1940s. With banks failing and businesses closing, more than 15 million Americans (a quarter of the workforce) became unemployed.

President Herbert Hoover, underestimating the seriousness of the crisis, called it a "a passing incident in our national lives," and assured Americans that it would be over in 59 days. A strong believer in rugged individualism, Hoover did not think the Federal Government should offer relief to the poverty-stricken population. Focusing on a trickle-down economic program to help finance business and banks, Hoover met resistance from business executives who preferred to lay off workers. Blamed by many for the Great Depression, Hoover was widely ridiculed: An empty pocket turned inside out was called a "Hoover flag;" the decrepit shanty towns springing up around the country were called "Hoovervilles." But Hoover was following the dominant thought of the free-market classical economists who predated Keynes' famous book of 1936.

Franklin Delano Roosevelt, the rich governor from New York, offered Americans a New Deal, and was elected in a landslide victory in 1932, three years before Truman arrived. He, unlike Hoover, took quick action to attack the Depression, declaring a four-day bank holiday, during which Congress passed the Emergency Banking Relief Act to stabilize the banking system. During the first 100 days of his administration, Roosevelt laid the groundwork for his New Deal remedies that would rescue the country from the depths of despair.

The New Deal programs created a liberal political alliance of labor unions, blacks, and other minorities, some farmers and others receiving government relief and intellectuals. The hardship brought about by the Depression affected America deeply. Since the prevailing attitude of the 1920s was that success was earned, it fallowed that failure was deserved. The unemployment brought on by the Depression caused self-blame and self-doubt. Men were harder hit psychologically than women. Since men were expected to provide for their families, it was humiliating to have to ask for assistance. Although some argued that women should not be given jobs when many men were unemployed, the percentage of women working increased slightly during the Depression. Traditionally female fields of teaching and social services grew under the New Deal programs. Children took on more responsibility, sometimes finding work when their parents could not. As a result of living through the Depression, some people developed habits of careful saving and frugality, others were determined to create a comfortable life for themselves.

African-Americans suffered more than whites, since their jobs were often taken away from them and given to whites. In 1930, 50 percent of blacks were unemployed.[2] However, Eleanor Roosevelt championed black rights, and New Deal programs prohibited discrimination. Discrimination continued in the South, however, as a large number of black voters switched from the Republican to the Democrat party during the Depression.

It hardly need be said, but the Great Depression and the New Deal changed forever the relationship between Americans and their government. Government involvement and responsibility in caring for the needy and regulating the economy came to be expected.

Roosevelt's New Deals

The First New Deal — that is, the legislation passed by the 73rd Congress, between 1933 and 1935 — did not end the Depression. Its great statutory pillars, the National Industrial Recovery Act (NIRA) and the Agricultural Adjustment Act (AAA), were struck down by the Supreme Court. When Roosevelt ran for reelection in 1936, the unemployment rate was 16.9 percent, almost twice what it had been in 1930. Yet Roosevelt won 523 electoral votes, and his opponent, Alf Landon, won only eight. When Roosevelt ran for the unprecedented third term, unemployment was 14.6 percent. Still, he carried 38 states, while Wendell Willkie carried only 10.

In its two-year life, the 73rd Congress raised tax rates, ended the tax-exempt status of corporate dividends, limited deductions for capital depreciation, and approved the exercise of eminent domain. It restored the banking system (after Roosevelt had closed it), increased federal unemployment assistance to the states, and authorized the President to negotiate tariff reductions in order to promote freer trade. It passed the AAA, which was designed to increase the purchasing power of farmers, and the NIRA, which mandated a minimum wage and maximum hours in certain businesses, asserted the right of workers to organize, and

---

[2] I am using the term "black," though "negro" was the operative noun of the day and for many days to come. Though he was an early champion of civil rights and was a friend of Mrs Roosevelt, Harry Truman usually used the N-word.

gave the Federal Government powers to oversee production and prices in some industries. In 1933 it passed the Glass-Steagall Act, which separated commercial and investment banking. (This provision of the Act was repealed in 1999, is what contributed to the financial meltdown of 2008.[3]) It also created the Securities and Exchange Commission, the Civilian Conservation Corps, the Federal Deposit Insurance Corporation, and the Tennessee Valley Authority.

The 74th Congress (1935–1937), the Congress of the Second Hundred Days, passed the National Labor Relations Act (the Wagner Act), which protected unions, created the Social Security Administration and the Works Progress Administration (WPA), and passed laws regulating railroads and public utilities and prohibiting unfair price discrimination. Senator Truman backed the New Deal legislation.

In the passage of this legislation, Roosevelt had what President Truman was to lack in congressional support in 1947–1949. In 1933, when Roosevelt came into office, there were 59 Democratic senators. In the next Congress, there were 69. In 1937, there were 80 Democrats and progressives in the Senate and 347 in the House of Representatives; only 16 senators and 88 congressmen were Republicans. Still, other Presidents might have squandered the opportunity that majorities gave Roosevelt; we cannot underestimate the power of his personality. The use of Executive Orders after 1939 and during WWII gave President Roosevelt still more leverage.

Background: The Jazz Age and the Great Depression

The 1920s and 1930s also comprised the age of Will Rogers, a homespun philosopher who began his career as an Oklahoma cowboy. He was a beloved and respected radio commentator, film actor, and author. He was the leading political wit during what has been described as a Progressive Era, the world's best known comedian. Harry Truman met him (and applauded his humor) shortly before Rogers died in a plane crash on August 15, 1935. The premature death greatly depressed Truman. After observing the 1928 Democratic convention, Rogers said, "I am not a member of an organized, political party. I am a Democrat." It was an aphorism that Harry Truman often quoted. Rogers, like Truman, favored

---

[3] For the full story of the meltdown and the Great Recession that followed, see E. Ray Canterbery, *The Global Great Recession* (Singapore, New Jersey, London: World Scientific, 2011).

the common man. As Rogers put it, "Everybody is ignorant, only on different subjects."

Popular culture did not stand still during the 1930s. After all, it was the one indulgence that the public could afford. The 1930s are often referred to as Hollywood's "Golden Age." Tickets were relatively cheap and Hollywood made movie after movie to entertain a Depression audience. Mainly the movies provided escapist fare. Movie goers swooned over such matinee idols as Clark Gable, Bette Davis, Greta Garbo, and Errol Flynn. Moreover, they laughed at W. C. Fields, Bob Hope, and the Marx Brothers. They fell in love with the little curly headed moppet Shirley Temple and flocked to see her tap dance and sing "The Good Ship Lollipop". Then, there was Busby Berkeley's dance numbers, and Fred Astaire and Ginger Rogers tapping and ballroom dancing across the screen. It was a time when many of America's most distinguished writers produced works of fiction. They included F. Scott Fitzgerald, Ernest Hemingway, and Thornton Wilder. Ogden Nash wrote light verse for the *New Yorker* magazine. Notable authors such as William Faulkner and F. Scott Fitzgerald were penning Hollywood screenplays. Fitzgerald was riding on his fame as the definer of the prior decade. Young people flocked to hear and dance to the big bands of Benny Goodman, Duke Ellington, Glenn Miller, and Tommy Dorsey. The title of a Duke Ellington tune, "It Don't Mean a Thing (if it Ain't Got That Swing)" summed up the 'in' music. All was not sweetness and lightness. John Steinbeck's *The Grapes of Wrath* bought to film the story of the Joad family and its migration from the Dust Bowl of Oklahoma to the agricultural fields of California. *Gone With the Wind*, one of the top money makers of all time, debuted in Atlanta, Georgia in 1939.

There was a migration of farmers from the Trumans' Midwest into the Southern Plains at the turn of the twentieth century. They were lured by a land lush with shrubs, grasses, and soil so rich it looked like chocolate. These farmers didn't realize that they were witnessing a brief respite in an endless cycle of rain and drought. Undeterred, they enjoyed great harvests and raced to turn every inch of the Southern Plains into profit. There was no conservation. These farming prospects changed when the rain stopped falling in the summer of 1931 and the "black blizzards" began. Powerful dust storms carrying millions of tons of stinging, blinding black dirt swept across the Southern Plains, the panhandles of Texas and Oklahoma, western Kansas, and the eastern portions of Colorado and New Mexico. Topsoil that had taken a thousand years per inch to build suddenly blew away in only minutes. The devastated region became the Dust Bowl of the 1930s. The decline in farm output would contribute to the Great Depression.

In 1932, the weather bureau reported 14 dust storms. The next year, the number climbed to 38. By 1934, the storms were coming with alarming frequency. The dust was beginning to make living things sick. Animals were found dead in the fields, their stomachs coated with two inches of dirt. People spat up clods of dirt as big around as a pencil. An epidemic raged throughout the Plains; they called it dust pneumonia. By the end of 1935, with no substantial rainfall in four years, some residents gave up. Neighbors and friends picked up and headed west in search of farm jobs in California. The fictional Joad family was among them. Still, three-quarters of the Dust Bowlers chose to stay. During the 1930s, adversity in agriculture eventually reached the Trumans' farm.

Truman: From the Farm to the Senate

Harry Truman had moved from the farm to the city of Washington, DC. As noted, he took his populism to the Senate with him. He was pleased at becoming one of 96 senators in a country of 130 million people. Still, Truman was aware of the precarious nature of the job; he thought it prudent to rent in Washington rather than buy. He also was aware of the challenges he faced. "I was timid as a country boy arriving on the campus of a great university for his first year," he recalled in his *Memoirs*.[4] Less charitable was the *New York Times* which described the new senator from Missouri as "a rube from Pendergast land."

At first Harry struggled with self-doubt about his fitness for the office. Veteran Senator J. Hamilton Lewis of Illinois put him at ease by telling him Harry not to start out with an inferiority complex. "For the first six months you'll wonder how the hell you got here, and after that you'll wonder how the hell the rest of us got here."[5] Truman came to believe, though there were some senators he held in high regard, he was no less qualified to hold his seat than most of his colleagues.

At age 50, he was a politician who did not take himself too seriously, a friendly, likeable, warmhearted fellow with a lot of common sense. He also remembered names, personal interests, family connections. Very retentive in

---

[4] Harry S. Truman, *Memoirs, Volume 1: Year of Decisions* (New York: Doubleday, 1955), p. 142.
[5] Quoted by Truman, *ibid.*, p. 144.

mind, he remembered things he had read or learned in school long before, often bringing them into conversation in a way that amazed people. He had come to Washington knowing almost no one there. Later, he would fondly remember Harry Hopkins, because Hopkins showed him kindness during difficult times in his life.[6] William Helm, Washington correspondent for the Kansas City *Journal Post,* showed him around. Carl Hatch of New Mexico and Lewis Schwellenbach of Washington, two new Democratic senators, befriended him. Especially important was Burton K. Wheeler, a lanky, independent-minded Montana Democrat, who ran the powerful Interstate Commerce Committee. And there were many others. He nonetheless remained under a cloud because of his close ties to the Pendergast machine.

He retained his farm life habit of rising early. He would be the first in the Senate. By the time his colleagues arrived, Truman had been through the morning mail, dictated several hundred letters, fixed up as many deserving Democrats with jobs as possible and was ready to go. On good weather days he walked the several miles to the Capitol, moving at the military clip of 120 paces per minute and stopping usually at Childs Restaurant for breakfast.

Still, he did not distinguish himself during his first years on Capitol Hill. When Truman arrived in January 1935, the Democrats held 69 of the 96 Senate seats, a majority that grew to 71 to 25 after Roosevelt's landslide victory in 1936. These large majorities diminished Truman's importance to the White House, which saw little need to court a freshman senator who was likely to vote with the President without much prodding. He was so sympathetic to Roosevelt's legislative agenda that, indeed, he needed few inducements.

He was assigned as a member of the powerful Appropriations Committee and the Interstate Commerce Committee. He also served on the Public Buildings and Grounds Committee and the Committee on Printing in his first term. On May 15, 1935 he introduced his first public bill. It was tied to farm interests, and was "a bill to provide for insurance by the Farm Credit Administration of mortgages on farm property, and for other purposes." The bill died later in committee. In 1937 he was named as vice-chairman of a subcommittee of the Interstate Commerce Committee to investigate American railroad finances. During this time he met with Justice Louis D. Brandeis, an enemy of big business, on several social occasions and discussed transportation

<hr>

[6] See, for example, Merle Miller, *Plain Speaking: An Oral Biography of Harry S. Truman* (New York: Berkley, 1974), pp. 198–199.

regulation. In 1938 he helped draft the Civil Aeronautics Act of 1938, His interest in airplanes proved to be way ahead of the times. In 1939 he introduced with Senator Burton Wheeler a bill to reorganize the railroads and place them under the regulation of the Interstate Commerce Commission. As a member of the Military Subcommittee of the Appropriations committee, he visited defense installations in the United States, Panama, Cuba, and Puerto Rico.

Railroads continued to fascinate Harry. As noted, he was co-chairman of a subcommittee investigating railroads which was headed by Wheeler. It was the committee headed by the redoubtable Burton Wheeler. Truman's populist antagonism to big business in the thirties fueled the committee hearings, which concluded that exploitative Wall Street bankers and lawyers were causing the railroad's problems. Bankers were once again his nemesis. Senator Truman led efforts to pass regulatory legislation that would make the railroads less vulnerable to wasteful and destructive competition. This flew in the face of the classical theory of the times that valued free market competition as always efficient. Unfortunately, conflicts between labor and business interests blocked passage of the bill.

He was more successful with another piece of legislation. He worked hard on what became the Public Utility Holding Company Act, designed as a blow against public power cartels. In the process he had his first brush with big time lobbying and high-powered witnesses. Witnesses for the public utilities included such prominent Wall Street figures as Wendell Willkie, president of the Commonwealth & Southern, and John W. Davis, the former Democratic presidential candidate. In June, the bill passed the Senate by a wide margin. It was a piece of populist legislation and another New Deal victory.

His smaller assignments included the aforementioned Public Buildings and Grounds Committee and the Printing Committee, headed by the formidable Carl Hayden and responsible primarily for the *Congressional Record*. He did not much care for his assignment to the District of Columbia Committee, because he thought the District ought to have self-government. He seldom missed meetings and was known for speaking rarely and listening much.

Throughout, Truman was a New Dealer. He repeatedly voted with President Roosevelt because he genuinely wanted to do what was best for the common people at a time when so many were desperate. He was one of them, and he knew they were suffering. He also knew the value of voting with the President, both as an article of faith and as a way ahead. He was praised by Alben Barkley of Kentucky, assistant to the majority leader, for voting right, which meant "left." Congress labored through the sweltering summer of 1935, the worst summer of the infamous Dust Bowl. President Roosevelt had told Congress it could not go home without passing his entire program.

Among those who Harry drew close to was Bennett Clark, also of Missouri. Like "Cactus Jack" Garner, the vice president, he enjoyed a social "libation" over lunch, or in mid-afternoon, or day's end, or most any time. Harry enjoyed the banter and storytelling that went with this social side of senatorial life. It was close to the comradeship of Army life which he had enjoyed. For special guests like Clark, Harry kept a supply of Tom Pendergast's best bourbon. In that office he heard plenty of criticism of Pendergast, but no senator raised his voice against the quality of Pendergast liquor. Other such supplies were kept by the Secretary of the Senate, Colonel Edwin Halsey in an office only a short stroll across the hall from the chamber. Unlike Clark, Harry had a rule of one stroll, one drink only.

Truman felt the cloud he was under begin to recede during the second half of his first term in the Senate. Not only was his standing among his colleagues improved, he was assigned more spacious offices. Truman was now perceived as dogged, productive, respectful of the opinion of others, good-natured, and extremely likable. This reputation soon would be tested.

Meanwhile, President Roosevelt would see highs and lows in early 1937. In his acceptance speech at the convention, Roosevelt said, "To some generations much is given. Of other generations much is expected. This generation of Americans has a rondevous with destiny." This masterful speech was followed by his second inaugural address in January 1937, when he become more specific. "I see one third of a nation ill-housed, ill-clad, ill-nourished." The Congress and the country waited in anticipation to see what new legislation he would demand.

Congress did not stand in his way; rather, it was the Supreme Court, which had found some New Deal programs unconstitutional. Roosevelt hatched a scheme in February to reshape the Supreme Court to his liking. Without consulting Congress, he decided to increase the size of the Court, to "pack it." The whole thing was a blunder, damaging to Roosevelt and ultimately to the Senate.

The opposition in the Senate was fierce, especially among Democrats! The opposition included not only conservatives like Carter Glass and Bennett Clark, but reliable Roosevelt men such as Connally, Wheeler, Barkley, and even Truman. Virtually every Democratic senator who had been a Roosevelt loyalist now found himself caught between vehement pressure from the White House on the one hand and outrage at home on the other. Garner, Roosevelt's own Vice President, had become so annoyed over the affair that he packed his bags and went back to Texas. Truman and Barkley ultimately decided to stand with the President, but without much enthusiasm. By a margin of 50 votes, the Senate sent the Court bill back to the Judiciary Committee, where it died.

On Monday, December 20, 1937, Senator Truman delivered the second of his assaults on corporate greed and corruption. In an earlier speech in June he had recalled how Jesse James, in order to rob the Rock Island Railroad, had to get up early in the morning and risk his life to make off with $3,000. Now, by means of holding companies, modern-day financiers had stolen $70 million from the same railroad. In his new speech he attacked the power of Wall Street and the larger evil of money worship, sounding very much like his boyhood hero, William Jennings Bryan. He proceeded to attack the gigantic receiverships and reorganizations that destroyed railroads, and named the powerful law firms involved. He went on,

> How these gentlemen, the highest of the high-hats in the legal profession, resort to tricks that would make an ambulance chaser in a coroner's court blush with shame? The same gentlemen, if the past is any guide to the future, will come out of the pending receiverships with more and fatter fees, and wind up by becoming attorneys for the new and reorganized railroad companies at fat yearly retainers, and they will probably earn them, because it will be their business to get by the Interstate Commerce Commission, to interpret, and to see that the courts interpret, laws passed by the Congress as they want them construed.[7]

The underlying problem was avarice, on which he elaborated:

> We worship money instead of honor. A billionaire, in our estimation, is much greater in these days in the eyes of the people than the public servant who works for the public interest. It makes no difference if the billionaire rode to wealth on the sweat of little children and the blood of underpaid labor. No one ever considered Carnegie libraries steeped in the blood of the Homestead steelworkers, but they are. We do not remember that the Rockefeller Foundation is founded on the dead miners of the Colorado Fuel & Iron Company and a dozen other

---

[7] Speech: *Congressional Record*, December 20, 1937, 2482–2495.

similar performances. We worship Mammon, and until we go back to ancient fundamentals and return to the Giver of the Tables of Law and His teachings, these conditions are going to remain with us.

It is a pity that Wall Street, with its ability to control all the wealth of the nation and to hire the best law brains in the country, has not produced some statesmen, some men who could see the dangers of bigness and of the concentration of the control of wealth. Instead of working to meet the situation, they are still employing the best law brains to serve greed and self interest. People can stand only so much, and one of these days there will be a settlement.[8]

Senator Truman saw the country's unemployment and unrest as the fault of too much concentration of power and population, too much bigness in everything. Full Employment would eventually become his goal. He thought the country would better off if 60 percent of the assets of all insurance companies were not concentrated in just four companies. He drove his points home:

Wild greed along these lines I have been describing brought on the Depression. When investment bankers, so-called, continually load great transportation companies with debt in order to sell securities to savings banks and insurance companies so they can make a commission, the well finally runs dry....There is no magic solution to the condition of the railroads, but one thing is certain — no formula, however scientific, will work without men of proper character responsible for physical and financial operations of the roads and for the administration of the laws provided by Congress.[9]

Not surprisingly, the speech was front-page news in *The New York Times*. After all, it included Truman's theory of the cause of the Depression. It drew the immediate attention of labor leaders and reform-minded citizens across the country. The vested interests urged him to call off the hearings. The hearings continued. Moreover, Truman's courage was visible again as he began to take positions on civil rights that belied his Missouri background. He supported legislation that would abolish the poll tax and prevent lynchings.

He was also outspoken on national defense preparedness. "We must not close our eyes to the possibility of another war," he told an American Legion Meeting at Larchmont, New York, in 1938, "because conditions in Europe have developed

---

[8] *Ibid.*
[9] *Ibid.*

to a point likely to cause an explosion any time." He decried the isolationists who refused to sign the Versailles Treaty and to join the League of Nations. He felt that the United States did not accept its responsibility as a world power.

In normal times, a one-term senator of a majority party running on the same ticket with a popular president would be the odds-on favorite for reelection. This, however, was not the case for Harry Truman in 1940. After six years, he had little legislation to his personal credit, and his close identity with Tom Pendergast of Kansas City was now a major liability. As luck would have it, Pendergast had been convicted of tax evasion and sent to prison for 15 months in 1939. Truman, who owed so much to Pendergast, refused to abandon his ally. Instead he stubbornly defended him. It made Truman look like an uncritical partisan turning a blind eye to his mentor's corruption. He thought of not running again, and told Bess, "The terrible things done by the high ups in KC (Kansas City) will be a lead weight on me from now on."[10]

He went on to oppose President Roosevelt's seeking a third term and said his own choice for President was Bennett Clark. Never mind that Clark was a conservative, isolationist, and alcoholic. His opposition to a third term for Roosevelt was sincere, but the Bennett Clark presidential boom-let came to nothing. Truman believed that Roosevelt was not well enough to last through another term.

Truman by now had a record to run on. Several years of investigations into railroad financiers had resulted in the Truman-Wheeler Bill, still to be passed, providing protection for the railroads as a mainstay of the nation's transportation system. He supported the Agricultural Adjustment Act of 1938 that gave farmers price supports. In 1939 he had voted for expanding the low-cost housing program, for increased funds for public works, increased federal contributions to old-age pensions. He was active in the passage of the Civil Aeronautics Act, to bring uniform rules to the burgeoning new aviation industry. He was basically running on the New Deal ticket.

On February 3, 1940, Truman announced formally that he was declaring his candidacy for reelection to the United States Senate.[11] FDR offered no support and the Missouri press opposed him. This made Truman the underdog in the primary against a popular Missouri governor, Lloyd Stark. It was destined to be a

---

[10] Letter from Harry S. Truman to Elizabeth Bess Truman, October 1, 1939, Harry S. Truman Library.
[11] For specific dates and chronology in this chapter as well as in other chapters, I have relied on 'Chronology: Harry S. Truman's Life and Presidency,' Harry S. Truman Library, available online at www.trumanlibrary. org/chron/index.html.

close shave: Truman won by not quite 8,000 votes of 665,000 cast. He did well with the farmers and black community. Importantly, he carried Jackson county once again. It was a minor miracle: His outspoken backing of the New Deal and his strong support of military preparedness in a time of international threats carried the day. Three days after this primary election, when Harry Truman walked into the Senate Chamber, both floor leaders and all the Democrats present rushed to greet him. In the general election in the fall Senator Truman failed to do as well as President Roosevelt but nonetheless won by 44,000 votes. He and Bess set off for Washington in a brand-new pearl gray, two-door 1941 Chrysler Royal.

Privately, Truman was in despair over Roosevelt, Pendergast, and the terrible state of the world. As if to punctuate his concerns, in late August 1939, Hitler and the Russians had signed a nonaggression pact. On September 1, Hitler invaded Poland. Britain and France declared war on Germany. Truman attended the Washington premiere of Frank Capra's *Mr Smith Goes to Washington*, art imitating life. He hoped it would cheer him up. The movie had a blanket portrayal of senators as crooks and fools. He was distressed too by the fact that the chief figure of corruption was a heavy-handed machine boss who acted much like Tom Pendergast and ruled a city called Jackson.

Meanwhile, abroad Hitler's *Luftwaffe* crossed the Channel to bomb British ports, airfields, and London. The first great air battle in history, the Battle of Britain, began in July of 1940. In Washington Franklin Roosevelt delivered by radio a "fireside chat" to be known as his "Arsenal of Democracy" speech. "We must become the great arsenal of democracy," he said. "For this is an emergency as serious as war itself...."

Radio reached its zenith of popularity in the 1930s, and Roosevelt had mastered it. By 1939 about 90 percent of the population owned a radio set. Americans loved to laugh at the attics of such comedians as Jack Benny, Fred Allen, George Burns and Gracie Allen, Amos and Andy, and Fibber McGee and Molly. There also were the heroics of the Lone Ranger, the Green Hornet, the Shadow, and Jack Armstrong, all-American boy, which thrilled listeners both young and old and sold countless boxes of cereal. Meanwhile, news broadcasts by commentators like H.V Kaltenborn and Edward R. Murrow kept the public aware of the increasing crisis in Europe. Truman particularly liked Murrow, and fearfully listened to the tirades of Adolf Hitler on the radio.

Before a joint session of Congress on January 6, 1941, Roosevelt delivered a second summons to action. A few days later came the Lend-Lease plan to send

Britain arms on credit, a prelude to the Marshall Plan. Truman listened intently for he was now a member of both the Military Affairs Committee and the Military Subcommittee of the Appropriations Committee. In September he voted for the first peacetime draft. The Army's Chief of Staff, General George C. Marshall, went before Congress and called for a force of 2 million men and another $1 billion (on top of $10 billion already awarded in defense contracts) to cover expenses. For his part, Senator Truman, now a colonel in the reserves, went to Marshal's office to enlist. Marshall told him he was too old and could better serve his country in the Senate. Marshall was quickly added to Truman's list of "great men."

Senator Truman was investigating again. The Truman Committee, as it was known, documented waste and mismanagement in the construction of Army camps among other things. Once again, Truman butted heads with big business. There was a shortage of aluminum, so vital for warplanes, too little copper, zinc, and rubber. The Aluminum Company of America, Alcoa, had a near monopoly on the manufacture of the lightweight metal, but kept claiming it could supply both domestic and defense needs, while not coming close. The production of magnesium was even more woefully inadequate. A secret arrangement had been made thorough an interlocking cartel, between Alcoa and the giant German firm of I.G. Farben. To safeguard the American market, Alcoa had agreed to hold back on producing magnesium, but also to sell what magnesium it owed to the Germans at a cut price. As a result, Germany had far more magnesium than the United States. Alcoa was colluding with a potential enemy.

The German company, I. G. Farben was involved in other schemes. Through its agreements with I.G. Farben, Standard Oil of New Jersey had intentionally delayed the development of synthetic rubber plants. Standard Oil had agreed with the German company that in return for Farben giving Standard Oil a monopoly in the oil industry, Standard Oil would give the Farben Company complete control of patents in the chemical field, including rubber. Therefore, when American rubber manufacturers made overtures to Standard Oil for licenses to produce synthetic rubber, they were either refused or offered licenses on very unfavorable terms. One thing was transparent: I.G. Farben's position was dictated by the German government. Big business was playing by its own rules. Beyond these matters, Truman worried about the shortage of steel. American automobile manufacturers had been allowed to do as they wished, which was to keep producing cars as usual in 1941.

The root of many of these troubles was the Office of Production Management (OPM). As noted, one of the accomplishments of the Truman Committee's first report was to persuade Roosevelt to replace the OPM with an all new War Production Board under a single head. The OPM had been dominated by executives from American corporations who were still serving the interests of big business.

By then, Pearl Harbor had been bombed. Thereafter, in early 1942 Singapore fell to the Japanese, then Bataan, with the surrender of General Jonathan M. Wainwright and some 75,000 American and Filipino troops, the largest surrender of an American fighting force since Appomattox. Leningrad was still under siege. German U-boats were sinking oil tankers almost at will along the eastern seaboard of the United States. It was a dark time. Later, the devastation of the Naval Fleet by the Japanese would be chronicled in the movie, *From Here to Eternity* (which featured Frank Sinatra in a comeback).

In a speech on the Senate floor that summer of 1942, Truman called for a second front in Europe to relieve the Russians. In another speech, this time at home in Jackson County he said the war was only a tragic continuation of "the one we fought in 1917 and 1918." The victors, he said, "had the opportunity to compel a peace that would protect us from war for many generations. But they missed the opportunity." It was a conclusion reached much earlier by John Maynard Keynes who had been at Versailles. Isolationism had brought on the present conflict.[12]

The Truman Committee continued its work. What Truman had said in the Senate in earlier years about the evils of big banks, big insurance companies, big corporations still had the ring of truth. The committee disclosed that Curtiss-Wright had manufactured faulty airplane engines for delivery to combat forces. There were problems with the B-26 bomber built by the Glenn Martin Company. Its wings were not wide enough. Glenn Martin executives said that did not matter, because they already had the contract. Truman said that if the wings were not fixed, the committee would see the contract at Glenn Martin ended. The company agreed to widen the wings. At the Irvin Works the Truman Committee found that at least 5 percent of the plant's production failed to meet Navy specifications, yet was being labeled and delivered as up to standard. The *Schenectady*, built by Henry J. Kaiser broke in two.

---

[12] John Maynard Keynes, *The Economic Consequences of the Peace* (London: Macmillan & Co., 1919). This masterpiece is worth reading today both for its literary style and for its historical vision.

The Truman Committee held hundreds of hearings and issued dozens of reports between 1942 and 1944. They won almost unanimous praise from the press and the public for saving billions of dollars and advancing the war effort. *Time* magazine called his committee's work America's "first line of defense." In a poll of journalists, Truman was among the ten most important contributors to the war effort in Washington, and the only member of Congress to win the accolade. Others described the committee's work as the most successful congressional investigative effort in American history. It succeeded in putting checks on big business, labor unions, and government bureaucracies.

Through it all, Truman radiated good health and youthful energy. He had greater vitality than ever, and had new confidence. Senator Harry Truman was having a great time as head of the Truman Committee. By 1943 the committee had produced 21 reports on subjects ranging from gasoline rationing, lumber, farm machinery, to the loss of American shipping to U-boats. The committee saved the country an estimated $15 billion. Truman was on the cover of the March 8, 1943 *Time* magazine.

Truman was the guiding spirit behind a Senate resolution for the establishment of the United Nations. He made a Midwest speaking tour in the summer of 1943 to spread the internationalist word under the sponsorship of the United Nations Association. In one speech he said, "History has bestowed on us a solemn responsibility....We failed before to give a genuine peace — we dare not fail this time. We must not repeat the blunders of the past."[13]

Truman's reputation was virtually spotless around the White House. In the summer of 1943, a year in advance of the Democratic National convention, Truman was being talked of as a candidate for Vice President. He had been asked what he thought of Vice President Henry Wallace. Truman smiled, tongue in cheek, and said Wallace was the best Secretary of Agriculture the country ever had. Though it was talked about with increasing frequency, Truman said he wanted to remain in the Senate. Truman explained to a friend, "The Vice President simply resides over the Senate and sits around hoping for a funeral. It is a very high office which consists entirely of honor and I don't have any ambition to hold an office like that."[14]

---

[13] Speech during Summer 1943, "The Evolution of an Internationalist," Harry S. Truman Library.
[14] Quoted in William Helm, *Harry Truman: A Political Biography* (New York: Duell, Sloan and Pearce, 1947), p. 220.

Senator Truman Speaks at Ground Breaking of Pratt and Whitney Plant in
Kansas City (undated).
Source: Harry S. Truman Library (78–949).

Mr Vice President

In 1944 speculation intensified about whether Roosevelt would retain Vice President Henry Wallace on the ticket. The meteoric rise of Harry Truman put him on everybody's short list for the second spot. As Senator, he had established himself as much more than the senator from Pendergast. Still, his nomination for the vice presidency in 1944 is one of those events shrouded in mystery, and we will never entirely understand it. President Roosevelt followed "a Byzantine course."[15] One

---

[15] For the whole story, including the fascinating intrigue, see David McCullough, *Truman* (New York: Simon & Schuster, 1992), pp. 292–314.

thing was clear; Wallace was a divisive force in the Democratic Party. Worse, he was in line to succeed an unhealthy President.

Journalist Allen Drury said, Wallace "looks like a hayseed, talks like a prophet, and acts like an embarrassed schoolboy."[16] The main charge against him was he was too liberal. He was intellectual, a mystic who spoke Russian, was remote, and controversial. Roosevelt showed his intention to dump Wallace by sending him on a fact-finding trip to China and Russia in the spring of 1944. From that distance, Wallace could not push for his candidacy. James Byrnes, former South Carolina senator and Supreme Court associate justice posed a similar problem. He had headed the Office of War Mobilization in 1943 and was known as the "assistant president." He was favored by the conservative wing of the party. Roosevelt also indicated possible interest in the Speaker of the House Sam Rayburn, Senator Alben Barkley of Kentucky, Supreme Court Justice William O. Douglas, as well as Wallace, Byrnes, and Truman.

In the end, Roosevelt and the party's bosses selected Truman as the best alternative. He had ties to conservatives and liberals and was a solid New Deal supporter from a border state. Moreover, his reputation for patriotism and honesty were unimpeachable. It was the second Missouri compromise. But to many did it matter all that much? Truman would serve in the shadow of a larger-than-life President who, at the end of a fourth term, could anoint anyone he wanted to succeed him. Like other vice presidents he would fall into obscurity.

Excerpt for a lone lunch meeting at the White House, Truman had no direct contact with the President during the campaign. Yet Truman traveled the length of the country by train and spoke warmly on Roosevelt's behalf. Still, it was a contest between Roosevelt and Governor Thomas E. Dewey of New York. Roosevelt won by 3.5 million out of 47 million popular votes, and topped Dewey by four to one in the electoral college.

Like during the campaign, Truman seldom saw Roosevelt after the election. Truman was alone with Roosevelt only twice during the 82 days he served as Vice President. Roosevelt never discussed the imminent development of an atomic bomb. Truman didn't know what was going on and Roosevelt was not going to tell him. This, despite Roosevelt's failing health: He had severe hypertension and congestive heart failure.

---

[16] Quoted by Alonzo L. Hamby, *A Life of Harry S. Truman: Man of the People* (Oxford, New York: Oxford University Press, 1995), p. 278.

Lord Moran, Winston Churchill's physician, concluded at Yalta in February 1945 that Roosevelt would not live for more than another few months. Despite all appearances, Truman was no more prepared for Roosevelt's sudden death than anyone else. He received an urgent call from the White House late on the afternoon of April 12, 1945. Brought up to the President's quarters, Truman found himself in the room with the First Lady, Eleanor Roosevelt. She said, "Harry, the President is dead."

A stunned Truman asked, "Is there anything I can do for you?"

Mrs Roosevelt replied, "Is there anything we can do for you, Harry? For you are the one in trouble now."[17]

Harry Truman was thrust onto the world stage with no national executive experience and was to replace the longest-serving and most revered President since Lincoln, in the midst of a World War. His experience as Vice President was short and shallow. Now it would be his task to bring the war to an end and demobilize for peace. The challenges were great; how would Harry measure up?

---

[17] Truman, *Memoirs, Vol. 1, op. cit.*, p. 5.

Chapter 4

The Economics of War and Peace

On April 12, 1945, Harry S. Truman was sworn in as the 33rd president of the United States upon the death of President Franklin D. Roosevelt. In the days immediately after becoming President, Alben Barkley advised Truman: "Have confidence in yourself. If you do not, the people will lose confidence in you."[1] He took the advice to heart, despite some initial doubts about himself.

He made clear his intent to fulfill Roosevelt's wartime and postwar plans. On his first day in office, he directed Secretary of State Edward Stettinius to announce that the United Nations organizing conference scheduled for April 25 in San Francisco would take place as planned. On April 16, the day after Roosevelt was buried in Hyde Park, Truman gave a speech before a joint session of Congress that was nationally broadcast on radio. He promised to pursue the aim of unconditional surrender by the Axis powers.

Events in Europe at the end of April and the beginning of May seemed to cooperate with the President Truman's wishes. Italy's dictator, Benito Mussolini, was assassinated by antifascist partisans, signaling the collapse of his regime. This was followed by Germany's unconditional surrender on May 7, 1945, following Adolf Hitler's suicide in a Berlin Bunker. The next day was Truman's 61st birthday.

---

[1] Alben Barkley, *That Reminds Me — The Autobiography of the Veep* (Garden City, NY: Doubleday, 1954), p. 197.

That day, he announced the end of the war in Europe over radio at 9:00am (V-E Day). There was little time to celebrate because left on the table was the situation in Japan.

He was not overwhelmed by Roosevelt's shadow. On his own, beginning in June, Truman enjoyed an 87 percent approval rating according to a Gallup poll. When Gallup asked, "What one thing do you like best about the way Harry Truman is handling his job?" A plurality of respondents said, "His honesty, sincerity, and friendliness."[2] The prompt and decisive end of the war in Europe helped his ratings.

In seeking a quick and complete Japanese surrender, Truman was mostly concerned with saving American lives. Nearly 400,000 troops had already died in the war. He worried too about the prospect of the Soviet Union entering the war against Japan. Part of Moscow's price for joining the Pacific fighting seemed to be Allied acceptance of its control of Eastern Europe, especially Poland, all of which was unacceptable to Truman. When Truman had met with Soviet foreign minister Vyacheslav Molotov at the White House on April 23, he insisted on adherence to postwar democratic arrangements in the nations under Soviet control. Later he described what he gave Molotov, "the one-two, right to the jaw." Still, Molotov gave no indication of allowing free elections in Poland or anywhere else in Eastern Europe. This was reinforced by a May 12 telegram from British prime minister Winston Churchill to Truman, "An iron curtain is drawn down upon their [the Soviet] front. We do not know what is going on behind."[3]

Truman, however, was determined not to break openly with the Russians. Harry Hopkins, with Truman's acquiescence, all but conceded Soviet control of Poland, while Stalin affirmed his decision to enter the war against Japan, while abandoning Soviet demands for a veto over Security Council agenda items in the United Nations. Moreover, Stalin agreed to meet with Truman and Churchill at Potsdam outside of Berlin in July. The conference site was chosen by Stalin and was inside the Red bloc. The conference, from July 17 until August 2, tested Truman's hopes. Churchill was weakened by the defeat of his Conservative Party in the British parliamentary election. (He was replaced as Prime Minister by the Labour Party leader Clement Attlee on July 29.) Truman and Attlee could not

---

[2] George H. Gallup, *The Gallup Poll, Public Opinion, 1935–1971* (New York: Random House, 1972), pp. 503–504, 512, 558.

[3] Quoted by David McCullough, *Truman* (New York: Simon & Schuster, 1992), p. 383.

command the respect Stalin had for Roosevelt and Churchill, his wartime allies in Europe. Upon his return to the US, Truman privately denounced the Soviets as running a "police government pure and simple. A few top hands just take clubs, pistols and concentration camps and rule people on the lower levels."[4] This was a private view: Truman continued to keep his doubts to himself.

The Potsdam Conference

For the conference at Potsdam, the State Department, War Department, Army, Navy, and Air Corps, the White House staff, and Secret Service were all involved. As were the British and the Russians. Flying there, Truman would witness from the air the appalling spectacle of shattered bridges, railroads, the wreckage of factories, entire cities in ruins, a scarred, burned land where, he knew, people were living like animals among the debris, scavenging for food. The threat of disease and mass starvation hung everywhere. It was a sight that would instruct Truman on the formulation of the Marshall Plan.

Oddly, the central issues to be resolved at Potsdam were no different than those at Yalta: The political future of Eastern Europe (and Poland in particular), the occupation and dismantling of Germany, and a commitment from Russia to help defeat Japan, which Truman viewed as his main purpose in going. He also had a pet proposal of his own for ensuring free navigation of all inland waterways and the great canals, an idea he was sure would go far to guarantee future peace in the world. Of course, there was still another reason for the meeting: Truman needed to get to know the other two of the Big Three, namely Stalin and Churchill. Indeed, if asked who in the world they most admired, now that Roosevelt was gone, most Americans would have said Churchill, and probably, after some thought, Truman would have, too. This, despite the fact that the great empire of England was no more.

Truman found Churchill to be a charming and clever companion. And he meant clever in the English not the Kentucky sense. Stalin, "the Man of Steel", was the single most powerful figure in the world. He was the absolute dictator of over 180 million people in a country representing one sixth of the earth's surface. He was, surprisingly, "a little bit of a squirt," as Truman described him, standing

---

[4] Quoted from Truman's diary in McCullough, *Truman* (New York: Simon & Schuster, 1992), p. 451.

about 5 foot 5. He had small, squinty eyes that were a strange yellow-gray and there were streaks of gray in his mustache and coarse hair. He was badly pockmarked, his color poor, a Kremlin complexion. Truman, dressed in his freshly pressed double-breasted gray suit and two-toned summer shoes, looked a picture of vitality by contrast.

Stalin said that as they had already agreed at Yalta, the Soviets were ready to declare war on Japan and attack Manchuria by mid-August. To be sure that Truman understood, Stalin repeated that the Red Army would soon be at war with Japan, "as agreed at Yalta." Truman had what he wanted. Churchill still considered Russia "a riddle wrapped in a mystery inside an enigma." He warned both Roosevelt and Truman repeatedly of the Russian menace to Europe, confessing that he still liked Stalin the man. Truman also found "Uncle Joe" to be a likeable person. A likeable man who had killed probably five million peasants and put 10 million in forced labor camps. The composer Shostakovich once remarked, "and all I saw was corpses, mountains, of corpses." Ivan the Terrible, who may have been worse, was Stalin's favorite czar.

Truman proposed a Council of Foreign Ministers to make the necessary preparations for a peace conference. Stalin was dubious. Truman submitted a draft on how the administration of Germany should be handled. He read a prepared statement on implementation of the Yalta Declaration, which pledged the three powers to assist the people of all liberated European countries to establish democratic governments through free elections. He said, "Since the Yalta Conference, the obligations assumed under this declaration have not been carried out."[5] Of particular concern to Truman were Romania, Bulgaria, and Greece. Churchill said he needed time to consider the document. Eventually, Churchill would express his agreement with the President.

It was Stalin's turn. Stalin wished to discuss acquisition of the German Navy (which was in British hands), German reparations, the question of trusteeships for the Soviet Union (by which he meant colonies), the future of Franco's Spain, and the future of Poland. He also turned to the question of including China in preparations for the peace conference. Churchill thought that was a needless complication. It was generally thought that Churchill talked too much while Truman was very business-like.

---

[5] Foreign Relations of the United States, *Conference of Berlin (Potsdam)*, 1945, Volume II, p. 643.

"We cannot get away from the results of the war," said Stalin.[6] Churchill insisted on defining what constituted Germany. To Stalin, the Germany of the moment was one with eastern boundaries being determined by the position of the Red Army. To Truman, it was the Germany of 1937. This turned out to be the starting point. The day was saved by a party that night. Truman played Paderewski's *Minuet in G*, the piece Paderewski had demonstrated for him in Kansas City 45 years earlier.

Meanwhile, back at the table in Potsdam, Churchill again grew extremely long-winded and though an outward show of friendship continued around the table, an edge of tension could also be felt. In a single sentence, Stalin hit on the hard reality underlying nearly every issue before them, the crux of much of the frustration and divisiveness to come was Germany.

Afterward, Truman went again to Berlin, to the American sector, to speak at the raising of the flag that had flown over the capitol in Washington the day Pearl Harbor was attacked. Speaking without notes, Truman concluded: "If we can put this tremendous machine of ours, which has made victory possible, to work for peace, we can look forward to the greatest age in the history of mankind. This is what we propose to do."[7]

Potsdam and the Atomic Bomb

The atomic bomb was one of the best-kept secrets of the war, at least in the US, Soviet agents had informed the Kremlin of American and British work on the bomb. Truman himself did not learn about the Manhattan Project until he was briefed by Secretary of War Henry Stimson, and did not receive substantial detail on the project until April 25, 13 days after taking office. Stalin knew about the atomic bomb before Truman. While he was at Potsdam, Truman received word of the bomb's successful test at Alamogordo in the New Mexico desert. On July 21, he received a full account of the weapon's devastating power. The flash at Alamogordo had been visible for 250 miles, the sound carrying 50 miles. Churchill agreed that Stalin should be told about the bomb, sooner rather than later, without the particulars. Thereafter Truman was firmer in rejecting Soviet demands. When Truman told Stalin of the bomb's power, Stalin was not the least

---

[6] *Ibid.*, p. 96.
[7] Public Papers, Harry S. Truman, July 20, 1945, p. 195, Harry S. Truman Library.

Winston Churchill, Joseph Stalin, and Truman shaking hands at the Potsdam Conference, 23 July 1945.

Source: Harry S. Truman Library (63-1457-29).

bit surprised. Stalin merely said, he hoped we would make "good use of it against the Japanese."[8]

The next day Truman confirmed an order to go forward with plans to use the bomb against Japan. He was focused on forcing Japan into a prompt and uncon-ditional surrender before the Soviets even entered the war against Japan. His

---

[8] Harry S. Truman, *Memoirs, Volume 1: Year of Decisions* (New York: Doubleday, 1955), p. 416.

decision was quick even though for more than half a century, an argument has raged over whether Truman needed to use the atomic bomb to end the war. Truman saw it as "the most terrible bomb in the history of the world," and thought its development might be the fulfillment of the biblical warning of "the fire destruction prophesied in the Euphrates Valley Era after Noah and the fabulous Ark."[9] Still, nothing weighed on Truman more heavily than the losses that American troops would suffer in an invasion of Japan's home islands. The US military chiefs estimated that between 250,000 and 500,000 American deaths would occur in an invasion, which would be roughly equal to all US troop losses to that point in the war. This is what led to Truman's decision to use the atomic bomb. The bomb had cost $2 billion. To Churchill, there never was a decision to use the bomb. It was simply a given.

A given? "There never was a moment's discussion as to whether the atomic bomb should be used or not," Churchill later wrote. "To avert a vast, indefinite butchery, to bring the war to an end, to give peace to the world, to lay healing hands upon its tortured peoples by a manifestation of overwhelming power at the cost of a few explosions, seemed, after all our toils and perils, a miracle of deliverance....The decision whether or not to use the atomic bomb to compel the surrender of Japan was never even an issue." Agreement was "unanimous," Churchill concluded. He never heard "the slightest suggestion that we should do otherwise."[10] At Potsdam, recalled the American diplomat Charles Bohlen, the "spirit of mercy was not throbbing in the breast of any Allied official."[11] In cost-benefit terms, it was a matter of American lives versus Japanese lives. However, it would have been American soldiers and it turned out to be mostly Japanese civilians. The ultimate choice was between sacrificing 250,000–500,000 US servicemen or 150,000 Japanese civilians. This was the cold economic calculus. The holding of the atomic monopoly left the decision in Truman's hands.

The attacks on Hiroshima on August 6 and then Nagasaki on August 9 eventually killed perhaps as many as 150,000 civilians. Some 10,000 Japanese soldiers also were killed. Truman received a Japanese offer to surrender on August 10, but assumed that this was a ploy and ordered a thousand-plane raid on Tokyo on August 13. The next day, Japanese radio read an address from the

---

[9] Quoted by McCullough, *Truman*, op. cit., p. 443.
[10] Winston S. Churchill, *The Second World War: Triumph and Tragedy* (New York: Bantam Books, 1962), p. 546.
[11] Charles Bohlen, *Witness to History, 1929–1969* (New York: W. W. Norton, 1973), p. 231.

emperor accepting the Allied peace terms. Truman announced the end of the war with Japan at a 7:00pm press conference. As Truman preferred, the Pacific War ended before Russia could attack Japan.

In just three months in office, Harry Truman had been faced with larger, more difficult, more far-reaching decisions than any President before him. Neither Lincoln after first taking office, nor Franklin Roosevelt in his first hundred days, had to contend with issues of such magnitude and also coming all at once.

The Spoils of War

Despite its promise, Potsdam produced little. The only consensus was the one reached by Truman and his aides regarding the use of the atomic bomb and the contradictory agreement by Stalin to invade Japan. It should have been a time of celebration. Truman had insisted on results, not just talk, something in the bag at the end of of every day, as Churchill observed. Most of all, he wanted the future of Germany settled satisfactorily. Germany was the key, but there also was the issue of free elections in Poland, Eastern Europe, and the Balkans. Truman made little progress with Stalin.

Meanwhile, the Red army was on the move; it had pushed to the Oder River and on to the Neisse and Sothoswe rivers. These were in western Poland and it was agreed that the rivers would serve as Poland's western frontier. Poland also was given the southern portion of East Prussia, including the port of Danzig, while the Soviet Union was granted the northern portion. Free elections in Poland were up in the air. What was to happen to Italy, Bulgaria, Finland, Hungary, and Romania was postponed, left to the Council of Foreign Ministers to resolve at some unspecified time. Germany, already portioned off into the four zones of military occupation — American, British, Russian, and French — was in effect divided down the middle, between East and West. The three powers had agreed to demilitarization of the German state and that Nazi war criminals would be brought to justice in Nuremberg. Meantime, the Soviet Union got the lion's share of reparations, mostly in capital equipment. Soviet occupation of Eastern Europe was a *fait accompli*.

As luck would have it, Russia was not finished with Japan. On August 9, a million Russian troops crossed into Manchuria. This despite a second atomic bomb having been dropped on the major Japanese seaport of Nagasaki. Truman should have been more careful in what he wished for. Less than 24 hours after Nagasaki, on August 14, the Japanese government accepted the Potsdam Declaration with the understanding the Emperor would remain sovereign. General Douglas MacArthur had been appointed the Supreme Allied Commander to receive the surrender.

No sooner than the Pacific War had ended did President Truman have to turn his attention to US-Soviet tensions. Moscow was as unyielding as ever on the control of Bulgaria, Romania, and Poland. In their East German occupation zone, they transferred territories to Poland. Moreover, the Soviets would not consider proposals for free elections in Korea that would unify the country under one government. They did not want to lose control of the area north of the 38th parallel, where they had installed a Communist regime. Nor would they agree to withdraw troops from northern Iran. Further, Truman believed that Russia intended an invasion of Turkey and the seizure of the Black Sea Straits to the Mediterranean. The only language the Russians understood was that of military might.

On top of the Soviet problems, in the fall of 1945, after Japan's surrender, China fell into a civil war. Once the Pacific War ended, the tensions between Chiang Kai-shek's Nationalist government and Mao Tse-tung's Communist Party could not be held in check. To stop the fighting in China, Truman asked General George C. Marshall, the former army chief of staff, to negotiate an end to the civil war. These developments in China, combined with a deterioration in Soviet-American relations, undermined the hopes of many Americans for a more placid postwar world. Truman's popularity suffered as isolationist sentiments resurfaced across the country.

On the domestic front, Truman proposed an economic bill of rights that would assure every American of a job, food, clothing, housing, and adequate medical care. He called for economic security in a September 6 message to Congress that aimed at a smooth transition from a wartime to a peacetime economy. There was widespread concern that the end of the fighting, the reduced defense spending, and the need to absorb 11.4 million of demobilized troops into the labor force would lead to another Great Depression. Truman remembered the postwar slump in 1920 that cost him his haberdasher's shop. To guard against a serious downturn, Truman called for full employment legislation guaranteeing everyone a job at a good wage, fair employment practices to ensure against racial discrimination in hiring, affordable housing, aid to small businesses and farmers, a strengthened social security system, and a national health insurance program to protect Americans against the costs of serious illness.

The Recession of 1945

To understand the difficulties of transitioning from a wartime to a peacetime economy we need to consider military expenditures during WWII. Table 4.1 shows total military expenditures and gross domestic product (GDP), as well as military expenditures as a share of GDP. The latter measure illustrates the dominance of the military, especially during 1942–1945. The military build-up was rapid after 1940, peaking at nearly half of GDP during 1943–1944. By that time and continuing into 1945, the USA was clearly a militarized economy. Private consumer expenditures were limited by rationing. Some 11 million out of a 66 million labor force was in the armed forces by 1945. By that time women comprised a large share of the civilian labor force.

The demand for war materials and enlistment in the armed forces ended the Great Depression, beginning around 1940. The effect of intentional federal deficits was purely Keynesian. The unemployment rate was 14.6 percent in 1940, but dropped to 9.9 percent in 1941, then to 4.7 percent in 1942. Great unused industrial capacity enabled the economy to switch to wartime production at high levels. In 1944, with military expenditures at 47.9 percent of GDP, the economy

Table 4.1 Military Expenditures and the Gross Domestic Product, 1940–1946.

Year	Military Expenditures ($, billion)	GDP ($, billion)	As Share of GDP (%)
1940	15.0	101.4	14.8
1941	26.5	126.7	20.9
1942	62.7	161.9	38.7
1943	94.8	198.6	47.7
1944	105.3	219.8	47.9
1945	93.0	223.0	41.6
1946	39.0	222.2	17.5

Source: U.S. Department of Commerce, Bureau of Economic Analysis.

was operating at full capacity and at full employment. With the Japanese war ending in August of 1945 (and in May in Europe), 1945–1946 would be a crucial transition period. The auto industry would have to shift from building tanks and jeeps into making automobiles. The aircraft industry would have to convert its production from the building of war planes to passenger airliners. Other industries would be freed to produce for the American consumer. The iron and steel industry would be moving to a peacetime platform.

Few seem to want to talk about it, but the recession of 1945 began in February, while Roosevelt was still in office, and ended in October. What caused the downturn? It was a *sui generis* end-of-the-war recession. It was the only purely fiscal recession during the past 100 years. The Pentagon rushed to cancel billions of dollars in war contracts — $15 billion in less than a month. Boeing aircraft laid off 21,000 workers, Ford laid off 50,000, at the same time that hundreds of thousands of soldiers were going home and expecting to find jobs. The cutback in military expenditures of $12.3 billion in 1945 was sufficient to topple the economy into recession. The slash in expenditures was the equivalent of a $4.7 trillion fiscal cliff (in today's GDP terms). The decline in GDP from its peak to its trough in October was 12.7 percent, which nearly matched the 11.7 percent fall in military spending. The unemployment rate rose only to 1.9 percent in 1945, then to a relatively modest 3.9 percent during 1946–1947. The recession was clearly a result of demobilization and the shift from a wartime to a peacetime economy. Thankfully, it was short, some eight months and not very painful for the labor force. It was short because during this time private sector GDP was surging in reaction to pent-up demand from wartime rationing. The Dow Jones Industrial Average rose 20 percent from the peak of the business cycle to the trough. By the end of the year, the GNP was higher than in 1944.

The recession of 1945 is not even mentioned by Truman's major biographers (Robert Dallek, David McCullough, and Alonzo L. Hamby). Perhaps this is because it seemed an unnatural event and it had roots in the Roosevelt Administration. But the recession continued for five months of the Truman years. The ultimate fault may lay with President Truman who fails to mention the recession in his *Memoirs*. As we and the National Bureau of Economic Research (NBER) have noted, it actually did occur.

The role of military expenditures in an economy raises some fundamental questions. Conventional economics treats a dollar of military expenditure the same way as a dollar of non-military government expenditure. There are nonetheless differences. Ordinary government expenditures either directly increase incomes or investment, especially domestic infrastructure. Such expenditures have a full Keynesian multiplier effect. Military expenditures have different effects. The purpose of munitions is consumption with full depreciation. The $2 billion spent on the atomic bomb went up in fire and smoke. Besides that, there was the negative externality in the way of 150,000 Japanese civilian casualties. There is no domestic Keynesian multiplier effect. On the other hand infrastructure investment has a long-term multiplier effect and positive externalities inasmuch as infrastructure supports private investment.

At the time of the recession, there was no Council of Economic Advisers; in fact, Truman had no economic advisers. Nonetheless, Secretary of Commerce Henry Wallace estimated that the drop in the gross national product in the coming months would be $40 billion, the drop in wages $20 billion, which by spring would mean 7 or 8 million would be unemployed. As it turned out, he was unduly pessimistic, especially regarding unemployment.

The Strike: The Ultimate Weapon of Labor

The year 1946 would be eventful and difficult. Truman left no doubt that he saw himself in the eye of the storm when he famously accepted responsibility for all the country's tensions and woes by putting a sign on his desk that said, "The Buck Stops Here." He would go on to show, not at once, but over time that he really meant it. A small frame also held a motto of Mark Twain's, in Twain's own hand: "Always do right! This will gratify some people and astonish the rest." Most everyone had expected a depression after the war, based on history.[12] Neither Truman or his advisers expected inflation and strikes to be the principal economic problems. Moreover, Truman was still unsure of himself and, which only made the problems appear larger.

Some thought that Truman's travails were self-made. Those argued that Truman had made things especially hard on himself by trying to walk a middle ground on every issue of the day. At worst, it made him look indecisive. Still, a Gallup poll in August 1945 found that 55 percent of respondents favored a

---

[12] At the time, the term "recession" had not been widely used. Only when downturns were compared favorably with the Great Depression did the term become popular. Economists and politicians are responsible for the shift in usage.

middle-of-the-road course, rather than a movement by Truman to the left or right.[13] He made an elemental mistake in his decision to make Edwin W. Pauley Undersecretary of the Navy. It deepened skepticism on the left about Truman's enthusiasm for party liberals. Interior Secretary Harold Ickes, one of two prominent New Dealers left in the administration, resigned in February 1946 to protest the appointment. This stumble left Truman open to ridicule: "To Err is Truman," conservatives began saying.

With the beginning of demobilization of America's armed forces came intense pressure to "bring the boys home." There were some problems with this. The private labor force could not accommodate a giant surge in supply without rising unemployment. Besides, there was the need to establish effective occupations of Germany and Japan. Worse, there lingered the Soviet threat. Truman called for compulsory military training for all able-bodied young men for a year to 18 months. He did this without confronting the country with the emerging dangers of Soviet aggression. He feared that a frank appeal might heighten international tensions and encourage isolationism. Still, a smaller military would reduce federal budget deficits, which, Truman believed, was feeding inflation. In the spring of 1946, he asked Congress to extend the Selective Service law for another year. This fell short of universal military training.

On top of this conflict over demobilization, domestic economic and social conflicts confronted Truman with hard choices. A populace that had been willing to accept shortages, inconveniences, ceilings on wages, and inadequate housing since 1941 now seemed desperate to make up for lost time, demanding everything at once. There was rising industrial strife in almost every major industry combined with the potential for runaway inflation. Truman described labor as making "power crazy demands" reminiscent of "arrogant industry" in the 1920s. Management, which would not "meet the situation halfway," was just as bad.[14]

The settlement of a historic steel strike for higher wages in February stimulated that inflation, provoking other unions to make new wage demands. The steel workers' union called for a wage increase of 19.5 cents an hour. Failing to come to an agreement with management, in mid-January 1946 some 800,000 steel workers at more than 1,000 mills across the country walked off the job in

---

[13] Gallup, *Gallup Poll, Public Opinion, 1935–1971*, pp. 499–500, 523, 558, 611.
[14] Quoted by Robert J. Donovan, *Conflict and Crisis: The Presidency of Harry S. Truman, 1945–1948* (New York: W. W. Norton, 1977), p. 164.

the biggest strike in history. The steel workers agreed to the 18.5 cents an hour suggested by President Truman. A coal strike followed in April and May and forced shutdowns in other industries, only to be followed by a national rail workers stoppage that disrupted transportation all over the country. Automobile workers, glass makers, telephone operators, electric utilities employees, and numerous other industrial laborers struck in protest against inadequate wages, fringe benefits, and working conditions. Some 175,000 employees of General Motors, workers in plants in 19 states, walked out in a strike that would last more than three months. Truman declared at a Gridiron Club dinner that General William Tecumseh Sherman had been wrong. "I'm telling you I find peace is hell...." These conditions led 70 percent of the country to support a moratorium on all strikes and lockouts for a year. As for Truman, he asked Congress to pass a law that allowed him to draft into the Armed Forces all workers who were on strike against their government. The House agreed to the request, but the Senate said it was unconstitutional. Indeed, it was!

Meanwhile, the President was being faulted for his ineffectiveness in controlling inflation. He had loosened price controls on some manufactured goods and food, gasoline, and clothes, and, it was alleged, prices would shoot up in an inflationary spiral. However, the Consumer Price Index (CPI) was very stable throughout 1945 (with its eight months of recession), registering zero inflation during most months. In the first half of 1946, Truman revisited the problem, calling for an extension of the Office of Price Administration (OPA), which was due to expire in June. There was a significant increase in the CPI in July (5.88 percent), followed by 2.02 percent in August, 0.99 percent in September, zero percent in November, and 2.40 percent in December. The average for the year was a robust 8.3 percent. People had been spoiled by the near-zero inflation rate made possible by wartime price controls. In the fall, the public nonetheless turned against price controls. By this time, however, Truman had already lost the public's trust on managing the economy. "I'm just mild about Harry," went a then-current Washington joke. To top things off, the CPI soared to 14.4 percent in 1947.

Labor problems grew steadily worse. On one hand, Truman called for reasonable pay raises through collective bargaining. On the other hand, he asked Congress to forbid strikes in large national industries for 30 days until the situation could be studied by a fact-finding board, something which pleased no one.

The Iron Curtain

Problems abroad multiplied. Joseph Stalin announced a new Five-Year Plan with a warning to Soviet citizens that they would have to sacrifice consumer goods to military ones, which would be essential in the coming conflict with the capitalist, imperialist West. This was tantamount to a declaration of war. Some, led by Truman's Secretary of Commerce, Henry Wallace, believed that Stalin's speech was a defensive reaction to America's refusal to give Moscow a generous reconstruction loan. Others, such as George F. Kennan, gave forceful expression to his fear in what became known as the "long telegram" of February 22, 1946. Kennan warned that there was no way to disarm Soviet hostility toward the West, for it was the product of a need to consolidate power at home by arousing fears of unrelenting foreign dangers. Truman approved of Kennan's conclusion that the West should resist Communist expansion and attempts at subversion of democratic institutions.

Truman's caution was obvious when he accompanied Winston Churchill to give a speech at Westminster College in Fulton, Missouri. Truman thought well of the speech in advance. Churchill's speech left no doubt about what Washington should do. "From Stetinn in the Baltic to Trieste in the Adriatic," Churchill famously orated, "an iron curtain has descended across the continent. Behind that line lie all the capitals of the ancient states of central and eastern Europe" that had fallen under Soviet control. Churchill called for an Anglo-American military alliance to act as an effective check on Soviet aggression. Afterword, Truman did not take an open stand on Churchill's remarks, which further undermined his public standing. Rather, Truman attacked Henry Wallace, leading to his resignation.

None of this was to help the Democrats' cause in the November elections. Liberal Democrats felt betrayed. Conservative southern Democrats objected to the Fair Employment Practices Committee and the continuation of the Office of Price Administration. They were also at odds over southern states claiming they and not the federal government, controlled offshore oil rights. The Republicans won a 58-seat margin in the House, 245 to 188, and a six-seat advantage in the Senate. The results were a decisive defeat for Truman's stewardship. Among Republican newcomers were Senator Joseph McCarthy of Wisconsin and Representative Richard Nixon of California. Among the Democratic freshmen was John F. Kennedy.

Truman bounced back from defeat, declaring himself ready to fight for what he believed right for the country. Congressman J. William Fulbright of Arkansas said that Truman should appoint the Republican senator Arthur Vandenberg of Michigan as secretary of state and then resign to make Vandenberg president. In response, Truman dismissed Fulbright as "Halfbright."

Truman felt a sense of freedom. He decided to do what he thought right and "let them all go to hell". He would go on to write a fine record during the next two years. It was to be another Truman comeback.

Popular Culture of the 1940s

War dominated the first half of the 1940s decade. The consequences of the war would linger beyond the next half decade. Genocide, the killing of about six million European Jews would never be forgotten. To some degree internal and external tensions in the post-war era were managed by new institutions, including the United Nations, the welfare state and the Bretton Woods system, accompanying the WWII boom, which lasted well into the 1970s. Meanwhile, advances in technology were made. Besides the atomic bomb, the first computer was built, radar was developed, as was ballistic missiles and jet aircraft, it was the decade of the Jeep and the development of commercial television, the microwave oven, the invention of Velcro, Tupperware, and the Frisbee.

War influenced such movies as *Casablanca* (1943), and *The Best Years of Our Lives* (1946). But some of Hollywood's most notable blockbuster films included *The Maltese Falcon* (1941) and *The Big Sleep* (1946), films making Humphrey Bogart a star. Then, there was Frank Capra's *It's a Wonderful Life* (1946) and Orson Welles's *Citizen Kane* (1941). Musicals included the delightful *Meet Me in St. Louis* with Judy Garland (1944) and *Yankee Doodle Dandy* (1942) with Jimmy Cagney. Film Noir, a film style that incorporates crime dramas with dark images, became largely prevalent during the decade, including Bogart's classic turns.

The most popular music during the 1940s was swing and it was imported by the Europeans. This was the age of the big bands with Benny Goodman and Glenn Miller leading the way. Popular crooners were Frank Sinatra, Bing Crosby, and Perry Como. It was a time too when we heard the sounds of the Andrews Sisters, Louis Armstrong, Harry James, Al Jolson, Duke Ellington, Ella Fitzgerald, Dick Haymes, Fred Astaire, Lauren Bacall, Ingrid Bergman, Charles Boyer, Gary Cooper, Bette Davis, Marlene Dietrich, Kirk Douglas, Ava Gardner, Greer

Garson, Cary Grant, Bob Hope, Katharine Hepburn, Gene Kelly, Hedy Lamarr, Bert Lancaster, Vivien Leigh, Carole Lombard, Myrna Loy, Marilyn Monroe, Mareen O'Hara Gregory Peck, Walter Pidgeon, William Powell, Tyrone Power, Ronald Reagan, Ginger Rogers, Mickey Rooney, Barbara Stanwyck, James Stewart (who also served in the Air Force), Elizabeth Taylor, Robert Taylor, Gene Tierney, Spencer Tracy, and Lana Turner. Leggy Betty Grable was the G.I.'s favorite pin-up. It was an era in which the movie stars were bigger than life. It was the era of the "star system."

Major advances were made in literature. In 1940 came Ernest Hemingway's *For Whom the Bell Toils*. Ayn Rand established herself as an icon of the far right with *The Fountainhead* in 1943. *The Diary of Anne Frank* by Anne Frank appeared in 1947. Arthur Miller penned *Death of a Salesman* in 1949. George Orwell followed with the classic *1984* the same year. Orwell's book is often turned to when there is concern with dictatorship.

The war also had an enormous impact on sporting events. Among the baseball stars who served during World War II were Joe DiMaggio, Bob Feller, Stan Musial, Warren Spahn, and Ted Williams. After the war many players returned to their teams, while the major event of the second half of the decade was the 1945 signing of Jackie Robinson to a players contract by Branch Rickey of the Brooklyn Dodgers. Signing Robinson opened the door to the integration of Major League Baseball, finally putting an end to the professional discrimination that had characterized the sport since the nineteenth century.

The glamor of the decade even touched Harry Truman, with Hollywood becoming part of the presidential image (this will be explored in the chapters to follow). However, despite the excitement and glamour of the 1940s, popular culture entered the 1950s not with a bang but a whimper.

Chapter 5

The Employment Act of 1946 and the President's Council of Economic Advisers

E very day, the change in the President became more obvious. Ironically, it had been the sweeping Republican triumph in the congressional elections that had given Harry Truman a new lease on life. At last, he was free from the shadow of Franklin Roosevelt. Charlie Ross told White House reporters, "The real Truman administration began the day after the elections." The President was now a free man and could write a fine record. Henceforth, Harry Truman would be guided by the simple idea that he would be for the welfare of all the people without regard to political considerations.

Despite all the labor strife of the past year, the country was prospering as it never had. This is what Truman declared in his State of the Union message on January 6, 1947. The national income was higher than ever before in peacetime. There was virtually full employment. Still, he called for far-ranging improvements in labor-management relations, a strengthening of the anti-trust laws, a national health insurance program, including support for mental health, child care, and hospital construction. He also wanted a fair level of return for farmers, aid to veterans, an aggressive program of home construction, and he promised new progress in civil rights.

Common sense told Truman that full production would be the greatest weapon against inflation. On September 6, 1945 he sent to the Congress full-employment legislation. His objective was to carry out, during the peacetime reconversion period, the economic bill of rights which had been formulated by President Roosevelt. By full employment he meant the opportunity to get a good peacetime job for every worker who was ready, able, and willing to take one. He felt it was the responsibility of the federal government to inspire private enterprise with confidence by giving assurances that all the facts about full employment and opportunity would be gathered periodically for the use of all; assurance of stability and consistency in public policy, so that enterprise could plan better by knowing what the government intended to do; assurance that every governmental policy and program would be pointed to promote maximum production and employment in private enterprise; and assurance that priority would be given to doing those things first which stimulated normal employment most.

The Employment Act of 1946 nonetheless was fashioned out of a much more radical (left) bill. When Senate Bill 380 was sent to the floor on January 22, 1945, it was called the Full Employment Bill of 1945. It was meant "to establish a national policy and program for assuring continuing full employment in a free competitive economy, through the concerted efforts of industry, agriculture, labor, State and local governments, and the Federal Government." That it was a Keynesian document was made clear in Section 1, which stated "This Act may be cited as the 'Full Employment Act of 1945'."[1] This bill mandated that the Federal Government do everything in its authority to achieve full employment, which was established as a right guaranteed to the American people. Despite a declaration of policy wherein the Congress makes it "the policy of the United States to foster free competitive enterprise and the investment of private capital...,"[2] it was passed through a Keynesian strategy but as the Employment Act of 1946, its language greatly changed.

Conservative Congressmen led by Republican Senator Robert A. Taft argued that business cycles in a free enterprise economy were natural and that compensatory

---

[1] Senate Bill 380, January 22, 1945, p. 1 Papers of Gerhard Colm, Box 1. Harry S. Truman Library. The papers of Gerhard Colm relate to his work in the Fiscal Division of the Bureau of the Budget and his service as an economist on the Council of Economic Advisers throughout the Truman Administration. While the majority of the documents consist of correspondence between Colm and various colleagues, the collection also includes reports to Congress and Colm's ideas on fiscal policy.
[2] *Ibid.*, p. 4.

spending should only be exercised in the most extreme of cases. Some also believed that the economy would naturally and automatically move toward full employment. Others believed that accurate employment level forecasting by the Federal Government was not practical or feasible. Some were uncomfortable with an outright guarantee of employment. Classical economics won the battle for the heart and minds of Congressmen in the final Bill.

The Full Employment Bill of 1945

The history of the fate of Senate Bill 480 is an interesting one because we need to consider what was lost to understand the final outcome. The Full Employment bill says that the

> estimated aggregate volume of investment and expenditure by private enterprises, consumers, State and local governments, and the Federal Government, required to produce such volume of the gross national product, at the expected level of prices, as will be necessary to provide employment opportunities for such labor force (such dollar volume being hereinafter referred to as the 'full employment volume of production'); and the estimated aggregate volume of prospective investment and expenditure by private enterprises, consumers, State and local government, and the Federal Government (not taking into account any increased or decreased investment or expenditure which might be expected to result from the programs set forth in such Budget). The estimates and information herein called for shall take account of such foreign investments and expenditures for exports and imports as affect the volume of gross national product.[3]

This paragraph can be summed up in a basic Keynesian identity, or

$$GNI = GNP = C + I + G + (X - M),$$

where GNI is gross national income, I is private business investment, G is total government spending, and $(X - M)$ is the trade balance. Changes in these variables determine economic growth and therefore can be expressed as percentages. In turn, in Keynes, there is positive relationship between GNI and employment.

---

[3] *Ibid.*

Lest there be any question about Keynesian fiscal policy and the role of Federal G, the original Act goes on to say,

> To the extent, if any, that such increased non-Federal investment and expenditure as may be expected to result from actions taken under the program set forth in accordance with subsection (b) of this section are deemed insufficient to provide full employment volume of production, the President shall transmit a general program for such Federal investment and expenditure as will be sufficient to bring the aggregate volume of investment and expenditures by private business, consumers, State and local government, and the Federal Government up to the level required to assume full employment volume of production.[4]

In other words, if C + I + non-Federal G + (X – M) was at an insufficient level to achieve full employment, then the gap is to be filled with increases in Federal G. In turn, in Keynesian economics there would be a multiplier effect whereby changes in G would augment C and I after some lag. (Later, we will be more specific about these multiplier effects.) It was stipulated that if and when the private GNI was growing faster than the capacity to produce, then anti-inflationary policies would be put into place, including a reduction in Federal G.

The original bill was read by many and commented on by about the same. Senator Robert F. Wagner (1877–1953) sent S. 380 to Harold D. Smith, Director of the Bureau of the Budget on March 3, 1945. (Wagner was a leading architect of the modern welfare state.) In the attached letter, Wagner asked Smith several questions, most of which were about the availability of statistics and economic forecasts inside and outside the Federal Government.[5] Smith's answers reveal a sophisticated understanding of Keynesian economics while expressing caution about the current availability of statistics and forecasts within the government and necessarily elsewhere. One comment could have been written today: "If governmental and private programs succeed in achieving full employment, many of the Government's most difficult problems would become more manageable."[6] He goes on to list the problems that would go away, a list that

---

[4] *Ibid.*, pp. 4–5.
[5] Letter from Robert F. Wagner to Harold D. Smith, March 3, 1945, Papers of Gerhard Colm, Box 1, Harry S. Truman Library.
[6] Long memo in reply by Harold D Smith to Robert F. Wagner, April 4, 1945, Papers of Gerhard Colm, Box 1 , Harry S. Truman Library.

would be valid today. For example: "If full employment is assured by means of maximum private activities, certain expenditures of Federal, State, and local governments could be avoided or reduced."[7] A concern at the time was the re-absorption of WWII veterans in the labor force.

Gerhard Colm (1897–1968) was the principal fiscal analyst and Assistant Chief, Bureau of the Budget, Fiscal Division (1940–1946) under Smith. As a Professor of Economics at the unconventional New School of Social Research (1933–1939), he was introduced to Keynes' economics. He was in Washington DC during Roosevelt's war years and he had a great influence on Smith. Moreover, he had a close relationship with Bertram M. Gross (1912–1997).[8] Although Smith and Colm provided valuable insights and advice on the Bill, Gross drafted the Roosevelt-Truman full employment bills of 1944 and 1945, leading to the Employment Act of 1946. From 1941 to 1945 he was a staff member of a number of Senate committees. From 1946 to 1952 he was executive secretary of the President's Council of Economic Advisers. Despite his historical role in the economics of the nation, Gross's academic degrees were a B.A. in English and Philosophy and an M.A. in English literature from the University of Pennsylvania. Although self-taught in economics as a Federal bureaucrat, he and Colm were influenced by Alvin H. Hansen of Harvard, one of the first among the American Keynesians, often referred to as "the American Keynes."

Hansen (1887–1975) was a professor of economics at Harvard (1937), a widely read author on current economic issues for laymen and professionals alike, and an influential adviser to the government during the Roosevelt and Truman years. He is best known for introducing Keynesian economics in the United States in the late 1930s. Later, he had help from colleague John Kenneth Galbraith (1908–2006), while influencing Paul Samuelson (1915–2009), James Tobin (1918–2002), and Robert Solow (1924–). Perhaps more effectively than anyone he explicated, extended, domesticated, and popularized the then controversial ideas embodied in Keynes' *The General Theory of Employment, Interest, and Money* (1936). He helped to create the Social Security System in 1935. While his book, *Fiscal Policy and Business Cycles* (1941) influenced government fiscal policies, his 1953 book, *A Guide To Keynes* (like student Paul Samuelson's

---

[7] *Ibid.*
[8] See, for example, Memorandum from Bertram Gross to Gerhard Colm, January 3, 1946, Papers of Gerhard Colm, Box 1, Harry S. Truman Library.

multi-edition textbook, *Economics*), promoted Keynesian economics in America and in many other countries after World War II.[9]

An attachment to a letter from Alvin H. Hanson to Colm (with a copy to "Bert Gross") on November 27, 1945 explains why the Federal budget should not be balanced on an annual basis, but rather on a cyclical one.[10] The attachment is written as an amendment to the original Bill. Hansen wrote:

> The Act provides for a program of taxation which shall be designed to prevent any net increase in the national debt over a reasonable number of years without interfering with the goal of full employment. This provision constitutes a complete rejection of the old concept [classical] that the Federal budget should be balanced every individual year. It also constitutes a rejection of the idea that even a long-range balance in the Federal budget is more important than full employment.[11]

Once again, the "full employment" phrase is used. He goes on to say,

> A planned program of taxation designed to finance investment and expenditure over a reasonable number of years represents an important forward step in public finance procedure in two directions: (1) it provides on a sound basis for the financing of a compensatory fiscal program over the [business] cycle; (2) it provides for long-term financing of public works and capital projects.
>
> In so far as federal investment and expenditures are used as a balance wheel to offset the larger swings of the business cycle, a reasonable number of years (if we may judge by past experience) lies in the range of 7 to 9 years. Thus 1920 to 1929, a period of 9 years, represented a full swing of the cycle, while the next swing, 1929 to 1937, covered a period of 8 years.[12]

The then prevailing classical view (in the academy) favors a regressive tax system in which income tax rates decline with income levels. Hansen displays a

---

[9] I never met Alvin Hanson, but I got to know James Tobin and Robert Solow as we served during various years as Presidents of the Eastern Economic Association. Need I say, John Kenneth Galbraith was a lifelong friend and influence. Tobin and Solow served on the staff of the Council of Economic Advisers under President John F. Kennedy, who befriended citizen Truman. Tobin may be best known for advocating the "Tobin Tax" on financial assets.

[10] Letter from Alvin H. Hanson to Gerhard Colm (copy to Bertram Gross), November 27, 1945, with attachment titled "A tax program to finance federal investment and expenditures over a 'reasonable number of years'": Papers of Gerhard Colm, Box 1, Harry S. Truman Library.

[11] *Ibid.*, Attachment, p. 1.

[12] *Ibid.*

sophisticated understanding of the true nature of the nation's income tax system in the following paragraph:

> Whenever a decline in income and employment occurs, it is not possible (unless tax rates were raised) to cover the regular, operating expenditures of the government with adequate tax receipts. This follows from the fact that our federal tax system is highly progressive. As is well known under such a tax system, tax revenues fluctuate percentage-wise far more than the national income. Moreover corporate profits fluctuate more than income; and this also results in volatile tax revenue. Thus with the 1944 tax structure, it is estimated that a 10 percent fall in income would cause about a 15 percent fall in tax receipts. Accordingly, if the tax rates were set sufficiently high so that tax receipts would cover the total operating expenditures over an entire [business] cycle, a progressive individual income tax structure together with a corporate income tax would produce a deficit in low income years, and a surplus in high income years.[13]

The above paragraph is an accurate description of what later became known as the "balanced budget multiplier." It would be a few years before this multiplier would be defined in economic textbooks. Hanson provides still more detail:

> It is evident therefore that temporary loan financing in depression years is necessary even in the case of the regular operating expenditures of the government. If there is going to be any reasonable assurance that these deficits will be covered over the [business] cycle by offsetting surpluses, some systematic plan subject to adjustment as experience warrants is necessary. Without this a reasonable degree of success in achieving a cyclical balance of the budget is not at all probable.[14]

He still was not finished with his lessons in basic Keynesian economics. This was easily understood by other students of Keynes such as the addressed Gerhard Colm and Bertram Gross. Doubtless, it would be much less understood by the members of Congress. As we will come to note, there would be enough understanding to pass some sort of employment bill. Meanwhile, we continue to sit at the feet of Professor Hanson:

> The goal that should be set to achieve a cyclical balance of the budget may be stated as follows: The tax rate structure should be fixed at a level which will

---

[13] *Ibid.*, pp. 1–2.
[14] *Ibid.*, p. 2.

cover the regular operating expenses of the government at a point intermediate between a full employment income and the minimum income level which we should set as the lowest level that we will tolerate within the swing of the [business] cycle. For example, if it is estimated that in the first postwar years a full employment income would come to $150 billion, the minimum income might be set at say $130 billion. As more and more experience is gained with a full employment program the range between the full employment income and the minimum income could be narrowed. The goal might be to keep the national income in most years within a range of $140 billion and $150 billion in the worst years.[15]

S. 380 does not specify which agencies would be responsible for carrying out the functions outlined in the Bill. Smith suggested that the Budget Bureau, located as it then was, in the White House, was the ideal coordinating agency. In fact, that was much of what it had been doing. However, this suggests the need for a new group of economic advisers. This, and other issues raised by the Smith document would make their way into the final Bill. Most of the Keynesian aggregates — C, I, G, (X – M) — had been estimated by various Federal government agencies. Truman's 1946 Budget included estimates of GNP for 1944. Still, one must admire Hansen's estimates of what later would be called full-employment national income. These aggregates were published in the first Economic Report of the President. The GDP for 1946 was $222.2 billion; national income figures were not given.

Needless to say, there were gaps in the estimates and in the forecasts. One problem was being up-to-date on a quarterly basis. Another problem had to do with estimates of net national income and disposable income. Harold Smith understood that consumer expenditures were directly linked with disposable income, though they were loosely correlated with net national income. This means that there was an understanding of Keynes' marginal propensity to consume and, by extension, the marginal propensity to save. The marginal propensity to consume is the ratio of changes in consumption to changes in disposable income. The marginal propensity to save is the ratio of changes in savings to changes in disposable income. Their sum is unitary. From the marginal propensity to save comes Keynes' famous investment multiplier, or at least, the first rudimentary estimate of the multiplier. It is 1/MPS. The higher the propensity to

---

[15] *Ibid.*, pp. 2–3.

save, the smaller the investment multiplier.[16] An MPS of 0.5 would yield a multiplier of 2, so that an increase of $10 million in private investment would lead to a $20 million jump in GNP. Public investment would have the same effect. In turn, employment would be increased.

There was no mention of monetary policy or the Federal Reserve System by Robert F. Wagner, the sponsor of the original S. 380. Smith did mention the use of "primary information" of, among others, the "Board of Governors of the Federal Reserve System." By "information," he probably meant data because he also mentions such agencies as the Bureau of Internal Revenue, the Bureau of Labor Statistics, and the Bureau of the Census. There are a couple of possible explanations for otherwise ignoring the Federal Reserve System: (1) During WWII interest rates on bonds were more or less fixed to keep borrowing costs down and monetary policy was taken off the table; (2) The experience of the Great Depression suggested to the Keynesians that there was a liquidity trap whereby the demand for money was perfectly elastic, meaning that regardless of how much the money supply was increased, the interest rate would remain stuck at one level, making monetary policy impotent. Besides that, interest rates were pegged at a low level to keep borrowing costs down during WWII. (Still, total interest was substantial because the war was fought mostly with Federal debt.)

There were references to a "Joint Committee on the National Budget," but no reference to a Joint Economic Committee of Congress. Moreover, there was no reference to a President's Council of Economic Advisers. These, and other issues, would be resolved in the final Act. Still, the references to absolutely full employment and to Keynesian ideas would be lost; this loss is as important as the Employment Act of 1946.

The Final Employment Act of 1946

To fill these gaps and to further its new goals the Act was to establish a joint congressional committee to study and report to the Congress on the president's recommendations regarding the employment program. It further established a Council of Economic Advisers (CEA) within the Executive Office of the President. The job of the Council was to help the President decide what

---

[16] Other multipliers were added to the Keynesian arsenal over time by the Keynesians, such as the tax multiplier, the employment multiplier, and the balanced budget multiplier.

the government should do to help the nation's economy function smoothly and prosperously. The CEA was also assigned the duty of assisting and advising the President in the preparation of an economic report to be submitted to the Congress within sixty days after the beginning of each regular session. Alvin Hansen has been referred to as the "father of the CEA."

Early on (October 29, 1945), in a letter to the Speaker of the House of Representatives, John W. McCormack (1891–1980), President Truman urged the speedy passage of the bill. He wrote, "It is time that the people be reassured by the Congress that the government stands for full employment, full production and prosperity, not unemployment and relief."[17] He still had full employment on his mind as a national goal, and he noted that the Senate had already passed such legislation. Truman signed the Employment Act of 1946 on February 20, 1946. While the bill had undergone some considerable changes in the process of being shaped into law, it still retained some essential features favored by Truman. It was a populist proposal through and through even though much of the magic of John Maynard Keynes was gone. Most importantly, the final Act's reference to the promotion of "maximum employment, production, and purchasing power" left the door open to interpretation. After all, even in Keynes, there are tradeoffs among these three goals and it is difficult to pursue all at once, especially if relying only on fiscal policy.

It is curious that David McCullough's exhaustive biography devotes only two sentences to the Employment Act of 1946 and the Council of Economic Advisers (CEA) among 1116 pages.[18] Not so surprising when we consider that virtually no economic analysis appears in a book laden with other details. Truman does slightly better; there are four pages devoted to the Act and the CEA among 596 pages of Volume 1 of his *Memoirs*.[19] Clearly, Truman had the experience of the early 1920s as his guide. No one really knew what would happen as far as American production and employment were concerned after WWII. And, the Great Depression was still on everyone's mind. Despite his lack of interest in pure economic theory, Truman would interpret the Act as a Keynesian document. As it

---

[17] Letter from Harry S. Truman to John W. McCormack, October 29, 1945, Harry S. Truman, *Memoirs Volume 1: Year of Decisions* (Garden City, N.Y.: Doubleday, 1955), p. 492. Democrat McCormack served as Speaker of the House of Representatives three times — 1940–1947; 1949–1953; and 1955–1961. He was a member of the House of Representatives from 1928 until his retirement in 1971.

[18] David McCullough, *Truman* (New York: Simon & Schuster, 1992), p. 485.

[19] Harry S. Truman, *Memoirs, Volume 1, op. cit.*, pp. 491–494.

Truman with the "Big Four" (from left to right): Sam Rayburn, President Truman, Ernest McFarland, John W. McCormack and Alben W. Barkley (standing), ca. 1951. *Source*: Harry S. Truman Library (97-1941).

turns out the Employment Act of 1946 opened the door for executive action with respect to the business cycle.

Before passage of the Act, Truman discussed plans for the CEA with the Director of the Bureau of the Budget (Smith), with whom the Council would have to work very closely. But it was not until July 1946 that its membership was named. Truman appointed Edwin G. Nourse (to act as chairman), Leon H. Keyserling, and John Davidson Clark. Nourse remained chairman until his resignation, accepted by President Truman on October 19, 1949.[20] Nourse was the vice-president of the Brookings Institution, a distinguished and highly respected research organization in Washington. Earlier he had spent several years teaching economics and agricultural economics in the Mid-West. Keyserling was a by-product of the New Deal. He was a Harvard law graduate, first come to

---

[20] Letter from Harry S. Truman to Edwin G. Nourse, October 19, 1949, Nourse Papers, Box 5, Harry S. Truman Library.

Washington in 1933, as a lawyer with the Agricultural Adjustment Agency (AAA). He was the general counsel of the National Housing Agency at the time of his new appointment to the CEA. Clark came to the White House from the University of Nebraska, where he had been dean of the School of Business Administration. He had a long career as a lawyer and had been a vice-president of the Standard Oil Company of Indiana. Truman liked the idea that the trio often sharply disagreed and were not all of one mind. Only later did Truman say that he hankered for a one-handed economist.

In his *Memoirs*, Truman sums up what he thought of his selections. In hindsight, Harry surprises us with his retrospective satisfaction. He wrote:

> These were eminently qualified men. They differed greatly in point of view and, in the years ahead, were to disagree sharply. I knew this when I appointed them. I believe that I was well advised in their selection by the very fact that they were not all of one mind.[21]

Truman understood that economists of different schools of thought do not always agree. He knew further that to the degree that he was dealing with political economy, the politicians making policy would disagree even more.

Secretary of the Treasury Fred Vinson (1890–1953) accurately appraised the importance of the Act[22]:

> Occasionally, as we pore through the pages of history, we are struck by the fact that some incident, little noted at the time, profoundly affects the whole subsequent course of events. I venture the prediction that history, someday, will so record the enactment of the Employment Act of 1946.[23]

Conflict within the first CEA would seem to belie this prediction. As noted, however, Truman knew what he was getting into.

The Employment Act of 1946 might be envisaged as a chart of the ocean of uncertainty in which the economic ship of state rests. The policy of abandoning the economy to depression no longer seems apropos. The Act was passed in the hope that national economic goals could be defined and a system devised

---

[21] Harry S. Truman, *Memoirs, Volume 1, op. cit.*, p. 494.
[22] Truman appointed Vinson in 1945, but one year later he was Chief Justice of the Supreme Court.
[23] Quoted by Harry S. Truman, *Memoirs*.

whereby they could be insured. It is mindful that the economic ship of state is partly guided by the disorganized mass of government agencies and institutions which independently and sometimes together formulate and implement national economic policy. The CEA is not only one of these agencies but one designed to coordinate the actions of the others. The passage of the Act and the creation of the CEA is an important landmark in economic history.[24]

There are three broad objectives or criteria of action outlined by the Employment Act, all of which have economic content: (1) Employment opportunities for those able, willing, and seeking work; (2) promotion of maximum employment, production, and purchasing power; (3) deference to other "needs and obligations and other considerations of national policy." Additionally, the Employment Act sought to accomplish three other purposes which are not entirely economic in nature. First, it states unequivocally the intention of Congress to maintain a free enterprise economy. This is perhaps the most paradoxical legislative statement of interventionism ever uttered by Congress. Second, it provides for technical assistance for the various sectors of the economy in the determination of price and employment policies and of intermediate or minor targets. Third, it attempts or intends to safeguard the right of the President and of Congress to make decisions on policy matters. Thus, economic goals are not to be attained at the expense of the free enterprise system, but only through its retention. The requirement that only the President and Congress be allowed to make decisions on policy matters also represents an attempt to assure the continuance of democratic decision-making. This leaves the quasi-public Federal Reserve System and monetary policy in limbo, but quite independent.

The President's Council of Economic Advisers

The Act created the Council of Economic Advisers (CEA) in the Executive Office of the President to implement the economic objectives. The CEA is composed of three members appointed by the President, by and with the advice and consent

---

[24] Much of the discussion in this chapter on the Employment Act of 1946 and the CEA is based on E. Ray Canterbery, *The President's Council of Economic Advisers* (New York: Exposition Press, 1961), especially pp. 13–31. For a history and analysis of the CEA's roles under three presidents beginning with Truman and ending with John F. Kennedy, see E. Ray Canterbery, "The Fine Line between Politics and Economics," *Challenge: The Magazine of Economic Affairs*, July 1963, pp. 28–31. See also E. Ray Canterbery, *Economics on a New Frontier* (Belmont, CA.: Wadsworth, 1968), pp. 127–152.

of the Senate. Their salary is similar to that of Cabinet members. The members are chosen as a result of their training, experience, and attainments in economics. According to the Act, their job is to analyze and interpret economic developments, to formulate and recommend national economic policy to promote employment, production, and purchasing power under free competitive enterprise. The fact that these three persons are assisted by a staff of economists does not make this assignment any less formidable.

It is also the duty of the CEA to assist and advise the President in the preparation of the Economic Report of the President and to gather information concerning economic developments and trends, to analyze and interpret such information in the light of the policy objectives of the Act, and to appraise the various programs and activities of the Federal Government in the light of this policy. The CEA is also ordered to make an annual report to the President in December of each year. These reports comprise a history of the advice of the CEA.

Political considerations are inevitable. What is considered acceptable to a majority of the electorate is as important as it is elusive. For example, perhaps farm subsidies are uneconomical; nevertheless, this is a part of our national economic policy because the farm bloc is so politically strong. Perhaps a planned economy in the Soviet Union temporarily produced a faster rate of economic growth than free enterprise would have; nevertheless, the desire for a faster rate of production is not enough reason to convince the majority in this country that the concomitant loss of freedom is counterbalanced by the economic gain. As a result, it is necessary to consider what the CEA can and cannot do in a political as well as in an economic sense.

One factor influences the attitude of the CEA toward politics far more than others: This is the role of the economist as seen and practiced by the different CEA chairpersons. This role affects the relationships of the CEA with Congress and the President. It appears that the role was least political when the chairperson most strongly believed that the role of the economist was objective, and when this belief was prevalent, there was a strong tendency to respect the will of the Congress.

What I am about to say suggests that the role of the CEA was not definitively spelled out in the Employment Act. Rather, it devolved upon the President and the CEA chairpersons to design the role of the CEA. What the CEA should do is based on value judgments. Of course, there was an outline of CEA functions in Alvin Hansen's Attachment. This presents several potential alternative roles for the CEA, each with a different shade of political meaning. The CEA could have an analytical, advisory, or a policy-making function. As an analytical agency, the CEA would gather data, process and analyze it, and distribute the results to the President, Congress, and other interested persons. In such a role the CEA would make no policy recommendations to the President or Congress. As an advisory agency, the CEA would, on the basis of materials it had analyzed, make policy recommendations to the President and Congress. As a policy-making agency, the Council would, on the same basis, perform some of the duties in the realm of economics now performed by the President and Congress with the judicial approval of the Supreme Court.

As it has turned out, the CEA has played the first two roles, while putting its feet in the water in the third role. The policy-making role is not legally prescribed. What the role of the CEA should be has important implications, not only for the Council, but for the use of economics. It raises some fundamental questions. Are desired economic and political objectives mutually attainable? Can economic "experts" make the policy decisions for a country that traditionally has had a laissez faire philosophy? Is the state of economic knowledge adequate to enable economists to cope with such problems as inflation, recessions, economic growth, and economic stability? Can economists forecast the future? Should economic policy be made by a select few (economists), or should political pressures upon the President and Congress from the majority determine the direction of national economic policy? What would be the economic and political implications of a central planning agency? All these questions are virtually axiomatic in a consideration of the issues involving the Council.

Above all, the CEA is an institution. It has institutional objectives, which are not always formulated by the Council, but are ofttimes derived for the CEA by existing institutions. Moreover, since it operates within the framework of a democracy, its economic and political objectives, consistent or not, are similar to the goals of many economists who cite either quantitative or normative goals. Part of the framework within which the Council operates is the state of economic knowledge. The ability of the Council to cope with problems of inflation, recession, economic growth, and economic stability is dependent not only on the abilities of the Council membership and its staff but also on the current level of economic knowledge. If we assume that such knowledge has been available to and properly used by the Council, the failures and successes of its recommendations also give us some clue as to the general level of economic knowledge within the Council.

All these are questions and issues that faced President Truman and the first CEA. Some of the answers were resolved by another institution established by the Employment Act. (In a draft of the original bill, Alvin Hansen referred to a Joint [Economic] Committee.) The Congressional Joint Economic Committee has seven members appointed by the President of the Senate, and seven members appointed by the Speaker of the House. Bipartisanship is attempted by requiring that party representation reflect the relative membership of the majority and minority parties in the Senate and House as nearly as possible. The functions of this Committee are to study means of coordinating programs to further the policy of the Act and to guide the several committees of Congress dealing with legislation relating to the Economic Report. Finally, the Joint Committee is required to file a report with the Senate and the House of Representatives containing its findings and recommendations with respect to each of the main recommendations made by the President in the Economic Report. As early as 1948 it was asserted that these documents had gone far beyond any previous Presidential messages in laying before Congress, and the country a full picture of what had been happening to the American economy, and in developing a comprehensive national policy geared to the maintenance of prosperity.

The interaction between the CEA and the Joint Economic Committee has varied as the composition of the Council has changed. For example, Edwin G. Nourse, the first chairman of the Council, did not cooperate very well with the Joint Committee, whereas Raymond J. Saulnier, a later chairman, was very cooperative.

The Nourse Council

The original interpretation of the powers of the Act by the Council was a literal one. The Act provides that the President shall, thorough a group of professionally trained economists, make a continuing study of the entire economic situation of the country. This includes a review of the activities of all agencies in the Federal establishment as they deal with economic matters and of all government policies and programs in order to determine whether they are doing their utmost to promote full utilization of the nation's economic resources or whether some of them are inconsistent or conflicting. Edwin G. Nourse conceded each of these points. Harry S. Truman stood aside; pressured by other duties, he was indifferent to the complexities of economic theory. His Executive Orders and actions as President belay a pragmatic, populist stance.

The distinctions and similarities between the CEA's and the President's reports should be made clear. There are three main types of Council reports in addition to weekly or monthly transmittals to the President and the statistical supplement to the Economic Reports, *Economic Indicators*: (1) An annual report *to* the President in December of each year, (2) an annual report *of* the President in January of each year, and (3) a midyear report of the President each year. Until Truman's midyear report in 1948, no attempt had been made to separate the opinions of the President and those of the Council in the Economic Reports. The reason given by Nourse for rejecting the separation of views was that it would be practically impossible to keep from revealing differences between the conclusions of the Council and the President's policy decisions.[25] President Truman had seemed to follow the advice of the Council in the early reports, but this advice had been limited in scope. The dual authorship form presents the material solely authored by the Council under the heading of "The Annual Economic Review."

The CEA's task, as Nourse saw it, is broadly comparable to the administrative policy and program-making that is carried on by the top executives of a great corporate business, in consultation with each other and with research staffs.[26] The analogy is not a perfect one because business bureaucrats have a tighter control over subsidiary agencies than government bureaucrats have over the policies and operations of the component parts of the economic system, but it does have illustrative value. The division of functions first contemplated by Nourse was in many ways analogous to the relations between the operating staffs of General Motors plants located in various places about the country and the broad policy-making organizational coordination and overhead financing which are in Michigan.

Nourse equated the "staff" functions of the corporation to the functions of the Council; that is, the Council was advisery and should not perform "line" functions. Decisions and implementation of policy should be retained in the hands of professional executives, if this analogy is followed through. The CEA is supposed to perform the functions of the scientist, who analyzes cause-and-result sequences or probabilities, or—at most—those of a "consultant." The CEA was

---

[25] Edwin G. Nourse, *Economics in the Public Service* (New York: Harcourt, Brace and Co., 1953), p. 217.
[26] Edwin G. Nourse, "The Employment Act and the Economic Future," *Vital Speeches*, XII (January 1, 1946), p. 179.

organized to analyze materials obtained through its own research or the research of other agencies. Nourse was a strict constructionist in his interpretation of the Employment Act. He has explicitly indicated that it should be a Council of advisers *to the President*. The analysis of economic trends and developments is to be prepared for the benefit of the President. The reports are to be transmitted to the President and quickly moved by him to Congress. The Council is to "assist and advise the President" in the preparation of his economic reports.

To fulfill the Nourse-like functions of the Council, it is only necessary to have a research staff. Nourse states in his tell-all book, *Economics in the Public Service*, that the first function of the professional staff is to piece together a complete and consistent picture of the economic state of the nation from official sources and from any unofficial sources which appear to be useful. The Council would merely detect errors of method, bias, or inconsistency in the materials. Nourse believes that a second function of the Council is to interpret all available facts into the soundest possible diagnosis as to the state of the nation's economic health and the causes which explain any evidence of unhealthy conditions. For this reason, he favored drawing many outside economic specialists into consultation on the special phases of the diagnosis during his chairmanship. This practice has continued unabated.

To maintain this level of academic objectivity, the first Council staff was established on a highly professional level. Nourse stated in 1948 that not one of its employees had been selected for political reasons.[27] Until this time, the Council had not been put in the position of having to resist political pressure on appointments. Even the Pendergasts could not get to Nourse. But even before he left the Council, Leon H. Keyserling, as a member, attempted to change some of the functions of the Council. Some of these changes were motivated by political considerations.

Nourse directed his attention to completing his staff of professionals before the first Economic Report was completed. The Employment Act put a ceiling of $300,000 on the staff payroll (outside of Council members' salaries). In practice, it had been about two-thirds of this amount until the completion of the first Economic Report. Nourse's purpose was to maintain a small "analytical agency." With this relatively small sum he began looking for men (no women were considered) with intellectual ability and a capacity to work with other agencies along

---

[27] Bertram M. Gross and Edwin G. Nourse, "The Role of the Council of Economic Advisers," *American Political Science Review*, 42 (April, 1948), p. 291.

problem lines. He was not overly concerned about the individual's doctrinal position, although he encouraged conservatives to join the staff.

The first chairman has given several illustrations to show President Truman's casual attitude toward the Council. A typical case was the Chief Executive's use of data in a presidential radio address in the summer of 1949. He stated that national income during the last 40 years "has increased more than ten times as fast as the population." These figures, he said, are a measure of Americans' "rising standard of living." However, he failed to consider that adjustment for price changes should be made when drawing conclusions about the standard of living from the size of the national income. Included in those years was the inflation of World War II and its aftermath! After receiving the draft of this speech, Chairman Nourse made several efforts to change this statement and was finally assured by White House aides that it had been altered. That evening the passage was used exactly as first written. When Nourse wrote to the spirited President to express his concern over the omission of the suggestion, Mr Truman replied, "...I am glad you wrote me because that indicates to me that you listened to the speech."

Much of the academic work of Professor Nourse echoes a cautious attitude toward governmental economic policy. His writings reflect conservatism in the sense that they advocate a minor role for the Federal Government in shaping the trend of the economy. Needless to say, Mr Truman had little difficulty finding fault with this philosophy. Moreover, Nourse believed that the economist must exclude from his bailiwick all factors that are noneoconomic — whether aesthetic, ethical, "subjective," or broadly "political." Economists are "scientists" studying the cause-and-effect sequence in the economic situation, and economic policy is not a science. Economic policy must be a choice among conflicting values and thus a judgment on what is "good" in a particular case. Nourse could not find "a single word" in the Employment Act about any responsibility of the Council to Congress. He considered the economist a scientist and therefore not the proper implement for policy making, whether for business firms or for nations. "Policy-making passes beyond the role of the economic scientist," observed Nourse, "to that of someone who can best be called an 'economic engineer.'"

Because Mr Truman always had ample political advice, Nourse believed the Council would be superfluous in plotting policy strategy. Apparently Truman disagreed with this stewardship when the presidential election of 1948 got under way. In that battle, two of Truman's favorite targets were high prices and high profits. Being significant only through his silence, Nourse intentionally kept out of this debate. But Keyserling and Clark saw a less passive role for the government in the economy and backed the administration wholeheartedly.

The Keyserling CEA: New Roles

Keyserling's interpretation of the role of the Council is practically a direct refutation of the position taken by Edwin G. Nourse. While the Nourse Council was an analytical agency, under Leon H. Keyserling the CEA was even more than an advisery agency. In fact, Mr. Keyserling was often an advocate for the President's proposals. Keyserling was a feisty Vice Chairman of the CEA during 1946–1949 under Nourse; later, during 1949–50, he was Acting Chairman, and in 1950–1953, he was Chairman. During the Keyserling years the Council was closer to the policy-making function than at any other time. For this reason, the question of whether an advisory agency should be an advocate of its own recommendations or of those of the President is sometimes raised. If so, it is possible for the President and his Council to be at odds. Later, under Arthur F. Burns and Raymond J. Saulnier, respectively, the Council performed the double role of analytical and advisory agency but seldom appeared as an advocate during the Eisenhower years. Soon, Leon H. Keyserling would move from membership on the CEA to its chairmanship. He had been a vociferous supporter of FDR's New Deal program. His style of leadership seemed to mesh with that of Truman, in sharp contrast to that of Nourse.

Keyserling believed that the Council should do more than merely assist the President, be an advisery body, and be politically neutral. Keyserling proposed that: (1) The Council be a Council *of the President, not to the President*; (2) the council should perform some of the functions of an administrative agency; and (3) the Council should be active in policy-making. In fact, to argue that there is only one way "to foster and promote free competitive enterprise" is to encourage accusations of demagoguery. It will surprise few to learn that the interpretation of the goals of the Act by Leon H. Keyserling differed from that of Nourse.

Keyserling, a Democrat by choice and inclination, is quite different from the interpretation by Arthur F. Burns, a Republican. Thus the role of the CEA was not cemented by legislation; in fact, there was no intention to do to. As a result of this definite lack of direction, the structure of the Council changed with the views of different Council chairpersons and Presidents.

The role of the Council, argues Keyserling, is the same as that of Cabinet officers or other agency heads in the executive branch. The contention of the Employment Act that the Council is an intellectual staff arm of the Presidency devoid of any responsibilities or privileges of sharing in the official enunciation or implementation of executive policy is challenged by Keyserling. Furthermore, to say that members of the Council are no different from Cabinet officers or other agency heads implies that they could be dismissed if they found themselves unable or not willing to support the President's policies before the Congress or publicly.

To Keyserling, the commitment of the Employment Act to full employment economics, rather than countercyclical economics, represents a valuable and virile shift in emphasis. Later, he contended that "here is unique opportunity for leadership by the CEA."[28] His Council determined what the objectives of national economic policy *should* be. As he later summed up the role of the CEA:

> ... the Council should realize that it is not primarily an economic research agency, nor a statistical refinement agency, nor an interpreter of past trends, nor a pure forecasting agency. Drawing of course upon these resources and techniques, it is primarily an agency to help determine needs and evolve policies and programs.[29]

The CEA under Keyserling began to perform some of the functions of an administrative agency. In this new role one major function of the Council as a "trustee for the President in the Executive Branch of the Government" was to go before the relevant congressional committees to explain and defend presidential proposals. Keyserling does not feel that this practice endangers the professional standing of the economists, nor does he feel that rapport between the Council and the President is impaired. This is consistent with a Cabinet-like role for the Council.

Keyserling contended that problems of appraising political acceptability enter even into the initial formulation and articulation of national economic policies during the writing of the Economic Report because sound policies depend upon the state of the economy, and what a free people will accept is part of their behavior pattern and is therefore a part of the economy in action. This

---

[28] Leon H. Keyserling, "The Council of Economic Advisers' Tasks in the Next Decade," in *The Employment Act Past and Future: A Tenth Anniversary Symposium*, ed. Gerhard Colm, Special Report No. 41 (Washington, D.C.: National Planning Association, 1956), p. 70.
[29] *Ibid.*, p. 71.

attitude does not prevent the Council from attempting to persuade the people of a particular course of action, for Keyserling argued:

> ... even after the Economic Report is written and transmitted to the Congress, the CEA should help to obtain acceptance of its recommendations.[30]

In the Council's Fourth Annual Report to the President, which had been drafted primarily by Keyserling, the intention was expressed that in the future the Council would have more direct and active participation in the deliberations of congressional committees. Keyserling, who was the acting chairman on November 2, 1949, after the official resignation of Nourse until he was named chairman, became increasingly conspicuous in Democratic Party affairs. This participation actually began during the last months of his tenure as vice-chairman. This new institutional character of the CEA became more and more significant as Keyserling increased his political activity.

In September 1949 he addressed the Western States Democratic Conference in San Francisco. Keyserling's address, "Prospects for American Economic Growth," was an expression of economic expansionism. He participated in the Southern Regional Conference of the Democratic Party at Raleigh on January 30, 1950. After being named chairman of the Council on May 10,1950, he participated in the "Jefferson Jubilee" of the Democratic Party in Chicago, where he made two speeches: "Toward an Expanding American Economy; and "The Federal Budget and the National Economy." The latter speech evoked so much criticism that is is difficult to obtain a copy. Edwin G. Nourse quotes the critical portion.

> [I]... believe profoundly that the budgetary policies of the Federal Government since the first administration of Franklin D. Roosevelt until the present moment have been basically right. And because they have been subjected to misrepresentation and sophistry, we must continue to fight for them to assure their maintenance.[31]

It is difficult to know where the Democrat ends and the economist begins.

---

[30] *Ibid.*
[31] Nourse, *Economics in the Public Service, op. cit.*, p. 293.

The danger of economic advisers following the advice of the President rather than vice-versa is illustrated by the chaos subsequent to Keyserling's appointment as chairman. He followed Mr. Truman's lead and advocated in the 1949 *Economic Report* a $4 billion *tax increase* to curb the inflation of "high profit levels." As the issue reached a heated peak, the Council apparently failed to notice that the economy was in the throes of its second postwar recession. The GDP contracted by 1.1 percent in the second quarter of 1949, 0.5 percent in the third quarter and 1.6 percent in the fourth. Truman and the Council had to reverse themselves when Congress rejected their program. Consequently, the 1950 Economic Report's appraisal of the preceding year is among the most ambiguous of Council reviews. A housing boom and robust private investment spending led to a robust recovery in 1950.

Keyserling participated in the Midwest and Western States Conference at Denver, Colorado, on May 23, 1951, and was no more politically neutral than his prior pro-Roosevelt quotation would suggest. Such statements do not reflect the type of conclusions reached by a purely analytical agency. It certainly is not purely objective to say that America should have had the same budget policy in 1951 as America had in 1932. The entire structure of the budget, the national debt, and much of the economy had changed greatly since 1932. Total government purchases of goods and services *from 1932 through 1939* was only $29.3 billion, which was less than the total expenditures in the year 1951. In 1951, $37.3 billion of that total was spent in the name of national security, while less than $50 *million* was spent for the *same reason* in 1932.

The Republican minority of the Joint Economic Committee used the changing character of the Council as a basis for political attack. Its report, issued in 1949, rejected the basic philosophy of the *Economic Report* which, it stated, recommended that we set up a planned and controlled economy and increase taxation for that purpose. The Committee Report expressed fear that the Economic Reports were becoming political propaganda rather than a scientific analysis.

The present Economic Report reads in many respects like a political argument. We see no reason why it should not be confined to economic discussions without entering into controversial political fields, or why it should not state the arguments on both sides where the economic issues are inextricably involved in politics.

The Economic Report in 1949 seemed to carry on a crusade for more executive power than initiated in previous reports of the President. The minority raised this same question:

> We, therefore, oppose broad grants of power to fix all wages, to impose compulsory allocations in every field, to impose production controls on farmers indiscriminately, and to modify the adjustments occurring from natural forces of demand, supply, saving and investment by economists claiming omniscience.

It is the kind of argument leveled at a CEA which assumes the responsibility of directing the national economy from an "ivory control tower" by those who still believe in the classical model of an economy as self-regulating. Some believe that economists are much more likely to make mistakes than the natural forces of economic adjustment in lieu of their belief that most minor maladjustments in the economy tend to correct themselves. If there is a maldistribution of the national income between capital expansion and consumer income (as the Council once alleged), economic forces would soon adjust to a proper relationship. Such a view precludes the advocacy of anti-cyclical fiscal measures because there is no serious danger of either inflation or deflation in an economy which is self-regulating and left alone.

The CEA had been transformed from an analytical staff of technicians serving the President into a far-reaching agency for the formulation and implementation of economic policy. It was suggested that the Council have meetings with representatives of business, labor, agriculture, and consumers and that it designate one or two special problems for consideration at another regularly scheduled meeting. A staff of such experts, as well as the Council's, undertook specific studies which were circulated in advance of discussion. Keyserling believed that there was a psychological advantage to working together as well as talking together. Keyserling also recommended that the CEA be more active in participating in discussions with the Joint Committee. As to work with other governmental agencies, the Council began to participate in developmental thinking about those policies and programs which were of central concern to the whole economy. This way the other agencies received the Council's assistance at an early enough stage for it to be effective, and in this way, the Council is brought in contact with their work at an early enough stage to comprehend it fully and benefit by their thinking and experience.

This new CEA orientation had several implications. It meant that the CEA, as well as the White House and the various administrative agencies, now had to be looked to for possible new policies affecting business. The Council did not intend to stop at giving business and the executive branch of the government the benefit of its advice; it made a pass at offering to tell Congress what to do about economic policy-making. Even on controversial questions of pensions, unemployment insurance, other Social Security measures, the CEA became bold enough to state a specific policy. Keyserling saw no distinction between the role of the Council members and the position of Cabinet members and other agency heads in their responsibility of sharing in the enunciation and implementation of presidential policy. It was by now understood that Truman's Council economists, like Cabinet members, were expendable if they were unable or unwilling to support the President's specific proposals before Congress and the public. Despite miscalculations by Keyserling, he, an ex-New-Dealer, was much preferred over Nourse by President Harry S. Truman.

Afterward

Some time later, Leon H. Keyserling was not included in the plans of the new Republican Administration. President Dwight Eisenhower nominated Arthur F. Burns, long-time Professor of Economics at Columbia University and Director of Research at the National Bureau of Economic Research, as a member of the Council. Burns held the unique title of "Economic Adviser to the President" for a short period until the Council was reconstituted by Eisenhower. Later he was designated chairman of the Council. Eisenhower had even toyed with the idea of eliminating the CEA. He doubtless was cautioned by the fact that this would violate the Employment Act of 1946. Conservatives had to live with the liberal ideas that remained and was interpreted for the Act.

The years 1945–1946 were busy years for President Truman. As we have already surmised, there was much more on his plate than getting the CEA up and running. Still, Truman must be given considerable credit for his interpretation of the Employment Act of 1946. After all, there was sufficient vagueness, especially regarding the role of the CEA, to open the door to various interpretations. The struggles with interpretation took new turns with Keyserling in 1949. But there was still more going on as early as 1946 because of a Communist threat at home and abroad. It is these concerns to which we next turn; they too would have economic implications on Truman's time in office.

Chapter 6

Communism and The Truman Doctrine

arry S. Truman was very busy during his first days in the White House. In 1946 it seemed that the Communist menace was everywhere. The Soviets were threatening Turkey and Greece. Moreover, they loomed over a devastated Eastern and Western Europe. In Asia, Communism in China was flexing its muscles. The immediate Communist threat was at home, or so it was thought. In any case, it was something President Truman could not ignore. The Republicans would not let him.

The Communist "Threat" at Home

By the summer of 1946, large majorities of Americans were convinced that the Soviet Union had spies at work in the United States and believed that Communist Party members should be barred from civil-service jobs. The loyalty of federal employees became a popular political issue. Truman had concluded that a Republican Congress would exploit these public fears by investigations aimed more at Democrats than at the handful of Communists who actually held or were applying for government jobs. Anti-communism would become more of a political bludgeon than a realistic campaign to preserve American values. An example of how vulnerable liberals could be to charges of Communist connections was

Congressman Richard Nixon's successful 1946 campaign in which he attacked his Democratic opponent, Jerry Voorhis, as a Communist sympathizer.

President Truman decided to do an end run around the Republican agenda on American communists. In November, he created the President's Temporary Commission on Employee Loyalty. This Commission quickly issued a Report to Congress.[1] The Commission members included A. Devitt Vanech, Special Assistant to the Attorney General, Department of Justice (Chairman); John E. Peurifoy, Acting Assistant Secretary of State for Administration, Department of State; Edward H. Foley, Jr., Assistant Secretary of the Treasury, Department of the Treasury; Kenneth C. Royall, Under Secretary of War, Department of War; John L Sullivan, Under Secretary of the Navy, Department of the Navy; and Harry B. Mitchell, President, Civil Service Commission. These men represented the departments of government most likely to be enmeshed in questions of loyalty. To facilitate the work of the Commission, a subcommittee was appointed to prepare and draft memoranda and agenda for the consideration of the Commission at its meetings.[2] Its representatives were drawn from the same departments as the Commission members.

What, the reader may ask, does a government loyalty program have to do with economics or economic policy? As it turns out, the disputes and the acrimony over this program as it evolved raised the question of whether the United States would survive as a democracy. Free markets which had been partly set aside during World War II cannot survive under dictatorship. Private property depends upon democratic protections. Moreover, the Populist agenda demands that a small minority not prevail, especially when employment issues are involved. The fragility of a great democracy is evident from a reading of the many letters and documents related to the loyalty executive orders. Ultimately, one man in the USA, Harry S. Truman, stood in the doorway that had been opened to tyrants. It was not easy, but with great political skill, he turned aside the anti-democratic voices and saved capitalism at home and abroad.

As the Report finds, loyalty to the Government of the United States was simply assumed prior to 1939. Qualification and character were the bases for employment. The Civil Service Commission prohibited inquiry into an

---

[1] The Report of the President's Temporary Commission on Employee Loyalty, 1947, Harry S. Truman Library.
[2] *Ibid.*, p. 2.

individual's partisan political affiliation and beliefs and placed federal employment on a non-partisan plane. On August 2, 1939, the Congress passed the original Hatch Act "to prevent pernicious political activity." Section 9A of this Act was designed to prevent any person employed from holding membership in any political party or organization advocating the overthrow of the USA's constitutional form of government. More broadly, the "traditional American way of life" was to be preserved. The element of employee loyalty became an issue, especially during wartime. On June 25, 1940 the Congress granted specific powers to the more sensitive agencies, the War and Navy Departments. President Franklin Roosevelt issued War Service Regulations in March, 1942 (acting through the Civil Service Commission) specifying that a person could be disqualified for employment if there was a reasonable doubt as to his loyalty to the Government. On July 5, 1946 the Secretary of State was given substantially the same authority of summary removal.

Earlier, J. Edgar Hoover got in on the action. In October 1941, the US Attorney General directed the FBI to investigate complaints made against federal employees alleged to be disloyal. The FBI continued to be heavily involved until February 5, 1943 when President Roosevelt set up a Committee composed of officials representing the Interior Department, Treasury Department, Commerce Department, Justice Department and the Federal Deposit Insurance Corporation. Although Roosevelt's Executive Order was still in effect when the Report was issued, it was advisory only.

In actual practice, the authority to remove or retain an employee rested solely with the head of the employing department or agency. No matter how much hearsay and innuendo was brought to the table by the FBI, court cases through the third branch of government provided considerable protection to innocents.

Statistics on the outcomes were provided by the Civil Service Commission. These are summarized in the Report.[3] For the period beginning with the fiscal year 1941 and ending on December 31, 1946, 392,889 investigated cases covering qualifications, character, and loyalty of applicants were closed out. Of these, 43,537 persons were rated ineligible, of which 1,307 were cases in which disloyalty was the major disqualification. Of the disloyal minority, 694 cases

---

[3] The Report of the President's Temporary Commission on Employee Loyalty, *op. cit.*, pp. 21–27, Harry S. Truman Library.

involved persons who were either Communists or followers of the "party line." Despite all the smoke, there was little fire, this during mostly an era of declared war. Of a total of 9,604,935 employed during the reporting period, a very small share was declared disloyal, much less Communistic. Despite the specter of Adolf Hitler, fascism apparently was not considered a threat to capitalism.

As it turned out, the Commission became a device for undermining confidence in the Truman Administration. In January 1947 it became evident that the Commission would be an instrument for turning aside liberal reforms and be a Republican launching pad for a 1948 anti-Truman presidential campaign. The movement was dominated by conservative Midwestern and western Republicans such as Robert Taft of Ohio, Kenneth Wherry of Nebraska, and William Knowland of California as well as racist southern Democrats such as Mississippi's Senator James O. Eastland and Congressman John Rankin. They had denounced the New Deal as "un-American" and "unconstitutional."

The conservatives on both sides of the aisle were unified by anti-communism and unpopularity of unions. Truman was pressed to head off more aggressive investigations by right-wing congressmen. He issued an executive order establishing a Federal Employees Loyalty and Security Program. Rather than the issue of spies in the government, it was a political problem. Sadly, the program did nothing to serve national security. Several thousand employees resigned under a cloud between 1947 and 1951, and 212 were dismissed, but no one was ever indicted or evidence of espionage ever uncovered. Truman was simply worried that doing nothing would lead to even greater misuse of power by a paranoid Congress and a repressive FBI (he compared the FBI to the Gestapo). Later, Truman characterized his actions as "terrible."[4]

Labor unions were taking a beating from the same sources. The 80th Congress went after that National Labor Relations Act of 1935, which had legalized collective bargaining and exempted unions from antitrust laws that courts had used to prohibit strikes. The provisions of a bill named for Senator Taft and New Jersey representative Fred Hartley Jr, who chaired the Senate and House labor committees, sharply curtailed union rights. The closed shop, a requirement that a new employee belong to a union, would be prohibited by state right-to-work laws. Moreover, union members had to sign non-Communist affidavits and

---

[4] See David McCullough, *Truman* (New York: Simon & Schuster, 1992), pp. 550–553 regarding Truman's views of the FBI and the justifications for his own actions.

unions could not make political contributions, while Presidents could act in an emergency to delay and impede a strike. The Senate and the House passed the Taft-Hartley Act in June 1947 by veto-proof margins. In a radio address, Truman told the nation that the Act was "bad for labor, bad for management, and bad for the country. We do not need — and we do not want — legislation which will take fundamental rights away from our working people." Truman's veto was predictably overwhelmed. Truman's actions nonetheless won renewed political backing from labor and liberals, many of whom now pledged to back him in 1948.

Still, natural allies of Truman had misgivings about the loyalty program. Philip Murray, the President of the Congress of Industrial Organizations (CIO) expressed his reservations regarding Truman's Executive Order on Loyalty (Number 9835) in an April 14, 1947 letter. He wrote:

> Our laws and processes have always been designed to protect the innocent. That they should be changed now is appalling. It is my sincere belief, Mr. President, that if Executive Order 9835 cannot be brought into conformance with this time-tried principle, without the institution of thought police and denial of due process, the Executive Order should be repealed outright.[5]

President Truman sent a short reply the next day in which he stated: "The Order was most carefully drawn with the idea in view that the Civil Rights of no one would be infringed upon and its administration will be carried out in that spirit. Of course, I am glad to have your views on it."[6]

The actions and rhetoric of the House Committee on Un-American Activities surely appeared as more of a threat than Truman did. Then, too, the President had to deal with J. Edgar Hoover, who had a knife in his back.

The struggle between Harry S. Truman and the Committee on Un-American Activities was intense during 1947–1948, and is well-documented by fiery exchanges of letters between Truman and J. Parnell Thomas, the Chairman of the Committee. An inflammatory letter in April 1947 came from Thomas. Among his lurid accusations, Thomas wrote:

> The Communist menace in America is serious. It is no myth, and it is no "bugaboo." As a member of the Committee on Un-American Activities for

---

[5] Letter from Philip Murray to Harry Truman, April 14, 1947, Harry S. Truman Library.
[6] Letter from Harry Truman to Philip Murray, April 15, 1947, Harry S. Truman Library.

eight years, and as its present Chairman, I am convinced of this, just as is Mr J. Edgar Hoover, the Director of the Federal Bureau of Investigation. It is a menace that is so serious, that unless it is dealt with by the law enforcement agencies of the Federal Government, the time may well arrive when the very security of our country will be impaired by this fifth column within our midst.[7]

Truman's brief, diplomatic reply came two days later, in which he wrote: "I think you will find the Attorney General will do his duty as it should be done and in the interest of the welfare of the United States."[8]

Another letter in 1948 in particular is sensational. At its beginning, Thomas states:

> For a long time the Committee on Un-American Activities has been striving diligently to unearth the facts of the Communist conspiracy in the United States and its infiltration into the government services .... The evidence of Communist espionage was laid on your desk more than three years ago. Since that time can you recall one action that has been taken to punish those guilty of spying in the United States? Where and when has your Attorney General prosecuted in public courts a single agent of the Russian espionage ring? The evidence has been gathered diligently by the FBI for many years. Why has it been allowed to gather dust in their files?[9]

The letter concludes in what is a foreshadowing of Senator McCarthy, and details the intended victims:

> As Chairman of the Committee of Un-American Activities, I do not intend to be deterred or intimidated by personal attacks upon me by the President of he United States, or by political-serving announcements by the Attorney General, for I shall continue to expose the participants in this communist conspiracy whether they be Government employees, scientists, diplomats, labor leaders, or movie stars.[10]

---

[7] Letter from J. Parnell Thomas to Harry Truman, April 23, 1947, Harry S. Truman Library.
[8] Letter from Harry Truman to J. Parnell Thomas, April 25,1947 Harry S. Truman Library.
[9] Letter J. Parnell Thomas to Truman, September 29, 1948, Harry S. Truman Library.
[10] *Ibid.*

Among the letters is a thoughtful, well-balanced one from the entire faculty of the Yale University Law School. They saw the liberties that so long distinguished the nation endangered from within, as well as from without. They wrote:

> … Under the cloak of Congressional immunity or the cloak of anonymity, high officials of the national Government are today acting in disregard and defiance of the American tradition of civil liberties and, in our considered judgment, in violation of the Constitution of the United States. It is, we believe, high time that the executive and legislative branches of the United States Government foreswear belief in witches and, by practicing democracy, set an example to those parts of the world which we hope to have embrace its principles. We, therefore, urge (1) that the House of Representatives immediately abolish its Committee on Un-American Activities and (2) that the President and Secretary of State revise their present policy with regard to governmental employees suspected as disloyal or as security risks, so as to bring that policy into conformity with both the spirit and the letter of the United States Constitution.[11]

Truman passed the Yale letter on to Seth Richardson, Chairman of the Loyalty Board, Civil Service Commission, Washington, DC. The loyalty boards were a special concern for the President as well as others such as Americans for Democratic Action.

Because they were luminaries in the media, movie stars and movie directors were particularly vulnerable. The stars themselves took sides for and against the Committee's motives. Several lost their livelihoods because of exposure by the Committee. Among the notables who sided with Truman were Humphrey Bogart and Lauren Bacall, whose star power blinded the Committee members. They testified in defense of colleagues before the Committee. Later, both (especially Bacall) would appear at campaign rallies. We will re-visit this in the next chapter.

These letters and counter-punches by Truman continued until the Korean War shifted the illusive Communist threat to its stark and unmistakeable reality abroad.

---

[11] Letter from the Yale University Law school to the President, Secretary of State, and the Speaker of the House of Representatives, November 26, 1947, Harry S. Truman Library.

Humphrey Bogart.
Source: doctormacro.com.

Lauren Bacall.
Source: Wikipedia.

The Truman Doctrine

Despite the perceptions of those who saw domestic Communists as the problem, Truman's potential supporters of his domestic programs had nowhere to go except to the Republicans who were especially shrill on the imagined problem. Then, there was the parallel foreign front, on which Harry S. Truman was to shine. His next boost in popularity came from a bold foreign policy initiative — the Truman Doctrine. Moscow's aggressiveness in Eastern Europe had provoked George Kennan's long telegram of February 1946 and Churchill's Iron Curtain speech in March. The Soviets moved in the summer to pressure Turkey into shared defense of her Black Sea Straits, an act that persuaded Truman to increase US naval presence in the eastern Mediterranean and to make clear to Moscow that the USA objected to demands on Ankara for a Soviet role in policing a Turkish sea-lane. Beyond this, it was a warning against Moscow's threat to Middle East oil supplies and its support of Communist parties in Western Europe.

Truman had expressed privately his concerns about Stalin (a dictator, pure and simple) and the Soviets. Now he was willing to take his case to the public, when Truman's principal aides gave him a lengthy report in the summer of 1946 on the threat of Soviet aggression and, more immediate, the growing danger of a Communist takeover in Greece. The British government informed Washington in February 1947 that strains on its economy from postwar shortages and the worst winter weather in decades compelled London to end its aid to Turkey and to withdraw its 40,000 troops from Greece, where they had been supporting an anti-Communist government. Britain's departure from the eastern Mediterranean left a power vacuum that the Soviets would likely fill. Worse, it could be a prelude to expanded Communist influence in Italy and France and the more general Soviet control of Europe.

The appointment of George C. Marshall as Secretary of State, replacing Jimmy Byrnes, was one of the best and most important decisions of Truman's presidency. History might have looked much different had Marshall been absent. At 66, Marshall was the first career soldier to become Secretary of State. Slightly under six feet, with sandy-gray hair and blue eyes, he was a figure of such flawless rectitude and self-command, so much so that he inspired awe. Churchill called him "the noblest Roman." Bill Hassett on Truman's staff spoke of the "reverence" Marshall inspired. Imperturbable under pressure, he was without a trace of petty vanity or self-serving ambition. He was the man most admired by Harry Truman, who described him as astute and profound. Most of all, Truman admired Marshall's rock-bound sense of duty, his selflessness and honesty. Marshall's high standing with Republicans on the Hill was frosting on the cake. By early February 1947 Truman's popularity in the polls, due in great part to Marshall's presence, was back up to 48 percent, having been near 30 percent in previous polls.

On February 24, Marshall and the under secretary of state Dean Acheson met with the President and urged "immediate action" to provide help for Greece, and to a lesser degree, for Turkey as well. To Marshall, the British announcement of a withdrawal from Greece was tantamount in foreshadowing British withdrawal from the whole of the Middle East. He saw the situation as extremely serious. The sum needed for Greece alone just for the remainder of 1947 was a quarter of a billion dollars. Truman agreed that Greece would have to be helped, quickly and with substantial amounts. But aid to Greece was only one aspect of a broader problem. The Soviets were determined to dominate Europe, the Middle East and Asia. The choice was acting with energy or losing by default.

The Soviets were maintaining excessively large military forces in the satellite countries. The Soviets already dominated Finland, Poland, Czechoslovakia, Hungary, Romania, and Bulgaria. In Austria only the presence of British, French, and American Occupation troops prevented a Soviet takeover. Moreover, Communist parties were growing in France and Italy. In a weak and divided China, the USSR was in a position to exert greater influence than any other country. The Soviets were supplying the Communist forces in China, while in Korea, the Soviets had shown that they would consent to the unification of the country only if assured of a "friendly" government. The menace was gathering as Russia was rapidly developing atomic weapons, guided missiles, materials for biological warfare, a strategic air force, and submarines of great cruising range.

Truman asked Marshall on February 27 to make the case to Congress for aid to Greece and Turkey. Marshall's standing as one of the architects of military victory in World War II gave him exceptional clout with Congress. He had a reputation as a nonpartisan patriot, who had sacrificed his personal comfort to serve in China. Marshall gave an impassioned plea for a costly commitment that gained a positive response from otherwise skeptical congressmen and senators. Dean Acheson followed Marshall with a dramatic call to arms that frightened the congressional leaders into seeing a clear and present danger. Arthur Vandenberg (1884–1951) a recent Republican convert to internationalism, declared himself in support of Truman's request. This was followed by a Truman speech to Congress on March 12 in which he characterized the crisis as part of a larger contest between freedom and totalitarianism, when he said:

> Totalitarian regimes imposed upon free peoples, by direct or indirect aggression, undermine the foundations of international peace and hence the security of the United States. I believe that it must be the policy of the United States to support free people who are resisting attempted subjugation by armed minorities or by outside pressures."[12]

Dressed in a dark suit and dark tie, he read from an open notebook slowly and with great force. His audience listened in silence. The speech set forth what became known as the Truman Doctrine. Clark Clifford insisted that Truman's name be attached to the Doctrine. Truman suggested that at the present moment nearly every nation must choose between alternative ways of life. One way of life is based upon the will of the majority, and is distinguished by free institutions, representative government, free elections, guarantees of individual liberty, freedom of speech and religion, and freedom from political oppression. The second way is based upon the will of a minority forcibly imposed upon the majority. It relies upon terror and oppression, a controlled press and radio, fixed elections, and the suppression of personal freedoms. Truman had made clear which way of life he preferred for Americans; he wanted the same for the Greeks and Turks.

His request for $400 million to aid Greece and Turkey did not meet with universal approval. While Congress agreed to the funding with the Senate vote of 67 to 23, the House vote of 287 to 107, and 56 percent of a poll supported Truman's request, while almost two-thirds of the country expressed a preference to have the United Nations take responsibility for the crisis in the Near East.

While it seemed so at the time, the Truman Doctrine was not an abrupt, dramatic turn in American policy, but a declaration of Principle. It was a continuation of a policy that had been evolving since Potsdam, its essence to be found in Kennan's "Long Telegram" and in a more emphatic Clifford-Elsey Report on the Soviet Union. It was an exciting and important time. In 1947 and 1948 Harry Truman and the United States saved the free world. The USA was the only free nation in a position to do so, and it did not have to. It owed a lot to the changed outlook of the President; this was the "new" Truman.

---

[12] Quoted by Robert J. Donovan, *Conflict and Crisis: The Presidency of Harry S. Truman, 1945–1948* (New York: W. W. Norton, 1977), pp. 279–285.

The Herbert Hoover Reports on European Conditions

Behind the scenes, a remarkable friendship between former President Herbert Hoover provided background material for further economic aid to Europe. The friendship was renewed with an exchange of letters between Truman and Hoover in January 1947. Truman noted how Hoover had, the year prior, taken a trip around the world at his request "to report on food needs at a time of critical shortage. The result was most helpful in meeting the acute problem which confronted us." Truman goes on to suggest that

> a serious situation in food still exists in certain areas, particularly those in Europe occupied by our forces and for which we, therefore, have a direct responsibility. I believe a food survey by you of these areas would be of great benefit to us in determining our policy in supplying food or funds for its purchase. The recent merger of the United States Zone in Germany with the British Zone for economic purposes makes the food conditions in the British Zone also of interest to us.

Truman then requested that Hoover undertake this mission and report to him upon it.[13]

In a return letter the next day, Hoover agreed to be of service, but suggested that the mission be broadened to "include inquiry into what further immediate steps are possible to increase their exports and thus their ability to become self-supporting; what possibilities there are of payment otherwise; and when charity can be expected to end."[14]

Herbert Hoover quickly provided three detailed reports. The first was on German agriculture and food requirements. Germany had been divided into four military occupation zones among the Russians, French, British, and Americans. The American and British Zones were administratively combined, each nation bearing one-half the expense. He proceeded to provide an overview and analysis of manpower available. Some 6 million of the most vital and most skilled workers in the population was subtracted by the war. Likewise, 90,000 Nazis are held in concentration camps and 1.9 million others are under sanctions by which they

---

[13] Letter from Truman to Herbert Hoover, The Waldorf Astoria, New York, N.Y., January 28, 1947, Harry S. Truman Library.

[14] Letter from Hoover to HST, January 19, 1947, Harry S. Truman library.

can only engage in manual labor.[15] He concluded that "the housing situation in the two zones is the worst that modern civilization has ever seen. About 25 percent of the urban housing was destroyed by the war." Furthermore "the average space among tens of millions is equivalent to between three and four people to a 12" × 12" room." Still further, "one consequence is the rapid spread of tuberculosis and other potentially communicable diseases."[16]

He continued: "The shortage of coal is, next to food, the most serious immediate bottleneck to both living and the revival of exports to pay for food."[17] The Ruhr, due to lack of skilled men and physical vitality in labor, was producing only 230,000 tons per day, as against a pre-war figure of 450,000 tons per day. Much of the output is exported to surrounding nations which are also suffering. This shortage leaves the two zones without sufficient coal for transport, household, and other dominant services, leaving little for export.[18]

He then turned to agricultural production and noted that some areas contributed nothing. About 25 percent of the German pre-war food production came from those areas taken over by Russia and Poland. What's more, millions of tons once flowed into the American and British Zones from these areas The Russian army was fed in their zone. The British and American armies and civilians were entirely fed from home.[19]

He considered the nutritional condition of the population:. "Over half of the 6,595,000 children and adolescents, especially in the lower-income groups, are in a deplorable condition .... In some areas famine edema (actual starvation) is appearing in the children,"[20] He further concludes that a considerable part of the "normal consumer" group of 17,910,000 is likewise in deplorable condition. They included the light physical workers and a large majority were women and many were aged. Some parts of the group were too poor to purchase even the 1,550 calorie ration. He finds the increased death

---

[15] Herbert Hoover, The President's Economic Mission to Germany and Austria, Report no. 1 — German Agriculture and Food Requirements, February 28, 1947, p. 2, Harry S. Truman Library.

[16] *Ibid.* p. 3.

[17] *Ibid.*

[18] *Ibid.* p. 4.

[19] *Ibid.*

[20] *Ibid.* pp. 7–8.

rate among the aged as appalling. For persons over 70, in three months in the autumn of 1946, the increase was 40 percent.[21]

Hoover went on to detail the amounts of foodstuffs and energy sources to be both imported and exported. Most importantly, he built a case for aiding America's former enemy, Germany, as necessary to rebuild a united Europe. For that reason, he concluded:

> Entirely aside from any humanitarian feelings for this mass of people if we want peace; if we want to preserve the safety and health of our Army of Occupation; if we want to save the expense of even larger military forces to preserve order; if we want to reduce the size and expense of our Army of Occupation — I can see no other course but to meet the burdens I have here outlined .... If Western Civilization is to survive in Europe, it must also survive in Germany. And it must be built into a cooperative member of that civilization. That indeed is the hope of any lasting peace.[22]

The main contribution of Hoover to what would become the Marshall Plan was to give rough estimates of the initial costs for restoration of Germany and Austria. Of perhaps equal importance, he laid out the basis for including Germany as one of the recipients of aid. As it turned out, without the Marshall Plan, Germany would *not* have emerged ultimately as the largest and most efficient of the European economies.

In Hoover's third report, he made even more explicit the means by which Germany could be made whole again and contribute her exports to the rest of Europe, the US and beyond. He outlined policies which would restore productivity in Germany and exports with which to buy their food and relieve the drain on the US and British Treasuries. In fact, Britain soon would cease to supply aid to Germany and France because of her own recovery problems. Hoover emphasized: "We desperately need recovery in all of Europe. We need it not only for economic reasons but as the first necessity in peace."[23]

---

[21] These and more extensive nutritional conditions are based upon surveys made by Dr. Wm. H. Sebrell, Jr., of the US Public Health Service, who was a member of Hoover's Mission. He also visited Italy, France, Belgium, Holland and Britain, and found the nutritional condition in those countries to be nearly "pre-war normal." See *Ibid.*, p. 9.

[22] *Ibid.* p. 21.

[23] Herbert Hoover, The President's Economic Mission to Germany and Austria — Report no. 3. The Necessary Steps for Promotion of German Exports, So As To Relieve American

He said that the German economic problems have two aspects: the long view and the immediate problems. The long view economic problems are greatly affected by war destruction, the boundary settlements for the New Germany[24], the plant removals for reparations, and the policies with respect to the war potential of industry. There was considerable destruction of non-war industry from the air and otherwise during the war. Moreover, the proposed annexations of the Saar Basin by France, would take from Germany, as compared to 1936, about 25 percent of her food supply, about 30 percent of her bituminous coal, and about 20 percent of her manufacturing capacity. There has been a demolition of all arms plants as part of disarmament. This destruction included some plants which could have been converted to peaceable production. In general, the attempt had been to convert Germany into a country mostly agricultural and pastoral. The absolute destruction or prohibition includes ocean-going ships, shipbuilding, aircraft, ball bearings, aluminum, magnesium, beryllium, vanadium and radio-transmitting equipment, together with synthetic oil, ammonia and rubber. Further, there are elaborate restrictions on heavy industry generally. For example, iron and steel production is to be reduced from 19 million tons (as in 1936) to a capacity of 7.5 million tons, with a maximum production of 5.8 million tons and only the "older plants" to be used.

There were consequences for the food supply. Germany in 1936 was, by intensive cultivation, able to produce about 85 percent of her food supply. This 85 percent had now been reduced by 25 percent through the Russian and Polish annexations; it was down to about 64 percent because even a larger population was to be concentrated in the New Germany. This production was greatly dependent upon the intensive use of fertilizers. Thus, the New Germany would require at least 500,000 metric tons of nitrogen and 650,000 tons of phosphoric anhydride, she having sufficient potash. However, under the "level of industry" agreement, the domestic production of nitrogen eventually would be reduced to under 200,000 tons; the production of phosphoric anhydride, would be reduced to about 200,000 tons. Thus there is a great discrepancy between minimum

---

Taxpayers of the Burdens of Relief and For Economic Recovery of Europe, March 18, 1947, p. 2., Harry S. Truman Library.

[24] "New Germany" is an idealized construct in which west and East Germany are fully integrated again. Hoover presumed that Stalin would be more cooperative than Stalin had ever intended or was. As a former ally during WWII, Stalin was trusted by many in the State Department and elsewhere.

agricultural needs and the possible fertilizer production under the "level of industry" plan. The level of industry was based roughly on pre-war production proportions. Unless there are large imports of fertilizer, Germany's food production was likely to drop under 60 percent of her requirements even with an austere diet. The New Germany would need, at 1947 prices, to import over $1,250,000,000 annually in food and animal feed alone. The fertilizer reduction in Germany not only led to losses in her own food production but in her export potential to supply food.

The now restricted "heavy industries" comprised between 60 percent and 70 percent of total German exports. Due to the prohibitions, she had of import all of her oil and rubber, and considerable nitrogen for fertilizers. The idea that exports from German "light industry," from coal and native raw materials, such as potash, could pay for her imports of food and other necessities was an illusion. To do so would require not only complete restoration of the pre-war level in "light industry" but much larger equipment than she had even before the war. If these industries expanded, Germany would be in competition with consumers' goods from all the rest of the world whose "light industries" have been little damaged by war. The overall illusion is that Germany could become self-supporting under the "levels of industry" plan within the borders envisioned at present for New Germany. Furthermore, Europe as a whole could not recover without the economic recovery of Germany.

Hoover's radical outline was only the beginning of Truman's bold internationalism. Secretary Marshall raised the stakes on the scope of the USA's commitment to Europe in June. Speaking for the Truman Administration in a commencement address at Harvard University on June 5, 1947, Marshall set forth a plan for repairing the devastated economies of all European nations. It was a plan brilliantly conceived. Soon, we will turn to the content of that speech and what it meant. We will also relate what was going on behind Truman's back as well as under his nose. All these actions were interrupted or at least slowed down by the Campaign of 1948 to which we next turn.

Chapter 7

The Populist Campaign of 1948

1 948. World War II was not far from memory but in its wake, another war was about to begin. While Truman was planning his Presidential Campaign, Stalin was to make a new play in Berlin which would require immediate, decisive action by the President.

Truman decided to run for President, on his own terms. He needed to kick-start the campaign. He quickly got the idea of a slow train trip across the United States. A planned speech at the University of California became the impetus for the cross-country foray. The train trip would allow ordinary people to see and hear the President. The train was dubbed the Ferdinand Magellan, suggesting an exploratory adventure. Truman spoke, worked, and lived from the last car of the train, which included a rear platform with a lectern and loudspeakers and space for some dignitaries to stand beside him.

The Warm-Up

It was a two-week trip that included five formal addresses. There were big cities, but the informal, seemingly extemporaneous talks at the "whistle stops," struck a responsive chord with the public. (Senator Robert Taft derisively called them insignificant communities.) One of Truman's biographers, Alonzo Hamby, described the typical scene:

> The president began a talk by alluding to some bit of local history..... [this after having introduced Bess (the "Boss") and Margaret (the "Boss's Boss")], he [gave]

the crowd a look at the womenfolk and a sense of his model middle-class family. He always displayed his customary smile and increasingly seemed to take a genuine delight in his fleeting contacts with the average American who came down to the station, many of them, in turn, saw someone who might be running a local bank or small business: decent, respected, well-traveled, but not much different from themselves.[1]

These were truly informal (with a capital 'I') talks, usually off-the-cuff (71 by Truman's count). Once, at a late-night stop in California, Truman appeared in bathrobe and pajamas. "Pour it on," someone shouted at a stop when Truman lambasted the "do-nothing" Republican Congress. It happened to be an apt description of this particular Congress. It was an exhausting two weeks that would be a model for what was to come. Yet *Time* described Truman as "full of bounce" when he got off the train at the return stop of Union Station in Washington on June 18, 1948.[2] He needed that as well as self-confidence. This turned out to be a warm-up for his train travels after the party conventions.

When the Republicans nominated Thomas E. Dewey, a poll showed the President at a continuing 11-point disadvantage.[3] Moreover, the Democrat Party was a fragmented party in which Southern stalwarts wanted no part of Truman, and liberals openly advocated drafting General Dwight Eisenhower as the party's nominee.[4] Some, such as Harold L. Ickes (1874–1952), privately urged Truman to drop out of the race, which he was losing.[5] Truman nonetheless remained confident that he could gain the nomination and win the election. This against great odds, for few, if any, agreed with him.

The 1948 Republican National Convention in Philadelphia came first. From the beginning on June 21 when Clare Booth Luce told a delighted crowd that Harry Truman was a "gone goose," the Convention hall smelled of victory. Governor Dewey of New York won on the third ballot and chose Governor Earl Warren of California as his running mate. These two popular, youthful progressive governors of the two largest wealthiest states made it a "dreamboat of a ticket." Warren's warmth compensated for Dewey's cold and self-assured manner.

[1] Alonzo L. Hamby, *Man of the People: A Life of Harry S. Truman* (New York: Oxford University Press, 1995), pp. 441–444.
[2] *Time*, June 28, 1948.
[3] Gallup, *The Gallup Poll: Public Opinion, 1935–1971*, p. 749.
[4] David McCullough, *Truman* (New York: Simon & Schuster, 1992), pp. 612, 632–636.
[5] Robert J. Donovan, *Conflict and Crisis: The Presidency of Harry S. Truman, 1945–1948* (New York: W. W. Norton, 1977), pp. 388–389.

Only a miracle, or so it was thought by *Time* and *Newsweek*, would make Truman the winner.

As it turned out, Truman had little time to contemplate the Republican coronation of Dewey. On June 24, 1948, the day Dewey won on that third ballot was also the day that the Russians set up a blockade on all rail, highway, and water traffic in and out of Berlin. Joseph Stalin (1878–1958) was trying to force the Western allies to withdraw from the city. As noted, post-war Germany had been divided into four sections with the allied parts controlled by the United States, Great Britain and France and the other part by the Soviet Union. Berlin, located in the eastern Soviet half was also divided into four sectors with West Berlin occupied by Allied interests and East Berlin occupied by the Soviets. Stalin's actions showed that the Soviet Union was attempting to control *all* of Berlin by cutting surface traffic to and from the city of West Berlin.

The Berlin Airlift

General Lucius D. Clay (1897–1978), then military governor of the US Zone in Germany (1947–1949), is the military hero who carried out the Berlin Airlift. Two days after the blockade Clay ordered the first phase. It was an act of defiance against the Soviets and, as we will see, an incredible feat of logistics.

President Truman reacted with caution and firmness. He rejected ideas bordering on outright aggression, but stated plainly that whether American forces would remain in Berlin was not open to question: "We stay in Berlin, period."[6] Clay did not have enough resources to continue the airlift alone. The next step depended upon Harry Truman, who took his own council. It took only two days for Truman to take decisive action: On June 26, he ordered a full-scale airlift to bolster Clay's improvised actions. He also sent two squadrons of B-29s to Germany, planes known to the world as the kind that dropped atomic bombs on Japan. That they were not modified to carry the bombs was a detail unknown to the Russians. This air-bridge to Berlin lasted until the end of September of 1949, despite the Soviet's lifting of the blockade on May 12, 1949.

There were only two airfields in Berlin at the time — Tempelhof with one runway in the US sector and Gatow with one runway in the British sector. At

---

[6] James Forrestal, *Forrestal Diaries* (edited by Walter Millis) (New York: Viking, 1951), pp. 454–455.

Tempelhof, before June 1948, US Army engineers had built a 12-foot thick rubber base runway and covered it with steel landing mats, adequate for US military needs before the airlift. Under the continuous pounding of heavy, loaded aircraft, however, the steel landing mats started to break. It took a force of 225 men working on the runway between plane landings to keep the field operational. In early July 1948, while the old runway was being constantly repaired, construction of a new runway began. This was followed in late 1948 by a third Tempelhof runway.[7] Cargo planes were landing at Tempelhof every four minutes, 24 hours a day.

The Berlin Airlift was a great American achievement. It affected the morale of Western, non-Communist Europe strongly, and the entire course of the Cold War, not to mention Truman's drive for election. Later, the airlift was the basis of a major motion picture.[8] Yet, it seemed to most observers at the time to be unrealistic to supply entirely by air for any but a very limited time the necessities of a major city. Had Truman consulted his staff, he probably would have been rejected. Clay is remembered for initiating and maintaining the airlift, which would have failed without Truman's actions.

General Clay reported to the White House on July 22, 1948 and confirmed Truman's thinking and actions. He said that the abandonment of Berlin would have disastrous effects upon allied plans for Western Germany. It would slow European recovery, the success of which depended upon more production, especially from Western Germany. (This echoes much of what Herbert Hoover had written.) At the same time, the allies should be prepared to go to any length to find a peaceful solution to the situation, but the US had to remain in Berlin.[9]

What was involved in the airlift operations? Initially, 52 C-54's and 80 C-47's were deployed. Each day two round trips were made with more than 250 landings. Later 75 additional C-47 planes would bring total tonnage to 3,500 tons per day. General Clay said he felt that the Russians would not attack the planes unless they intended to go to war, which he thought unlikely.[10] There was a lot at stake.

---

[7] See D. M Giangreco and Robert E. Griffin, "From Airbridge to Berlin," Harry S. Truman Library.
[8] The movie was *The Big Life* (1950) and it starred Montgomery Clift and Paul Douglas as two US Air Force Sergeants who participated in the Berlin Airlift. The movie gives us the flavor of the times.
[9] Harry S. Truman, *Memoirs: Years of Trial and Hope, Volume 2* (New York: Time, Inc., 1956), p. 124.
[10] See *ibid.*, especially pp. 124–125.

The Democratic Convention

Despite the economic and strategic heroics, the whole Democratic Party — the Roosevelt coalition of labor, intellectuals, city bosses, and southern segregationists was coming to pieces. On the eve of the Democratic Convention, Truman's chances for nomination in his own right seemed slim. The doctrinaire New Dealers favored a draft of Dwight D. Eisenhower, the WWII war hero. This despite Eisenhower's determination to stay out of politics. "If you can't stand the heat, you better get out of the kitchen," Truman liked to say. He was certain that Eisenhower was not a candidate; Ike knew the temperature of the kitchen. On July 9, Eisenhower again said "no way."

A keynote speech by 71-year-old Senator Alben Barkley (1877–1956) of Kentucky gave a spark of life to the convention gathering in which he recalled Franklin Roosevelt's years of the New Deal in contrast to Republican failings. Moreover, the speech won Barkley the vice presidential nomination. Truman's first choice had been the liberal Supreme Court Justice William O. Douglas, but Douglas opted to stay on the Court with its lifetime appointment. Again, despite the odds and the doubts, Truman was nominated on the first ballot. Token opposition came from the southern delegates supporting Senator Richard Russell of deep-South Georgia.

When Truman accepted the nomination, he did so with the same approach as on his western-bound train trip. He adopted the same informal style in a speech that lambasted the Republicans for offering empty promises and surprised the delegates with a call for a special congressional session on July 26. He sought to challenge the Republicans to fulfill Dewey's promises to halt inflation, ease the housing shortage, aid education, and enact civil rights reforms. The latter was in response to a successful convention challenge from Hubert Humphrey (1911–1978), the young and voluble mayor of Minneapolis, who led an impassioned revolt against what he saw as an ambiguous, restrained statement on the subject of civil rights.

Truman's was one of the best acceptance speeches in political history. He too must have thought well of it, as it is heavily quoted in the HST *Memoirs*.[11] He began, "Senator Barkley and I will win this election and make these Republicans like it — don't you forget that." And he meant it; the delegates knew that

---

[11] Truman, *op. cit.*, pp. 207–210. The speech is exactly like he gave it.

and they were brought to their feet. He recalled the benefits derived from Democratic Administrations. "Never in the world were the farmers of any republic or any kingdom of any other country as prosperous as the farmers of the United States; and if they don't do their duty by the Democratic party, they are the most ungrateful people in the world." He continued in Populist fighting mode. Truman suggested that wages and salaries had increased from $29 billion in 1933 to more than $128 billion in 1947. "That's labor," he added, "and labor never had but one friend in politics, and that is the Democratic party and Franklin D. Roosevelt. And I say to labor what I have said to the farmers: They are the most ungrateful people in the world if they pass the Democratic party by this year."

Then Harry tore into the 80th Congress, emphasizing that "the Republican party favors the privileged few and not the common, everyday man. Ever since its inception that party has been under the control of special privilege, and they concretely proved it in the 80th Congress....They proved it by the things they failed to do. ..." He listed in detail the failures of the Republican-controlled Congress, pulling no punches. Then, toward the end of the speech, he played what he called his "trump card."

"On the twenty-sixth day of July, which out in Missouri we call 'Turnip Day,' I am going to call Congress back and ask them to pass laws to halt rising prices, to meet the housing crisis — which they are saying they are for in their platform." He goes on, "At the same time, I shall ask them to act upon other vitally needed measures, such as aid to education, which they say they are for; a national health program; civil rights legislation, which they say they are for; an increase in the minimum wage, which I doubt very much they are for; extension of the Social Security coverage and increased benefits, which they say they are for, funds for projects needed in our program to provide public power and cheap electricity. By indirection, this 80th Congress has tried to sabotage the power policies the United States has pursued for 14 years. That power lobby is as bad as the real estate lobby which is sitting on the housing bill."

He was not finished with the Republicans. "Now my friends, if there is any reality behind that Republican platform, we ought to get some action from a short session of the 80th Congress. They can do this job in 15 days, if they want to do it. They will still have time to go out and run for office. They are going to try to dodge their responsibility. They are going to drag all the red herrings they can across this campaign, but I am here to say that Senator Barkley and I are not going to let them get away with it." It was a Populist speech through and through. Truman had said as much to Alben Barkley just prior to delivery.

Truman was calling the bluff of the Republicans, and the announcement of a special session of the Congress electrified the Democratic convention. The party had new hope. The stage was set for the most active part of the 1948 campaign. Truman picked Labor Day (September 6) to speak at Cadillac Square in Detroit. It set the pace for the campaign to follow. "As you know," he told a nationwide audience, "...I speak bluntly sometimes. I am going to speak plainly and bluntly today. These are critical times for labor and for all who work. There is great danger ahead. Right now, the whole future of labor is wrapped up in one simple proposition.

"If, in this next election, you get a Congress and an administration friendly to labor, you have much to hope for, if you get an administration and a Congress unfriendly to labor, you have much to fear, and you had better look out....

"If the Congressional elements that made the Taft-Hartley Law are allowed to remain in power, and if these elements are further encouraged by the election of a Republican President, you men of labor can expect to be hit by a steady barrage of body blows. And, if you stay at home as you did in 1946, and keep these reactionaries in power, you will deserve every blow you get....

"Remember that the reactionary of today is a shrewd man. He is in many ways much shrewder than the reactionaries of the 1920s. He is a man with a calculating machine where his heart ought to to be. He has learned a great deal about how to get his way by observing demagogues and reactionaries in other countries. And now he has many able allies in the press and in the radio.

"If you place the government of this country under the control of those who hate labor, whom can you blame if measures are thereafter adopted to destroy the powers, prestige, and earning power of labor?

"I tell you that labor must fight now harder than ever before to make sure that its rights are kept intact....

"I know from my own experience with labor leaders and unions that the ability of labor to discipline itself and to cooperate with other groups in the country is steadily growing....

"Labor has always had to fight for its gains. Now you are fighting for the whole future of the labor movement. We are in a hard, tough fight against shrewd and rich opponents. They know they can't count on your vote. Their only hope is that you won't vote at all. They have misjudged you. I know that were going to win this crusade for the right!"

Truman had not forgotten the farmers, who constituted the original motive for the American populist movement. Labor then was soon to follow. Of course, farming consists of labor as well. He was pitting the lowly against the privileged.

The Whistle-Stop Campaign

After the convention and the Detroit speech, it was time to get on the road again. The beloved train was the way to go. Again, the Ferdinand Magellan was the railroad *car* of choice, about which more should be said. It was the only private railroad car ever fitted out for the exclusive use of the President of the United States. Built originally in 1928, it was 83 feet in length and weighed over 142 tons. The weight came from three-inch, bulletproof glass and its armor plate so that it weighed as much as a locomotive. During the war only the word "Pull-man" appeared on the outside; in 1948, the only distinguishing exterior features were the presidential seal at the rear platform and three loudspeakers on top of the platform roof. Inside, everything was designed with comfort in mind. To Truman, it was the perfect way to travel.

The Magellan began its new adventure on the morning of September 17, 1948. While in June he had gone 9,000 miles, Truman now would travel 21,928 miles in his famous Whistle-Stop Campaign. And, it was all Harry Truman's idea; he wanted to see the people. Still, it was a campaign and would consist of three major tours. First, he went cross-country again to California, for 15 days; then there would be a six-day tour of the Middle West; this followed by a hard-hitting ten days in the population centers of the Northeast and then a return trip home to Missouri. Truman wanted to go to all 48 states, thus including the Deep South; in reality, given the demands of the presidency, he had to go where the electoral votes were. For 33 days the Magellan was center stage for a fast-paced political show, which consisted of one act and one 64-year-old performer. The heavy-weight campaign car would be Truman's campaign headquarters, home, office, presidential command center, and the place where he would keep hope alive. The Signal Corps, in a separate car, provided continuous contact with Washington, DC and hence the rest of the world. Truman had become more and more uneasy over the situation in Berlin, and wrote privately, "I have a terrible feeling that we are very close to war."[12]

People who had met Truman were impressed with his speed of movement and speech. As to speed, the train was no exception. While the infirm Roosevelt preferred the easy pace of no more than 35 miles per hour, Truman liked to go about 80.

At the start, in Union Station in Washington, DC the moderate crowd outside the Magellan rivaled that on the inside. The complete entourage, including the Secret Service, numbered some seventy persons. Truman took along Charlie Ross, Clark Clifford[13], Mart Connelly, George Elsey, Charlie Murphy, White House physician Wallace Graham, and Rose Conway, the President's secretary. Besides those, there were some new speechwriters, and Bill Boyle, an old friend from Kansas City and aid who had been on the Truman Committee. Boyle, would, along with Connelly, be doing the political chores. Barkley and Truman posed for a few last pictures.

"Mow 'em down, Harry," Barkley said.

"I'm going to fight hard. I'm going to give 'em hell,"[14] replied Truman, sounding the campaign's theme.

At this auspicious start, the odds were definitely against Truman's election in his own right. The Democrats and Henry Wallace had split the Party into several pieces. New York and the South already were presumed lost. Since the Civil War, the off-year election winner had always been the President's Party. Contrary to this mid-term linage, the Republicans had won the Congress in 1946; meanwhile, the dinner party talk in Washington was all about Dewey Cabinet selections. Prominent Democrats were putting their homes on the market. In the West, despite his June foray there, predictions were that he could win only 17 of

---

[12] Harry S. Truman Diary, September 13, 1948, Harry S. Truman Library. Again, the speech is exactly as he gave it.

[13] We should note one special role played by Clark Clifford as early as November, 1947. He wrote a long memorandum to Truman in which, among other things, he predicted that the Republican nominee would be Governor Thomas Dewey. He also said that "President Truman will be elected if the Administration will successfully concentrate on the traditional Democratic alliance between the South and West.," and "Henry Wallace will be the candidate of a third party." He also warned: "It is dangerous to assume that labor has nowhere else to go in 1948. *Labor can stay home.*" Furthermore, "The liberal and progressive leaders are not overly enthusiastic about the Administration." See Memorandum, Clark Clifford to Harry S. Truman, November 19, 1947, pp. 1–4. 6, 10. Political File, Clifford Papers. Harry S. Truman Library. The entire 26 pages is worth reading.

[14] *Time*, September 27, 1948.

the 71 electoral votes at stake. A Gallup Poll of farm voters, who Truman had to have, gave Dewey 48 percent to Truman's 38. Perhaps the farmers had not heard what Truman said about them at the Democratic Convention. Worse, the latest Roper Poll showed Dewey leading by an "unbeatable" 44 to 31 percent.[15] The widely respected Elmo Roper (1900–1971) said he would discontinue polling since the outcome had already been decided. Since a picture is worth a thousand words, *Life* had a picture of Governor Dewey and his staff with the headline: "Albany Provides Preview of Dewey Administration."

Despite the predictions, Truman drew tremendous crowds as the train and motorcade rolled through Grand Rapids, Lansing, Pontiac, and Flint. From Detroit to Pontiac, there were people along the highway, a lot of people. The turnout at Truman's six stops in Michigan was estimated at more than half a million people. Then came Davenport, Iowa City, Grinnell, and Des Moines, all in the Republican stronghold of Iowa. Iowa had a Republican governor and eight Republican Iowa representatives in Congress, plus both senators. But Truman noted that most of his audience were farmers and he knew that Iowa farmers had voted for Roosevelt during the Depression.

In Dexter, he laced into the Republicans:

> You remember the big boom and the great crash of 1929. You remember that in 1932 the position of the farmer had become so desperate that there was actual violence in many farming communities. You remember that insurance companies and banks took over much of the land of small independent farmers — 223,000 farmers lost their farms....
>
> I wonder how many times you have to be hit on the head before you find out who's hitting you?...
>
> The Democratic Party represents the people. It is pledged to work for agriculture.... The Democratic Party puts human rights and human welfare first.... These Republican gluttons of privilege are cold men. They are cunning men.... They want a return of the Wall Street economic dictatorship.[16]

He was sounding much like that other great Populist, William Jennings Bryan. However, 1948 was a year of general prosperity. What Truman was

---

[15] Gallup, *The Gallup Poll: Public Opinion, 1935–1971*, p. 757.
[16] Public Papers of the Presidents of the United States, Harry S. Truman, Containing the Public Messages, Speeches and Statements of the President, 1945–1953 (Washington, D. C.: Government Printing Office, 1961–1966), p. 504.

appealing to was the relative income position of farmers and labor compared with the fat cats on Wall Street or more broadly, the top one percent in the income distribution. In Dexter and elsewhere he made clear that he too had once been a working farmer who could easily relate to their needs. His concern at the time was not with the GNP (which was about to grow nicely) but with the income distribution, which was lopsided. There had been six stops prior to Dexter; after Dexter came Des Moines, Melcher and Chariton, Iowa. The crowds at the rear platform of the train were larger than the towns' populations.

In Chariton he said, "You stayed at home in 1946 and you got the 80th Congress, and you got just exactly what you deserved. You didn't exercise your God-given right to control this country. Now you're going to have another chance."[17] He was referring to the 1946 mid-term Congressional elections.

He was on a crusade against the Republicans who were standing astride the road to progress for the everyday man. At Trenton, Missouri, he said as much. He made an unscheduled stop at Polo, Missouri; where he gave his 13th speech of the day. After a brief pause in Independence the next day, the train raced across Kansas. Truman spoke to 25,000 people spread across the lawn of the State Capitol in Denver. There he made clear the difference between the average Republican voter and the policies of the Republican Party:

Republicans in Washington have a habit of becoming curiously deaf to the voice of the people. They have a hard time hearing what the ordinary people of the country are saying. But they have no trouble at all hearing what Wall Street is saying. They are able to catch the slightest whisper from big business and the special interests.[18]

It was September 20, 1948.

Truman's attack on the Washington Republicans was relentless at Grand Junction, Colorado and at Helper, Springville, and Provo, Utah. To a standing-room-only crowd in the gigantic Mormon Tabernacle in Salt Lake City, he charged "selfish men have always tried to skim the cream from our natural resources to satisfy their own greed. And their instrument in this effort has always been the Republican Party." Still Truman was at his best talking without notes to

---

[17] *Ibid.*, p. 501.
[18] *Ibid.*, p. 518.

small crowds. Nearly always he had something to say about local history, local achievements and interests. At Mojave, he said:

> They tell me that in 1883 — that was the year before I was born — that a gentleman by the name of Webb built ten grand, big wagons here in this town, bought himself a hundred head of mules, and began to haul borax out of the Mojave Desert — and that was the origin of Twenty-Mule Team Borax which we always kept in the house when I was a kid. I never thought I would be here as President at the place where it originated and talking to you people about your interests in the welfare of the country.[19]

He said again and again that he stood for a government of and for the people, not the "special interests." "You don't get any double talk from me," he declared at Sparks, Nevada, "I'm either for something or against it, and you know it. You know what I stand for."[20] He was full of fight but remained cheerful and friendly.

Biographer David McCullough vividly paints a typical scene:

> The crowds would be gathered at station stops often from early morning, waiting for him to arrive. Men and boys perched on rooftops and nearby signal towers for a better view. There would be a high school band standing by, ready to play the national anthem or "Hail to the Chief," or to struggle through the Missouri waltz, a song Truman particularly disliked but that it was his fate to hear repeated hundreds of times over. His train would ease into the station as the band blared, the crowd cheered. Then, accompanied by three or four local politicians — usually a candidate for Congress or state party chairman who had boarded the train at a prior stop — Truman would step from behind the blue velvet curtain onto the platform, and the crowd, large or small, would cheer even more. One of the local politicians would then introduce the President of the United States and the crowd would cheer again.[21]

People had heard of his promise to Barkley. "Give 'em hell, Harry!" would come a shout from out of the crowd. Often more than once, the shout would go up, followed by more whoops, laughter, and acclamations of approval, especially when he tore, as he so often did, into the 80th Congress.

---

[19] *Ibid.*, p. 554.
[20] *Ibid.*, p. 544.
[21] David McCullough, *Truman, op. cit.*, p. 663.

Much later, he would tell the *New York Times* (December 27, 1972): "I never gave anybody hell. I just told the truth and they thought it was hell."

At Gilmore Stadium in Los Angeles Truman had screen stars Lauren Bacall, Humphrey Bogart and young Ronald Reagan seated beside him. He liked to rub elbows with the stars that were liberal Democrats. (Reagan became a conservative when he started making "The Speech" for General Electric.) These stars were ardently opposed to the Nazis, Warner Brothers and Bogart having made a film attacking a New York mob of American-grown Nazis. Truman used the occasion to attack presidential candidate Henry Wallace. Truman envisioned Communists guiding and using Wallace's third party to abort peace. Besides a vote for Wallace was a vote for the Republican "forces of reaction." There was some irony is this call for liberal unification; J. Edgar Hoover was fingering American Communists among the Hollywood stars and screenplay writers.

Besides Wallace's Progressive Party Truman had to contend with Strom Thurmond and the Dixiecrats. Thurmond had called Truman's Fair Employment

Truman with Celebrities (from left to right): Gower and Marge Champion, Jack Benny, Dorothy Lamour, Truman, Jo Stafford, Liberace, and Wally Cox (undated).
Source: Harry S. Truman Library (59–19).

Practices Committee "communistic," and said that integration of the armed forces was "un-American." In truth, Truman, almost alone, did not see either candidate as a serious threat. Moreover, he never referred to Thomas E. Dewey, the Republican nominee, by name.

The Dewey Campaign

Two days after Truman had departed Washington, DC, Governor Dewey boarded his own campaign train at Albany. He, too, delivered his first major speech in Iowa two days after Truman spoke in Dexter. The Governor told the Des Moines audience, "Tonight we enter upon a campaign to unite America."[22] At the time Dewey was leading in the polls, 51 to 37 percent.

The cards were so stacked against Truman and his country-fried campaign that no one on Truman's train believed that he would win. In contrast to the Truman effort, the Dewey campaign was described as "slick" by journalists. Dewey had roughly twice the number of newsmen on his train than did Truman and they were drinking martinis while Truman offered his favorite drink, bourbon. Martinis said "sophisticated," while bourbon said "country." Dewey never even mentioned "the farm problem." Farmers did not exist in his America. His text lacked the color of Truman's. There being no farmers, government must help industry and industry must cooperate with government. He was banal: "America's future is still ahead of us," as if it could be elsewhere. Still, his voice was deep and resonant; Truman's was not.

There were other contrasts. Truman was a late bloomer who had had his share of failures. Dewey achieved fame as the crusading district attorney of New York while still in his thirties. He was a national hero, a Gangbuster. At age 36, he made his first run for governor of New York. Then, in 1942, four years later, he became New York's first Republican governor in 20 years. Running for his second term in 1946, he won by the largest margin in the state's history.

His record as Governor established him as a liberal Republican. His economic record was almost Trumanesque. He cut taxes, doubled state aid to education, raised salaries for New York state employees, reduced the state's overall indebtedness by over $100 million, and got through the first state law in the

---

[22] Irwin Ross, *The Loneliest Campaign: The Truman Victory of 1948* (New York: New American Library, 1968), p. 193.

country prohibiting racial discrimination in employment. No wonder he did not mention Truman by name during his campaign.

Unlike Truman, Dewey was so cautious as to seem mechanical. Journalist Richard Rovere said he was "like a man who has been mounted on casters and given a tremendous shove from behind." Unlike Truman, he had a hard look in his dark eyes, a stare that no doubt served him well as a prosecutor. In the Age of Adolf Hitler, his mustache did not serve him well. Actress Ethel Barrymore said he looked "like the bridegroom on the wedding cake," a remark widely quoted. Unlike Truman, Dewey was stiff and formal, like a wind-up toy. Truman was often described as the "little man" from Missouri, but Dewey was an inch shorter at 5 feet 7 inches. Unlike Truman, who never wanted to be President, Dewey started running for the job as early as 1939. He believed it was his destiny to be President. There was nothing in the 1948 campaign to change his mind about that.

There were others trying to guarantee his win. Dewey and J. Edgar Hoover (1895–1972) were old friends.[23] Hoover was secretly supplying Dewey with all the information the FBI had that could hurt Truman. As luck would have it, despite J. Edgar's best efforts, there was little that could be used against Truman. About the worst thing was that Truman drank bourbon and played poker whereas Dewey drank Martinis and played bridge. Besides, no one in the FBI believed that Truman would win. Dewey's greatest enemy was hubris. A widely repeated remark attributed to the wife of a New York Republican politician was: "You have to know Mr Dewey well in order to dislike him."[24] This happened to be not quite true.

It was in the stars. This was literally true at the Hollywood Bowl where Dewey was flanked by Gary Cooper, Janette MacDonald, and Ginger Rogers, all right-winged Republicans. Ginger Rogers was the other famous persona from Independence. Truman preferred to play piano for liberal Democrat Lauren Bacall. Echoing J. Edgar Hoover, Dewey charged, "Communists and fellow travelers [have] risen to positions of trust in our government... [and yet] the head of our own government called the exposure of Communists in our government 'a red herring.'"[25] It was a trifle chilling.

---

[23] Hoover was Director of the FBI from its inception in 1935 until his death in 1972. He was famous (infamous) for black-mailing Presidents.

[24] Ross, *The Loneliest Campaign*, p. 32.

[25] Quoted in *Time*, October 4, 1948.

Lauren Bacall on piano with Truman, 10 February 1945.[26]
Source: Harry S. Truman Library (64-13-02).

The Whistle-Stop Campaign Resumes

Meanwhile, Truman's train was headed for Texas. Like John F. Kennedy in 1963, Truman expected a cold reception. Beneath it all, Texas bordered the Deep South. Like John F. Kennedy, Truman received a warm reception. Some 25,000 stood at the station in El Paso to greet him. He had breakfast with John Garner, the former Vice President and a good friend. He met with the Governor of Texas, Beauford Jester, and Sam Rayburn. Old friendships and loyalties trumped the dreadful civil rights records of Garner, Jester and Rayburn. In San Antonio, some 200,000 people filled the streets. That night Truman spoke at the Gunter Hotel, speaking spontaneously and simply. "Our government is made up of the people. You are the government. I am only your hired servant." He said the most important thing in the world was peace. "That is much more important than whether

---

[26]After this famous photo was taken, Bess told Truman that it was likely to be the last time he would play the piano in public. True enough, Truman mostly played the piano in the White House thereafter.

I am President of the United States."[27] Later, at Rayburn's home and reception, Truman could be seen sipping now and then on bourbon and water. Truman was winning much-needed Texas votes with his human touch.

Truman gave his 100th speech at Eufaula, Oklahoma. The rest of the journey would take him through Missouri, Illinois, Indiana, Kentucky, and West Virginia. He was the first Chief Executive to campaign in southern Illinois. In Carbondale he talked about how different the economy was under his leadership after WWII compared with post-WWI. It was part of the history that he had made. The combination of a Democratic administration and a Democratic Congress had engineered the swift reconversion of industry in 1945, achieving more jobs and higher standards of living than ever before. A sharp, but short economic recession did follow, beginning in February (before Roosevelt's death). (Truman did not mention the recession, though it would be the equivalent of a $4.7 *trillion* fiscal cliff in today's GDP terms.) He recounted the enactment of the Employment Act of 1946 which pledged resources and efforts to the maintenance of prosperity. He returned to Union Station in Washington, Sunday morning, October 2.

Truman press releases were translated into various foreign languages — Polish, German, Spanish, Italian, Russian, Swedish. They comprised about 25 percent of the population of whom 11 million were eligible to vote. The Truman Doctrine, the Marshall Plan, and Truman's policy on immigration resonated with the foreign born. It helped to win their votes. He pushed on to a three-day swing through eastern Pennsylvania, New Jersey, and upstate New York, an extra effort.

The train trips were not over. Next would be a crucial swing into the Mid-West, highlighted by Ohio. Biographer David McCullough selected one day, October 11, 1948, as the classic day of passage in the whistle-stop odyssey. Truman was barnstorming through the key state of Ohio with its twenty-six electoral votes.[28] The day began early in the morning in Cincinnati where it was cold and raining. Beyond the gloom, Truman headed north on the B&O Railroad to Hamilton and Dayton, then to a string of little towns, Sidney, Lima, Ottawa, and Deshler. Then, the train turned east to Fostoria, Willard, Rittman, and that

---

[27] Public Papers of the Presidents of the United States, Harry S. Truman, *op. cit.*, September 26, 1948, p. 210.
[28] See McCullough, *op. cit.*, pp. 688–694.

night, stopped at industrial Akron. Dewey did not bother to speak in the little towns, but, he, of course, assumed that Ohio had already decided in his favor. Moreover, that is what the polls showed. It was somewhere on this trip that Bess told Harry that if he called her "the Boss" one more time, she would get off the train.

Beginning with Hamilton and continuing, the crowds were huge and Truman was enthused. The paradigmatic speech was given to a large throng in Willard on the same day.

I have had a most wonderful reception in Ohio today. It has been just like this all across the state of Ohio..., and now we are headed for Akron, and it seems as if everybody in the neighborhood and in every city has turned out, because they are interested in what is taking place in the country today and in the world.

It is good to be here in Willard this afternoon, even for a short stop. You people... have a great tradition, ... set by Dan Willard many years ago when he was President of the Baltimore and Ohio Railroad... he was the man who believed in the common people of the nation. He liked and respected the people who worked for him, and he recognized their right to join a union and bargain collectively.

Now, Dan Willard did not sneer at the 'whistle-stops' of our country. He trusted people, and people trusted him. I think that is a good principle. It is a good way to run a railroad, and it is a good way to run a country. That is the way I have tried to run the country, but the Republican Congress would not cooperate, this 80th Congress.

Now, that is the way we, with your help, we are going to run the country for the next four years.

The Republican candidate and Republican Congress do not trust the people. They just work along at their old problem of trying to fool the people into voting for the interests of the few. They try to do it without telling you what they think. I have been out among the people now for nearly a month. I believe you have got a right to know what I think, and I have been telling you....

Tonight, in Akron, I am going to talk over the radio about the Republican Taft-Hartley law. I am really going to tear the mask off the Republican Congress and the Republican candidate... this morning,... I talked about housing. I told the people... how your President had tried for three years to get a decent housing bill passed. At other places we stopped at in Ohio, I talked about prices. I told the people how your President had twice called Congress into special session in an effort to get something done about inflation that is picking your pockets.

Since I have been in the White House, there has not been a moment of doubt about where I stood on issues which are of concern to the people of America today. I have always spoken out and I have taken a stand on every issue as it has come up. I don't wait for any polls to tell me what to think. That is a statement some of the Republican candidates cannot make.

You know since I started this campaign, I have talked to over three million people in various communities. They have come down to the train, just as you did this afternoon, because they were interested in this election. They know that the peace of the Nation and the peace of the world depend, to a large extent, on this election. They know that the continued prosperity of our Nation depends upon this election, and they want to know where the candidates stand on the issues. And that is what I have been telling you as simply and as plainly as I know how.

There is not a single, solitary man or woman in the United States today who can't find out in two minutes where I stand on the important matters like foreign policy, labor, agriculture, social security, housing, high prices, and all the other problems we as a nation have to face.

But there is not a single, solitary man or woman in the United States who has been able, within the last two months, to find out where the Republican candidate stands on these issues.... Now, that will be entirely to your interests. You will have a Congress who believes in the people, and you will have a President who has shown you right along that he believes in the welfare of the country as a whole, and not in the welfare of just a few at the top.[29]

This speech, if nothing else, places Truman alongside Stonewall Jackson, William Jennings Bryan, Theodore Roosevelt, and Abraham Lincoln as a Populist. And, though he continues not to mention him by name, Thomas Dewey is squarely with the elite special interests; he is on the side of Wall Street.

In Akron, Truman provided the biggest political show in the city's history; an estimated sixty-thousand showed up, wildly cheering. Truman noted that in his 64 years he had never seen such a turnout.

The Historic Election

Truman had said more than once that he did not believe the polls and paid little attention to them. It had been known for a long time that *Newsweek* was taking a poll of 50 highly regarded political writers, asking which candidate they thought

---

[29] The Public Papers of the Presidents of the United States, Harry S. Truman, *op. cit.*, p. 740.

would win. In an issue dated the same day as the Willard speech, *Newsweek* reported the results. Not one of the 50 thought Truman would win. The vote was 50 for Dewey and 0 for Truman. The next day Clark Clifford managed to get a copy of the magazine, which he tried to to hide from Truman. It was to no avail. "What does it say?" Truman predictably asked. Truman looked at the results in the *Newsweek* issue. He said, "I know every one of these 50 fellows. There isn't one of them (who) has enough sense to pound sand in a rat hole."[30]

Truman, and only Truman, was optimistic. At St. Paul's Municipal Auditorium an overflow crowd of 22,000 to 27,000 heard him say, "But we are bound to win and we are going to win, because we are right! I am here to tell you that in this fight, the people are with us."[31] Dewey drew only 7,000 in his Municipal Auditorium appearance two days later. Yet, among professional gamblers, the odds against Truman averaged 15 to 1. The majority of editorial opinion was heavily against him. Dewey was endorsed by *The New York Times*, the *Los Angeles Times*, the *Washington Star*, the *Kansas City Star*, the *St. Louis Post-Dispatch*, and, of course, *The Wall Street Journal*. Yet, by Truman's count he would win with 340 electoral votes to Dewey's 108.

The crowds grew in Chicago, Boston, and during nine more speeches in Massachusetts, Rhode Island, and Connecticut. On October 28, the Truman campaign reached New York. Over a million people turned out for a rip-roaring, ticker tape tour of the city to see Truman sitting atop the back seat of an open car. Later, at the Waldorf-Astoria, the band played "I'm Just Wild About Harry." For his part, Harry evoked the memory of Al Smith, Robert Wagner, and Franklin Roosevelt while expressing his faith in the New Deal and his support of Israel. In a first for a major party candidate, he gave his only civil rights speech of the campaign in Harlem. He was back home at 219 North Delaware Street on Halloween, October 31.

Though Truman did not mention it, the Berlin airlift was succeeding, it too against all odds. He had authorized another 26 giant C-54 planes for the airlift on October 22. Winter supplies for the city were assured. The plan was to continue the airlift until the blockade ended.

In a final Gallup Poll, Dewey's lead was cut to a still substantial five points. The news predictions provided the great constant. *The New York Times* predicted

---

[30] From an interview by David McCullough with Clark Clifford, as reported in McCullough, *Truman*, *op. cit.*, pp. 694–695.
[31] The Public Papers of the Presidents of the United States, Harry S. Truman, *op. cit.*, p. 774.

that Dewey would win with 345 electoral votes. The *Wall Street Journal* began to refer to "President Thomas E. Dewey." *Time* and *Newsweek* envisioned a Dewey victory. The latest issue of *Life* carried a full-page photograph of Dewey as "the next President." Alistair Cooke and the *Manchester Guardian* referred to "Harry S. Truman, A Study in Failure." Kiplinger's *Changing Times* had in bold, block type, "What Dewey Will Do." Walter Lippmann and Drew Pearson had nothing but praise for Mr Dewey.

In the early hours of election day, Dewey led in such key eastern states as New York and Pennsylvania, but Truman led in the popular vote nationally. Governor Dewey was relaxing with family and friends at the Roosevelt Hotel (along with the head of the secret service), waiting to go to the packed Roosevelt ballroom to embrace his victory. Truman was alone (except for a secret service detail) in the Elms Hotel in Excelsior Springs. Among others, Franklin Roosevelt, John D. Rockefeller, and Al Capone had at one time or another eluded public view at the Elms. By 11:00pm, several commentators and the Republican chairman were still predicting a Dewey victory even though Truman was still ahead in the popular vote. At midnight Truman was ahead in the popular vote by one million votes. About that time, Truman awoke and switched on his radio to the sound of the authoritative voice of prominent political commentator H. V. Kaltenborn saying that Truman was undoubtedly beaten despite being ahead in the popular vote. Truman turned off the radio and went back to sleep. The secret service agents, who were also tuned into NBC radio, awakened Truman about four in the morning. Kaltenborn was now saying that Truman was ahead by two million votes, though he still would not concede the election to Truman because in key states like Ohio and Illinois the rural vote was not in. Since Truman fully expected to carry the farm-belt vote, he knew he had won.

By 6.00am, Truman had returned to an exhausted team at his campaign's headquarters. By 8.30am, Ohio went for Truman, putting him over the top with 270 electoral votes. At 9.30am he was declared the winner in Illinois and California. It was now also clear that the Democrats had won control of both houses of Congress. At 10.14am, Dewey finally conceded the election. All in all, Truman carried 28 states with a total of 303 electoral votes (not quite as many as Truman had predicted) and defeated Dewey in the popular vote by just over 2,100,000 votes. However, the electoral contest was closer than these numbers suggest. A cumulative shift of just 333,000 votes apportioned to Ohio, Illinois, and California would have won the electoral vote for Dewey. The victory margins were that narrow in those three states. The same could be said in the other direction. Dewey barely won New York with its 47 electoral votes; it could have gone the other way. Henry Wallace and Strom Thurmond, not Dewey, cost Truman perhaps 85 electoral votes.

Irrespective of the electoral details, the popular vote went for Truman in *the greatest comeback in political history.* The victory celebrations were short-lived. Economic variables do not always respect the "time out" for political campaigns. Soon, there was to be the economic recession of 1949 which actually began in November 1948 and ended 11 months later in October 1949. It was a brief economic downturn at a time when much worse was expected. The Great Depression of the 1930s was still fresh in the minds of economists. There ensued a 1.7 percent contraction in real GDP. The nominal GDP decline was accompanied by a 1.6 percent *decline in the price level.* It was very much a Keynesian downturn with private business investment leading the way with the sharp drop of 8.5 percent. As Keynes would have predicted, consumption expenditures held their own with an increase of 3.3 percent. The likely cause of the recession was the tight monetary policy at the Federal Reserve where inflation (of all things) was predicted as the economic problem. Thus began a pattern for the Federal Reserve which was to continue, even during the supply-side shocks from oil and agricultural prices during the 1970s.

The second macroeconomic policy available during the Truman years was fiscal policy. Cutbacks in military expenditures had led to federal budget surpluses, comprising a tight (albeit unintended) fiscal policy. An income tax cut in 1948 partially offset the cutbacks in military expenditures. Unplanned military expenditure increases on 1949 once again reduced the budget surpluses. The White House and the President's Council of Economic Advisers were caught off-guard. Most everyone was focused on the presidential campaign. This did not prevent President Truman from blaming the Federal Reserve for the debacle. He would continue to privately call the Fed and J. Edgar Hoover at the FBI his "enemies."

At the heart of Populist economics is an easy money policy and low interest rates, something the Federal Reserve was reluctant to provide (until after 2008). The US Treasury was an uncertain ally of the President. It wanted low interest rates for cheap financing of Federal deficits, but contrarily wanted to reward bondholders with the appreciation in bonds (which went along with low interest rates) but wanted bondholders to enjoy higher rates of interest. The bondholding class, as I have called it, has always complicated monetary and fiscal policy with its contradictory demands.[32]

Foreign affairs ignore Presidential campaigns. As noted, Stalin interrupted the Truman Campaign, the famous Berlin Airlift being the consequence. Meanwhile, aid to Greece and Turkey was on track and the Marshall Plan, to which we now return, was ongoing.

---

[32] For much more on the bondholding class, see E. Ray Canterbery, *Wall Street Capitalism: The Theory of the Bondholding Class* (Singapore: World Scientific, 2000).

Chapter 8

The Marshall Plan

Much was going on during the Campaign of 1948, including the laying of the groundwork for what would be called "The Marshall Plan." Next, we focus on the forces that led to the Plan as well as re-visiting a famous speech. As already noted, Secretary of State George C. Marshall (1880–1959) was the key player, though there were others. Still, a good place to begin is with Marshall's speech at Harvard in which he said, "Our policy is directed not against any country or doctrine, but against hunger, poverty, desperation and chaos. Its purpose should be the revival of a worldwide working economy promoting the survival of free institutions." The Soviets and their Eastern European satellites were not to be excluded from the program but rather, were invited to participate. While the Communist bloc countries could opt out of the plan, the burden of dividing the continent would fall exclusively on them. In short, it was going to be virtually a global plan, with ripple effects throughout the world community.

The goal was European self-sufficiency. The US had already provided $6 billion in postwar aid to Europe. The Marshall Plan was scheduled to cost $16.5 billion over four years, a huge amount of aid in 1947 dollars. Among the promises greatly expanded US-European trade, with a recovered Europe prosperous enough to finance purchases of American goods. The positive effect on the trade balance with its multiplier consequences was irresistible to Congress and to the country. It was a plan that would guard an unstable Western Europe from Communist subversion while also promoting the prosperity of both Europe and the United States.

The speech was delivered at 2:00pm in Harvard Yard at a luncheon given for alumni, parents of alumni and select guests. No one at the time had anticipated its import. Marshall had told Harvard President James Conant that he would simply make a few remarks — and perhaps "a little more." No one had seen the final draft of the speech, not even President Truman. It nonetheless was an address that would transform Europe, dramatically change the international political landscape, and launch America as a modem superpower with global reach. Of course, it was not simply the speech, but everything that had taken place before and after it that would be transforming. The "before" picture included the influence of Hoover's reports.

Marshall spoke of Europe's dire economic condition. The time for action was now. Then, Marshall outlined the elements and the contours of the Plan that would quickly bear his name. Those in the audience who did not grasp its significance were not alone. *The New York Times* and most other national papers led with other stories the next day. But there was one who understood. British Foreign Secretary Ernest Bevin listened to a broadcast of the speech on the BBC. He is quoted as saying: "It was like a lifeline to sinking men. It seemed to bring hope where there was none. The generosity of it was beyond my belief."[1]

For this and other reasons, the Marshall Plan belongs to Europe as much as it does to the United States. Beyond Bevin, the story of the Marshall Plan revolves around eight US statesmen who, more than others, were indispensable to the genesis and ultimate success of the Marshall Plan. They are — besides Herbert Hoover, Harry S. Truman, and George Marshall — Will L. Clayton (1880–1966), Arthur Vandenberg, Richard Bissell, Paul Hoffman, and W. Averell Harriman. The Marshall Plan story is shared by them.

From June 1947 to its termination at the end of 1951, the Marshall Plan performed much as it was designed. The Soviet Union and the Eastern European states refused to participate, but that placed the blame for the deepening European divide on Moscow. In the end, only $13 billion of the $16.5 billion was needed to restore Western European living standards, which in turn undermined Communist parties and made Europe a major trading partner of the United States.[2] The Marshall Plan provided the Europeans with dollars that

---

[1] Quoted by James Chase, *Acheson: The Secretary of State Who Created the American World* (New York: Simon & Schuster, 1998), p. 179.

[2] For an excellent analysis of the Marshall Plan, see Greg Behrman, *The Most Nobel Adventure: The Marshall Plan and the Time When America Helped Save Europe* (New York: Free Press, 2007).

would be recycled as they bought American goods and services. As a comparable share of today's GDP, that would be in excess of $500 billion. In a virtuous cycle, as American goods and services were bought, the US export earnings were used in turn to buy European goods, and so on. This illustrates the power of the Keynesian multiplier effect.

Clark Clifford originally suggested that the plan be called the Truman Plan. Truman dismissed the idea. He said, it would be called the Marshall Plan. Truman insisted that Marshall would always be be given full credit.

It had all began with the March 5, 1947 trip of George Marshall to Moscow. Marshall had been appointed secretary of state six weeks earlier. Dean Acheson was asked to stay on as Marshall's under secretary; to him Marshall's appointment seemed "an act of God." As Marshall mulled over his subordinates' briefings from January and February before leaving for Moscow, it seemed a "get tough attitude had become and end in itself."[3] He agreed and was concerned that the Soviet Union had been behaving aggressively. But when the Allies stormed Normandy, the Soviets attacked in the East, as promised. In other words, Stalin had done what he had said he would do on the eastern front. Stalin once said, "I trust Marshall as I would trust myself."[4] Marshall believed that cooperation with Stalin was possible. Still, Marshall suffered no illusions about the difficulties that lay ahead, though he was hopeful.

Economic Conditions in Europe

On the way to Moscow, Marshall got a bird's-eye view of Western Europe. As Hoover had reported, the war had destroyed much of Europe. (Marshall had read Hoover's reports.) Physical destruction and human dislocation matched by post-war misery and dispiritedness. Much of the population of Germany felt shamed and powerless. Marshall stopped in Germany and France. In wartime France, the

---

See also Niall Ferguson, "Dollar Diplomacy: How Much Did the Marshall Plan Really Matter?" *The New Yorker*, August 27, 2007.
[3] Quoted by Daniel Yergin, *Shattered Peace* (Boston: Houghton Mifflin, 1977), p. 297.
[4] Quote is from a speech by Averell Harriman delivered at Ceremonies Commemorating the 20th Anniversary of the Marshall Plan, Lexington, Va., Marshall files, Harry S. Truman Library.

French were pitted against themselves and their experience left undercurrents of antipathy, suspicion, and ambiguity in the national psyche.

Winston Churchill had summed up the condition in Europe in an address in Zurich, Switzerland, in May 1946, one year after the war. "What is the plight to which Europe has been reduced? Over wide areas a vast quivering mass of tormented, hungry, careworn, and bewildered human beings gape at the ruins of their cities and homes, and scan the dark horizons for the approach of some new peril, tyranny, or terror. Among the victors there is a babel of jarring voices; among the vanquished a sudden silence of despair." In his diary, Henry Stimson said in simple terms, the war and the destruction it had sown were "worse than anything probable that ever happened in the world."[5]

Despite its poverty, Western Europe had been staging a remarkable industrial recovery. From the second half of 1945 to the last quarter of 1946, 15 European countries had advanced industrial production from 50 percent to 83 percent of 1938 levels. This relativity great achievement was helped by the billions of dollars in US loans and aid. However, as luck would have it, a storm tore off the mask over deeper dislocations in the economies. The winter storm of January 1947 rolled across Norway, with the front settling over Britain, bringing ferocious winds and a biting cold. Snow fell on London. In the next few weeks Western Europe experienced the most punishing weather in living memory. Coal in short supply but desperately needed sat frozen in carts attached to trains rendered immobile by the piled up snow. A number of power stations shut down. The storm did what German bombing had never been able to do, it effectively stopped industrial production for three weeks. Snow fell in St. Tropez, France. It was difficult to know which was worse, the cold or the hunger. Wheat crops were ravaged by the storm.

There were longer-term problems. During the 1930s–1940s, Great Britain and France had not been modernizing and replenishing their physical capital. There was no new net investment in French industry from 1929 to 1938. The economy was in a Keynesian liquidity trap. The war further destroyed and depreciated factories, machinery, and other physical capital. There were human losses of skilled labor, generations of know-how and intellectual capital. As a result, postwar labor productivity dropped to 40 to 50 percent of prewar levels. But net investment in physical and human capital is required for sustained economic growth.

---

[5] Quoted by Yergin, *Shattered Peace*, op. cit., p. 304.

Stagnation in capital and labor that squeezes productivity is a condition conducive to inflation, if the money supply is increased. Worse, there was little faith in the value of currencies. Government expenditures fueled by money supply increases led to inflation in France and Germany. In France, wholesale prices rose an astounding 80 percent during 1946. Inflation was worse in Germany. Through the black market, 24 cartons of cigarettes could purchase a 1939 Mercedes-Benz. Cigarettes and other commodities (especially silver and gold) were more dependable mediums of exchange than were D-marks.

Internationally there was a "dollar gap." The United States enjoyed a trade surplus with respect to Europe in 1946. Europe's trade debt was $5 billion and growing. This was viewed as the key problem by many. This dire circumstance stood in the way of economic recovery. Since the United States was the only power whose economy had flourished during the war, she was looked to for the goods and natural resources that Europe needed. Though there seemed to be little chance for reciprocity, the Marshall Plan would change the odds.

February was a fateful month for Great Britain: Besides the storm, in mid-month Britain referred Palestine to the United Nations, ceding not only some of its responsibilities but its clout in the Middle East. It also announced that Britain would hand over its responsibilities to India before June 1948. That same month Britain's Cabinet also agreed that aid to Greece and Turkey would be suspended, forever downsizing its Mediterranean influence. The British Empire was rapidly shrinking. There was the question of whether the United States was prepared to take Britain's place, especially at a time when Communism was offering Europe's suffering masses equality, material gains, dignity and peace. After all, capitalism had failed Europe during the 1920s and 1930s.

The Russian Threat

Unlike in the USA, the communist threat was real abroad. Elections in Czecho-slovakia in 1946 gave the Communists just under 40 percent of the vote and a popular front. In France, the Communist Party won 29 percent of the vote, the greatest of any party (just as in 1945). In Italy, dominated by mass unemployment and 20 years of pent-up-anti-Fascist sentiment, 40 percent of the vote went to the Communist Party and the Socialist Party in the June 1946 elections. George Marshall flew over this landscape on the way to the Moscow conference.

In mid-afternoon on March 9, 1947, George Marshall and his entourage landed at Moscow's General Airport. The large delegation included economists, generals, Foreign Service officials, aides and others. Marshall appeared tired. The agenda for the conference would include a peace treaty for Austria, border issues in Eastern Europe and claims for war reparations. Again, the number one issue would be Germany, considered to be the biggest obstacle to a genuine European peace. The four-part control of postwar Germany had the United States, the Soviet Union, Great Britain and France responsible for administration in one sphere, and these powers collectively responsible for administering joint national policy on the Allied Control Council (ACC). Much of the trouble with this arrangement rested with the Soviet Union and the division of natural resources.

Administered by the Soviet Union, the eastern zone was rich in foodstuffs and agriculture but poor in industrial development. As luck would have it, the western zone administered by Great Britain contained most of the Ruhr. The Ruhr had large coal resources, was Germany's industrial heartland and the center of its war-making potential. Besides stripping resources from its own zone, the Soviets sought reparations from the zones controlled by Great Britain and the United States. Without foodstuff and with France insisting that German industrial production remain low (to reduce its future military threat), the United States and Great Britain ended up with most of the bill for feeding and caring for the German population. The reparations in real terms had been reversed. In an early response, Lucius Clay, occupying the position of US authority, cut off all reparations from the US zone in May 1946. At the same time, the Soviets were consolidating their economic and political ties in the eastern zone.

By January 1947, the scenario most dreaded was Soviet control of Germany and its industrial capacity. To repeat, Germany was the key. The Soviets and economic adversity were making the Germans looks like saints. But, now, France feared not Germany, but a Germany under Soviet control.

A new view emerged in the spring of 1947. President Herbert Hoover's February 1947 report was quoted by the War Department and others such as Averell Harriman, then secretary of commerce, "We can keep Germany in these economic chains but it will also keep Europe in rags." In other words, Germany was the key to future European prosperity. German production would save Europe. France, who had been at war with Germany three times, preferred a wasteland for Germany. The French view, however, was superseded by the reactions of the Soviets. In mid-1945, then Secretary of State James Byrnes had proposed a 25-year demilitarization treaty, with a demilitarized Germany. Soviet Foreign Minister Vyacheslav Molotov rejected the treaty.

As the conference proceeded through March, Marshall argued that if the Soviets cooperate to achieve German economic unity, Germany could produce more, and all of Europe would benefit from revitalized German production. He further noted, "We cannot accept a unified Germany under a procedure which in effect would mean that the American people would pay reparations to an ally."[6] Still, Molotov demanded $10 billion in reparations.

Behind Molotov was Stalin. Stalin sought short-term peace with reparations to revitalize the Soviet Union. In this, he had to have all of Germany. We now know that his ultimate goal was communist domination. Though Marshall gave up on the prospect of mutual agreement, he was not aware of Stalin's overall plan. Marshall nonetheless was to side with Herbert Hoover. On his way back to Washington, Marshall stopped at Tempelhof Airport in Berlin to consult with Clay, instructing him to move to revive Germany's industrial production without delay. Meanwhile, he talked of the importance of finding some initiative to prevent the complete breakdown of Western Europe.

At the time of Marshall's trip to Moscow, alarms were going off at the State Department. The undersecretary of state for Economic Affairs, Will Clayton, was increasingly concerned at Europe's condition. In a March 5, 1947 memorandum, Clayton writes, "The reins of world leadership are fast slipping from Britain's competent but very weak hands. These reins will be picked up either by the United States or by Russia." The American people will be shocked into action by "the whole truth."[7] A holdover from the Roosevelt Administration, Clayton had built the largest cotton brokerage firm in the world and was a multimillionaire, called "King Cotton" by the cover of *Time* magazine. At State, Clayton would take on the principles of Cordell Hull, the former Secretary of State. Truman quickly pulled Clayton into his "inner circle" because Clayton was also beloved at State. There he assembled a talented cast of young economists in the economic affairs department.

Sue Clayton, Will's wife, probably assured that George C. Marshall would succeed Hull as Secretary of State. In the spring of 1946, when Truman was

---

[6] Foreign Relations of the United States, Volume 2, 1947, p. 256.
[7] Quoted by Gregory Fossedal, *Our Finest Hour: Will Clayton, the Marshall Plan, and the Triumph of Democracy* (Stanford, Ca.: Hoover Institution Press, 1993), pp. 216–217.

William L. Clayton arrives for the Potsdam Conference, 24 July 1945.
Source: Harry S. Truman Library (63–1456–62).

considering Clayton for the position, Sue convinced the 66-year-old man to turn it down. Marshall was given the nod. Earlier, in August 1945, Clayton came close to resigning with Truman's ill-conceived decision to end Lend-Lease, in some cases recalling shipments in mid-ocean. Later, Truman called it one of the worst decisions of his presidency. As luck would have it, there was an alternative to Lend-Lease. The United Nations Relief and Rehabilitation Administration (UNRRA) had in place an aid vehicle, which was meant to supplant Lend-Lease. It was to provide humanitarian relief to people suffering due to the war. The US committed about $4 billion in aid, approximately $2.5 billion going to Europe.

By 1946, however, suspicions arose that the Soviet Union was using the United Nations Relief and Rehabilitation Administration (UNRRA) aid to compensate for supplies it had plundered from Eastern Europe. Moreover, it was reported that Marshal Tito's army in Communist Yugoslavia was consuming much of the aid. UNRRA's policy was a nonpolitical, needs-based-aid-provision one. But by this standard, roughly two-thirds of the aid went to eastern and central Europe, including not only Yugoslavia, but Poland and the Soviet Ukraine. Though the agency was founded by 44 nations, the United States provided about 75 percent of the funding while having only 1 out of 17 votes. At the same time Congress was hostile to expensive foreign aid programs. Clayton was selected as the executioner, and by the summer of 1946 he was shutting the agency down. Then, he turned his attention more and more to Western Europe's economic condition.

The Plan

Earlier, in the spring, Clayton had been plowing a different path of aid. He was spending a lot of time with Lord John Maynard Keynes, who was negotiating a loan with Great Britain: Keynes was seeking $6 billion to avoid "an economic Dunkirk." So, in the end, Keynes got a great part of what he was after. Clayton negotiated a $3.75 billion loan at a very low interest rate that was to be paid back over 50 years. It was a virtual grant. At the same time he provided a multibillion-dollar forgiveness of Lend-Lease obligations held by Britain. Churchill's trip to the US and his "iron curtain" speech at Fulton in March 1946 were aimed at securing the loan. With support from key congressmen, Clayton secured the loan's passage in July 1946. It was insufficient to turn Britain around. Keynes was right to demand more.

In drafts of speeches for Harry Truman, Clayton often worked alongside Dean Acheson. Truman did not always use Clayton's words, but clearly they were on the same page. As noted, in mid-March, President Truman proposed what became known as the Truman Doctrine. Therein, as also noted, military and financial aid would be provided to Greece and Turkey. It was the role that the British had ended in the Mediterranean. Truman spoke in sweeping rhetoric that seemed to support any government anywhere that would strand against "Communist subversion."

Marshall was back in Washington from Moscow on April 29, while Clayton was surveying European capitals. Marshall kept George Kennan informed, though Kennan had little knowledge of, or experience in, economics. However, Kennan brought in the best and brightest economists for consultation, including Charles Kindleberger and Walt Rostow. All had been influenced by Will Clayton. In early May Kennan wrote in a memorandum: "To talk about the recovery of Europe and to oppose the recovery of Germany is nonsense. People can have both or they can have neither."[8] This reflected the advice of the economists. Speeches, whether by Truman, Acheson, or Marshall received much wider and deeper notice in Europe than in the United States. Still, by the middle of May 1947, the State Department was fully behind a policy of European recovery, and the media began picking up on it. Among those favoring aid was the influential Walter Lippmann. Upon Will Clayton's return from Europe, a concrete plan began to take shape.

Clayton's plan seemed to be an oxymoron. The ball would be in Europe's court, but the United States would dominate the game. It was to be Europe's plan but the play would be on the part of the United States. As Clayton put it in a memorandum, *"the United States must run this show"* (italics original).[9] The memorandum provided Marshall with the substance he needed. The remaining question was whether or not to invite Russia to participate. Kennan wanted to invite Russia to participate because, he calculated that Stalin would not accept the offer. Kennan's view ultimately prevailed. Still, it was a big gamble.

In Chapter 6 we highlighted much of Marshall's Harvard speech, which later was considered the basis for the Marshall Plan. As we have just noted much work from the State Department had preceeded the actual speech. Now, we return to the speech in some detail. As noted earlier, Marshall was invited to give the commencement address at Harvard for June 4. The speech, based in part on memoranda from Clayton and Kennan, had not been read by Truman. The ongoing work had been approved by Truman, but he considered it a State Department project. Truman was kept abreast and was supportive. That Marshall felt that he could proceed without Truman's direct approval is a reflection on both Marshall and Truman, and the relationship they shared.

Marshall is said to have spoken in a staccato voice, with little emotion. The war, he said, had caused tremendous damage, but "the visible destruction was probably less serious than the dislocation of the entire fabric of the European economy.... The modern system of division of labor upon which the exchange of products is based is in danger of breaking down."[10] The objective of his plan is

---

[8] Quoted by Charles Mee, Jr., *The Marshall Plan: The Launching of the Pax Americana* (New York: Simon & Schuster, 1984), p. 90.

[9] Memorandum by Undersecretary of State for Economic Affairs, Will Clayton, "The European Crisis," May 27, 1947, Foreign Relations of the United States, Volume 3, 1947, pp. 230–232.

[10] The following excerpts from the speech are from the "Address of Secretary of State George C. Marshall at Harvard University, June 5, 1947," Harry S. Truman Library.

"the revival of a working economy in the world so as to permit the emergence of political and social conditions in which free institutions can exist. The assistance "must not be on a piecemeal basis ...." This would be a break with past policies, including the loan to Britain. European recovery would depend on Europe meeting its "requirements for ... foreign food and other essential products." The US would provide essential aid only to bridge Europe to self-sustainability. American self-interest was to be served: "The consequences to the economy of the United States should be apparent to all," for "there can be no political stability and no assured peace" as long as the European economy was desperate. And, any European state could participate, even Russia. However, he implied that any person or any country that wasn't for the Marshall Plan was promoting "hunger, poverty, and desperation."

The program would be a joint one. "The initiative," said Marshall, "I think, must come from Europe." His final lines were delivered impromptu: "We are remote from the scene of these troubles. It is virtually impossible at this distance merely by reading or even seeing photographs and motion pictures to grasp at all the real significance of the situation. Yet the whole world's future hangs on a proper judgement ... of just what ... can best be done, what must be done."

At home, Truman believed it was essential to modernize national security. He felt that the United States needed a separate air arm not subordinated to either the army or the navy, though navy aircraft carriers would still be necessary. Moreover, he wanted a separate intelligence service that could avert the kind of surprise attack suffered at Pearl Harbor. This national security bureaucracy was to be built without setting up a secret police that spied on citizens and jeopardized their democratic freedoms. The positive response was to widespread fear of another war with an aggressive Soviet Union. So, in July 1947 Congress passed the National Security Act. While falling short of Truman's original request, the Act nonetheless established three military departments administered by separate secretaries for the Army, the Navy and Air Force. The 1947 legislation also established a National Security Council and a Central Intelligence Agency (CIA). Only in 1949, when the ineffectiveness of this arrangement had become apparent, did Congress agree to Truman's insistence on a full-fledged defense secretary, who, in Truman's judgment, would have to be "the hardest, meanest son of bitch I could find."[11]

---

[11] Quoted by David McCullough, *Truman, op. cit.*, p. 483.

In the early winter of 1947, Humphrey Bogart and Lauren Bacall were in Washington testifying in protest before the House Un-American Activities Committee's investigation of "suspected" Communists in Hollywood. About the same time, it was becoming increasingly plausible that the Marshall Plan would pass Congress, at least in some form. On November 17, President Truman had addressed the first special session of Congress convened since Roosevelt had summoned the 76th Congress in 1939 (over war in Europe). In the 5,000-word address, Truman said that the US had achieved great power, and now must assume great responsibility. "The future of free nations in Europe hangs in the balance," he exclaimed, and urged Congress to pass interim aid and the long-term program for European recovery. Meanwhile, to control inflation, Truman asked for consumer rationing, wage controls and other price controls. For the year 1947, the inflation rate was 8.8 percent. There would be some American sacrifices to save the world. The prediction, by Robert Taft, Republican, that the Marshall Plan would be inflationary proved not to be true. In the years to follow, the inflation rate was 3.0% (1948), 2.1% (1949), and 5.9% (1950).

Mostly, opponents to the $17 billion bill followed Taft's line. American taxpayers, it was said, had sacrificed for enough years. Moreover, billions in foreign aid had failed to save Europe. Why would it work this time? Still, in the first two months of congressional debate, more members of Congress supported the Marshall Plan than were against it. Taft and the others could only seek to limit the amount of aid and the scope of commitment to Europe. George Marshall went on the road to defend the full Plan. In late January, he went to the Midwest, where the opposition to the Plan was strongest. Via radio in Iowa, Marshall said the American people face "the greatest decision in our history," a decision to set the course of history for a long time.[12] As Marshall's message became more urgent, it also became more anti-Soviet. Others were promoting the Plan. The Committee for the Marshall Plan called a conference in Washington on March 5 to convene more than 250 delegates, prominent leaders from a wide range of American life. The combined efforts of Marshall and the Committee elicited engagement from all parts of American civic life.

Marshall arrived back in Washington just in time to find Czechoslovakia ceding control to the Communists. About the same time, the Soviets made

---

[12] Quoted by William Blair, "Marshall Sees 'Great Hope' in Plan for European Union," *New York Times*, February 14, 1948.

threatening pokes at Finland, Norway and Austria. Meanwhile, in Britain, the $3.75 billion loan of 1946 had gone dry in May, just as the government published a White Paper predicting drastic cuts in food and raw materials as well as large-scale unemployment. Europe faced perilous times and could be rescued only with the Marshall Plan. In mid-March, Charles de Gaulle emerged to offer himself as a "a man of iron" for France, and said for the first time that he would be proud to accept aid from the United States. Some 70 percent of the French people now felt that the US would do more than any other country to aid the French. The Red Tide had turned; only 7 percent said that the Russians could do more. Meanwhile, in Italy the Marshall Plan was being defended.

To many, a war between the United States and the Soviet Union seemed inevitable. On March 13, the Joint Chiefs of Staff presented Defense Secretary James Forrestal with an emergency war plan to meet a Soviet invasion of Western Europe and the Middle East. A *Newsweek* poll showed a majority increasingly supportive of a preemptive nuclear strike against the Soviets. Truman and those closest to the President knew that the Soviet Union was still recovering from the effects of World War II. Truman would take mostly defensive actions in Europe (despite the coup in Czechoslovakia). Cooler heads saw the Marshall Plan rather than nuclear war as the better option. There was only mild comfort in having the atomic monopoly.

The Jewish State and Civil Rights

Two other problems bedeviled Truman in 1947. First was Middle East tensions over Zionist pressures for a Jewish homeland in Palestine. He was sympathetic to the Jewish plight, but was frustrated. In October 1946, he complained that "the Jewish and Arab situation in the Near East ... has caused us more difficulty than most any other problem in the European Theater." Still, he resented the unrelenting pressure on the White House from Jewish Americans. "Jesus Christ couldn't please them when he was here on earth, so how could anyone expect that I would have any luck?" he said at a cabinet meeting, venting his frustration. Nonetheless, against State Department advice, he issued a public expression of support in the fall of 1946 for the partition of Palestine into Arab and Jewish states. Meanwhile, the British asked the United Nations to assume responsibility for a decision on the future of Palestine. When a UN committee endorsed partition as the most equitable solution to the Arab-Jewish demands, Truman restated his support for this solution, despite again strong opposition from the State Department.

At the same time there were compelling pressures at home to act justly toward African Americans, a notoriously abused minority. At a time when Congress was dominated by southern senators and representatives with outsized influence over key committees, congressional action was out of the question. In December 1946, Truman had established a Committee on Civil Rights by executive order that was to suggest means of reducing, if not eliminating, racial discrimination and assuring African Americans of greater equality of opportunity in every facet of American life. In October 1947, Truman's committee issued an unequivocal call for equal treatment of blacks under the law in a report titled "To Secure These Rights." It urged a federal anti-lynching statute and federal action to abolish poll taxes and other bars to black voting as well as integration of the US armed forces and a halt to segregation on all public interstate transportation. Despite warnings from Democratic Party leaders that his stand on civil rights was political suicide, Truman did what was ultimately good for the country as a whole rather than for his party or any special interest. He believed such actions would ultimately also be to his best political advantage.

Truman, beset by a myriad of demands at home and abroad, put into motion much of what would emerge as the modern Jewish state. The separate Palestinian "state" would remain a vexing problem largely unresolved to this day. At the same time, he addressed many of the black-white issues that has long bedeviled American civilization. His moves against lynching of blacks and poll taxes were universally opposed by a southern-dominated Congress, justifying direct executive actions. Ultimately, the Supreme Court would decide affirmatively on the constitutionality of these measures. Meanwhile, under the leadership of Secretary Marshall, the Truman Doctrine stopped Communist expansion in Greece and Turkey. By the same token, the Marshall Plan succeeded in stopping the Soviet advance in Western Europe while helping to define what would become the Cold War borders for Washington and Moscow.

Chapter 9

Truman's Defining Test: The Korean War

In springtime 1948, the President was in good high humor, cheerful, chipper, but also very busy. Among new appointments he named Perle Mesta to be the new minister to Luxembourg, an appointment of no great importance but remembered fondly because it inspired a hit Broadway musical, *Call Me Madam,* with music by Irving Berlin and starring Ethel Merman.

Bad news was beginning to follow. The wave of anti-communism that had been gathering force since the charges against Alger Hiss erupted the previous summer now grew more serious, with Cardinal Spellman, of New York among others, saying that America was in imminent danger of a Communist takeover. In December 1948, Hiss was indicted for perjury. But was he a Communist spy? And, how many more like him were in the State Department?

By midsummer the outlook became dramatically worse. Truman would enter a time of severe trial. The news from China had been grim all year. The Chinese Nationalist regime of Chiang Kai-shek had been crumbling fast before the onrush of the Communists. It was thought that only the active participation of United States troops could effect a remedy. In April a Communist army of a million men crossed the Yangtze River, south into the last provinces still loyal to Chiang. The complete fall of China to the forces of Mao Tse-tung had become a foregone conclusion.

The Calm Before the Storm

The United States had poured more than $2 billion into support for Chiang Kai-shek since V-J Day, money and arms to help destroy Communists in China. It had not been enough. A lot of it had to do with the rampant corruption and lack of leadership of the Nationalist regime. In the end it was a civil war over which the US had little control. At home, the China Lobby contended that Truman and Acheson had "lost" China, as though China had been America's to lose. John F. Kennedy joined the Republicans in the attacks on Truman and Acheson.

Shortly thereafter, it was discovered that the Russians had detonated an atomic bomb. The news was three to five years ahead of predictions. The four-year American monopoly on the atomic bomb was over, and fears and tensions of the Cold War were greatly intensified. By October 1949 discussion at the Atomic Energy Commission began on the subject of a thermonuclear or hydrogen weapon — a Super Bomb. It would have more than ten times the destructive power of the bombs dropped on Hiroshima and Nagasaki. The atomic competition was about to escalate. The scientific advisory committee expressed its opposition to the project on both technical and moral grounds. General Omar Bradley was for it. It would up to the President.

More should be said of Dean Acheson (1893–1971). None of the nine members of Truman's Cabinet was so conspicuous or had more influence than the elegant polished Acheson, Secretary of State. Truman considered the office to be only second in importance to his own. Unlike his two predecessors, Byrnes and Marshall, Acheson had assumed the responsibilities of the office after years of experience in the department and after having played an important part in two landmark achievements of Truman's first term — the Truman Doctrine and the Marshall Plan. It was hard to believe that Truman, product of the Prendergast machines, could possibly have anything in common with Dean Acheson, who was a product Groton '11, Yale '15, Harvard Law '19, or feel at ease in such a partnership. But the President often surprised people. Acheson looked more like an English actor, cast for the part. He had his beautiful, chalk stripe English flannel suits, his striking carriage, his bristling guardsman's mustache, and his luxuriant eyebrows. He was tall, slim, imperious, emphatically English-like, complete with expensive English shoes rubbed to a fine gloss, the correct quantity of cuff showing spotlessly. He was just over six feet tall, but seemed taller. Like Truman, Acheson liked to walk, enjoy a convivial drink and a good story.

Dean Acheson at a meeting of President's consultants on foreign affairs, 8 July 1965. *Source*: Lyndon B. Johnson Presidential Library (A808-5).

In early November, Truman named Acheson, Johnson, and Lilienthal to act as a special committee of the National Security Council, the Z Committee, to advise him whether to proceed with the Super Bomb. Physicists Edward Teller and Ernest Lawrence were lobbying hard for the bomb, as was Karl T. Compton. At the State Department, George Kennan argued against proceeding. There were essentially three voices against the Super Bomb — those of Kennan, Lilienthal, and Oppenheimer. For one thing they did not think such a bomb was technically feasible. Paul Nitze's view was that since the Russians had the atomic bomb, the US must proceed with work on the H-bomb (Super Bomb).

On January 7, 1950, Truman presented his annual budget. The total sum of $42.4 billion included an increase of $1 billion for domestic programs. But most, some $30 billion, was used to pay for wars past and for the present national defense, listed to cost $13.5 billion. The budget did not balance, but the economy needed the boost. Truman asked for a "moderate" tax increase to bring in an additional $1 billion. It was pure Keynesian economics. In Keynes, when private investment is not adequate, the gap is to be filled with government deficit spending (or smaller surpluses). Any tax increases must be modest; ideally, a tax reduction might substitute for part of the government spending.

Amidst all this was the fuss over Alger Hiss, who had been found guilty of perjury a second time. Worse, Acheson came to his defense. Senator Joseph McCarthy seized on this "fantastic statement" by Acheson as only he could. McCarthy pointed to other (unnamed) Communists in the State Department being protected by Acheson. Soon, there was news from London that Klaus Fuchs, a former atomic scientist at Los Alamos, had confessed to being a Russian spy. In response, Senator Joseph McCarthy said that he had in his possession a list of more than 200 known Communist employees of the State Department. The loss of China, the Russian bomb, Alger Hiss, the treason of Klaus Fuchs — all in six months.

Meanwhile, Truman had decided in favor of the H-bomb. He issued the following statement:

> It is part of my responsibility as Commander in Chief of the Armed Forces to see to it that our country is able to defend itself against any possible aggressor. Accordingly, I had directed the so-called hydrogen or super bomb....[1]

McCarthy continued his wild and unsupported charges; he had no names, and produced no new evidence. He was a hard-drinking demagogue and political brawler. By then he was virtually friendless in the Senate; he was voted the worst member of the Senate in a poll of Washington correspondents. He now appeared a hopeless failure and drunk. As for Truman's judgment: "I think," he said with a hard look "the greatest asset that the Kremlin has in Senator McCarthy." As to Truman's future, on April 9, 1950, he drafted a statement to be released two years hence that he had decided not to run for another term. He would then be 68.

Popular Culture During the 1950s

The Red Scare dominated the decade. The Cold War and its associated conflicts helped create a politically conservative climate in the country. Fear of Communism at home caused public Congressional hearings in both houses in Congress while anti-Communism was the prevailing sentiment in the US throughout the

---

[1] Public Papers, Harry S. Truman, January 31, 1950, p. 138. Truman's words are not altered by the author.

era. Conformity and conservatism characterized the social mores of the time. Accordingly, the 1950s are noted as a time of complacence, conformity and also, to a lesser extent, of teenage rebellion. The teenage rebellion was epitomized by the angst-driven James Dean in movies and by rock-and-roll in music, led by the torso-twisting of Elvis Presley. The continued popularity of crooners Bing Crosby, Perry Como, and Frank Sinatra satisfied the more conservative tastes of the adult audience. They were joined by a popular Dean Martin.

The McCarthyism of the early 1950s included the speeches, investigations, and congressional hearings of Senator McCarthy; the Hollywood blacklist, associated with hearings conducted by the House Committee on Un-American Activities; and the various anti-communist activities of the Federal Bureau of investigation (FBI) under Director J. Edgar Hoover. McCarthyism became a widespread social and cultural phenomenon that affected all levels of society and was the source of a great deal of debate and conflict in the United States. Investigating private citizens for alleged Communist affiliations in government, private industry, and in the media produced widespread fear and destroyed the lives of many innocent American citizens. Using innuendo and intense interrogation methods, the "witch hunt" produced blacklists in several industries; this included notable citizens in Hollywood's Motion Picture industry who were persecuted, with certain directors, actors and screenwriters being prohibited from further employment. In the course of the investigations, Julius and Ethel Rosenberg were charged with the passing of information about the atomic bomb to the Soviet Union, and they were convicted of conspiracy to commit espionage. On June 9, 1953, they were both executed, the first of civilians for espionage in United States history.

In the area of consumerism, Americans were not conservative. Unions were strong, comprising almost half of the American work force, wages were high, and there was a large-scale expansion of the middle class in the 1950s. The need for more and better goods emerged rapidly during the era. People bought big houses in the new suburbs and bought new time-saving household appliances. The buying trend was influenced by many unique American cultural and economic elements such as advertising, the rising popularity of television, cars, and consumer installment credit. Everything made it possible to immediately have what one wanted; achieving a perceived better life. This new consumerism was satirized by John Kenneth Galbraith's best-selling *The Affluent Society.* Another popular book was John Updike's *Rabbit, Run.* Through it was not published until 1960, it was written during the 1950s and exemplifies the culture of that decade.

It was an era of fashion evolution as well. At the beginning, fitted blouses and jackets with rounded (as opposed to puffy) shoulders and small, round collars were very popular. Narrow pant legs and capris became increasingly popular, often worn with flats, ballet-inspired shoes, and Keds/Converse type sneakers. Thick, heavy heels were popular for low shoes. Socks were sometimes worn. Circle skirts (like the classic poodle skirt) were very popular. They were often hand decorated with various patterns, or beads to make them unique and worn over petticoats. Early 1950s women wore small hats over hair cut short, *à la* Audrey Hepburn. By the end of the 1950s, the Jackie Kennedy A-line look was in style. Loose-fitting dresses became more and more popular, and jackets took on a boxy look. Kitten heels and metal/steel stilettos became the most popular shoe style. Later, large hair styles became popular along with Liz Taylor.

Such performers as Bill Haley (of Bill Haley and the *Comets)* singing *Rock Around the Clock,* and Fats Domino singing *Blueberry Hill* became popular by the mid-1950s, again with the teens. The older crowd went with Tony Bennett, Patti Page, Patsy Cline, Judy Garland, Johnnie Ray, Rosemary Clooney, Maurice Chevalier, Eddie Fisher, Dinah Shore, Loretta Lynn, Nat King Cole, and the Mills Brothers, among others. Meanwhile, Rogers and Hammerstein were popular on Broadway with such hits as *Carousel, Oklahoma!, South Pacific, The King and I,* and *The Sound of Music.* Lerner and Loewe created *Paint Your Wagon* and *My Fair Lady.* Other popular musicals included *Guys and Dolls, The Pajama Game, Damn Yankees, The Music Man,* and *West Side Story.* All of these musicals made it to the big screen. It was the Golden Era for musicals on Broadway.

One should not forget the jazz stars who came into prominence during the 1950s. They also ushered in Bebop, Hard bop, Cool jazz and the Blues. These included Charlie Parker, Dizzy Gillespie, Miles Davis, Oscar Peterson, Cannonball Adderley, Stan Getz, Dave Brubeck, Ella Fitzgerald, and Ray Charles. I recall one magical evening in an elegant Boston nightclub, listening to the Cool jazz of Dave Brubeck (somewhat later, in the mid-1960s).

There were also some award-winning dramas. They included Tennessee Williams's *The Rose Tattoo,* Arthur Miller's *The Crucible,* William Inge's *Picnic,* John Patrick's *The Teahouse of the August Moon,* William Inge's *Bus Stop,* Tennessee Williams's *Cat on a Hot Tin Roof,* and Eugene O'Neill's *Long Day's Journey Into Night.*

Television began to successfully compete with the movies. Truman was the first US President to hold televised press conferences. Some 77 percent of households purchased their first TV set during the decade. The social mores about sex were particularity restrictive, characterized by strong taboos and a nervous attitude for prudish conformity, to the point that even the attempt at softcore pornography on TV avoided describing it. Still, Hugh Hefner (1926–) managed to launch *Playboy* magazine in 1953 with Marilyn Monroe (1926–1962) nude on the cover. However, much of TV was dominated by depictions of the ideal family, the ideal schools and neighborhoods. These included *Lassie*; *Father Knows Best*; *The Adventures of Ozzie and Harriet*; and *I Love Lucy*. The sit coms steered clear of controversy. Variety shows included *The Ed Sullivan Show* and *Disneyland*.

Marilyn Monroe in *The Prince and the Showgirl*, 1957.
Source: Wikimedia Commons.

General Douglas MacArthur's Strategy for "Winning" the War

On June 24, 1950 Dean Acheson called Truman from his country house in Maryland. "Mr President," he said, "I have very serious news. The North Koreans have invaded South Korea."[2] The North Koreans had crossed the 38th parallel in a heavy attack, never before seen. Acheson asked the Secretary General of the United Nations to call a meeting of the UN Security Council. The attack constituted an all-out offensive against the Republic of Korea. It was a total surprise. "By God, I am going to let them have it," was one of Truman's first reactions.[3]

The UN Security Council adopted an American resolution calling for immediate cessation of "hostilities" and the withdrawal of North Korean forces to the 38th parallel. There was no Soviet vote. According to Dean Rusk, the USA had occupied South Korea for five years and had therefore a particular responsibility of it, which, if absorbed by the Communists, would be "a dagger pointed at the heart of Japan."[4] The possibility of Russia's active intervention greatly troubled everyone. Truman asked for an intelligence report on possible next moves by the Soviets.

Truman told General Douglas MacArthur (1880–1964) to send arms and supplies to South Korea (from Japan) as swiftly as possible. The Seventh Fleet would proceed from the Philippines to the Formosa Straits. Truman did not take the time to consult Congress. Later, Truman provided American air and naval support to the forces of South Korea and pressed for immediate United Nations support. No action would be taken north of the 38th parallel, at least, not yet.

On June 27 North Korean tanks swept into the South Korean capital of Seoul. The government had already fled and its President, Syngman Rhee (1875–1965), bitterly described American help as "too little, too late." Communist Premier Kim Il Sung vowed to crush South Korea as swiftly as possible. At the United Nations a resolution to back the American decisions was passed and for the first time in history, a world organization had voted to use armed force to stop armed force. White House mail and editorial opinion ran strongly in favor of the President's actions. Though he did not hesitate at the time, later Truman would say that committing American troops to combat in Korea was the most difficult decision of his presidency, more so than the decision to use the atomic bomb against Japan.

---

[2] Harry S. Truman, *Memoirs, Volume 2, op. cit.*, p. 332.
[3] This was a privately expressed comment.
[4] Dean Rusk as told to Richard Rusk, *As I Saw It* (New York; Norton, 1990), p. 162.

Syngman Rhee, first President of the Republic of South Korea, ca. 1956.
Source: http://www.syngmanrhee.or.kr/.

The demographics were daunting. The Korean peninsula was almost half again the size of Greece. From the Yalu River, which formed North Korea's border with Manchuria, to the southernmost tip of the peninsula, was about 500 miles, while the distance across varied from 125 to 200 miles. The Republic of South Korea — everything below the arbitrary dividing line of the 38th parallel — was slightly larger than the state of Indiana. Its population of 20 million was double that of North Korea, and its economy was chiefly agricultural, whereas most Korean industry was in the north. The 38th parallel has no basis in Korean history, geography, or anything else. It had been settled on hastily in the last week of WWII, as a temporary measure to facilitate the surrender of Japanese troops. Those troops north of the line had surrendered to the Soviets, those south, to American forces.

In the first week of July, General MacArthur, now in overall command of the UN Forces, requested 30,000 American ground troops, to bring the four divisions of his Eighth Army to full strength. Just days later, the situation had become so critical that MacArthur called for a doubling of his forces. Four more divisions were urgently needed, he cabled Washington.

All was not well in the Congress. Senator Taft called for Dean Acheson to resign. Owen Brewster wanted MacArthur to use the atomic bomb "at his discretion." This was like waving a red flag in front of a bull. On July 19, in a special message to Congress, Truman called for an emergency appropriation of $10 billion — the final sum submitted would be $11.6 billion, or nearly as much as the entire $13 billion military budget originally planned for the fiscal year. Meanwhile, he stepped up the draft and called up certain National Guard units. Congress amazingly appropriated $48.2 billion for military spending in fiscal 1950–1951, then $50 billion for fiscal 1951–1952. These were nominal dollars. The nation was on a war footing. Even as the war ended, the real (1982 dollars) military expenditures never got much below $150 billion yearly.

As for MacArthur, Truman's private views seems to have been no different from what they had been in 1945, at the peak of MacArthur's renown, when, in his *Journal,* Truman described the General as "Mr Prima Donna, Brass Hat," a "play actor and bunco man." Elsewhere, John Foster Dulles told Truman that MacArthur should be dispensed with as soon as possible. Retire him before he caused too much trouble. He called him a "supreme egotist" who thought himself "something of a god."

In the first week of August, American and Republic of Korea (ROK) forces, dug in behind the Naktong River, had set up the final defense line to be known as the Pusan Perimeter, a thinly held front forming an arc of 130 miles around the port of Pusan. It was a bare toehold on the peninsula. Meanwhile, Averell Harriman returned to Washington, bringing the detail of a daring new MacArthur plan. It was a plan to win the war with one bold stroke.

This was the idea. Make a surprise amphibious landing on the western shore of Korea at the port of Inchon, 20 miles northwest of Pusan. Inchon had tremendous tides, of 30 feet or more and no beaches on which to land, only sea walls. Thus an assault would have to strike directly into the city itself, and only at full tide could landing craft clear the sea wall. There would be only two hours of high tide. To Omar Bradley, it was the riskiest military proposal in history. Admittedly, where was the element of surprise? The North Koreans knew about the tides and when high tide would occur. Meanwhile, at the Pusan Perimeter, desperate fighting raged on with huge American casualties.

Truman decided to give MacArthur his backing for the Inchon assault. On August 28, the Joint Chiefs sent MacArthur their tentative approval. MacArthur himself called it a 5,000 to 1 shot. But Truman as Commander in Chief was the

General MacArthur greeting Truman upon his arrival at Wake Island, 15 October 1950.
Source: NARA File: 111-SC-353136.

one with the final say on Inchon. The landing was to take place on September 15 at high tide. It went as planned and caught the enemy by complete surprise! The invasion force numbered 252 ships and 70,000 men of the Tenth Corps, with the 1st Marine Division leading the assault. Inchon fell in little more than a day. In eleven days Seoul was retaken. By September 27 more than half the North Korean Army had been trapped in a huge pincer movement. By October 1 UN Forces were at the 38th parallel and South Korea was in UN Control. It had become an entirely different war.

The Americans were emboldened. The next question was whether to carry the war across the 38th parallel and destroy the Communist army and the Communist regime of the north and thereby unify the county. Not surprisingly, MacArthur favored "hot pursuit" of the enemy, but so did the Joint Chiefs, the press and politicians of both parties. On September 27 the decision was made to make MacArthur's military objective "the destruction of the North Korean

Armed Forces," a very new objective. He was authorized to cross the 38th parallel, providing there was no sign of major intervention in North Korea by Soviet or Chinese forces. Also, he was not to carry the fight beyond the Chinese or Soviet borders of North Korea. After Inchon, MacArthur was regarded with "almost superstitious awe." Now, he was unleashed.

On November 4, 1950, MacArthur wrote a "top secret" message to the Department of the Army which read:

> It is impossible at this time to authoritatively appraise the actualities of Chinese Communist intervention in North Korea. Various possibilities exist based upon the battle intelligence coming in from the front.
>
> First, that the Chinese Communist Government proposes to intervene with its full potential military forces, openly proclaiming such course at what it might determine as an appropriate time; second, that it will covertly render military assistance, but will, so far as possible, conceal the fact for diplomatic reasons; third, that is is permitting and abetting a flow to more or less voluntary personnel across the border to strengthen and assist the North Korean remnants in their struggle to retain a nominal foothold in Korea; fourth, that such intervention, as exists, has been in the belief that no UN Forces would be committed in the extreme northern reaches of Korea except those of South Korea. A realization that such forces were insufficient for the purpose may well have furnished the concept of salvaging something from the wreckage.
>
> The first contingency would represent a momentous decision of the gravest international importance. While it is a distinct possibility, and many foreign experts predict such action, there are many fundamental logical reasons against it and sufficient evidence has not yet come to hand to warrant its immediate acceptance.
>
> The last three contingencies or a combination thereof, seem to be most likely condition at the present moment.[5]

President Truman decided that he wanted a face-to-face meeting with MacArthur. It would be on Wake Island. Two men, strikingly different in nature,

---

[5] Memorandum from Tokyo, Japan to the Department of War, Washington, D.C. from General MacArthur, Nov. 4, 1950, Harry S. Truman Library. Any mis-spellings are corrected by the author, but the language is unaltered.

would be able to appraise one another by looking each other in the eyes. Truman was dressed in a dark blue, double-breasted suit and gray Stetson. MacArthur assured him victory was won in Korea and that the Chinese Communists would not attack. The war would end by Thanksgiving. The North Korean capital, Pyongyang would fall in a week. By Christmas the Eighth Army would be back in Japan. By the first of the year the UN would be holding elections. There would be no need for military occupation.

As usual, the Russians were a question-mark. They had an air force in Siberia and could put a thousand planes in action. A combination of Chinese ground troops and Russian air power could pose a problem. But coordination of the two would be extremely difficult.

Despite MacArthur's assurances, the Chinese launched a furious counterattack, with a force of 25,000 men. MacArthur called for reinforcements of the greatest magnitude, including Chinese nationalist troops from Formosa. He wanted a naval blockade of China. He called for bombing the Chinese mainland. He wanted the authority to broaden the conflict.

On November 28, the National Security Council (NSC) met to decide whether the Korean War was to escalate into World War III. "We can't defeat the Chinese in Korea," said Acheson. "They can put in more than we can." Also, he was leery of air strikes against Manchuria. The Russians were likely to come to the aid of their Chinese ally.

Since the Chinese onslaught of November 28, the Eighth Army had fallen back nearly 300 miles, to a point just below the 38th parallel, and for a while, its new commander, Mathew Ridgway, had no choice but to continue the retreat. On January 25, 1951, the eighth Army began "rolling forward," advancing relentlessly to the Han River, to Inchon, then Seoul, retaking what was left of the capital city on March 15. With a force of 354,000 men, Ridgway faced an enemy of more than 480,000. By the end of the month the Eighth Army was again at the 38th parallel. While Ridgway fought the enemy, MacArthur fought the Pentagon. MacArthur considered the military position in Korea as untenable. He called on Truman to recognize the "state of war" imposed by the Chinese, then drop 30 or 50 atomic bombs on Manchuria and the mainland cities of China. The Joint Chiefs agreed. Truman refused to go down that trail.

Truman declared a national emergency. He announced emergency controls of prices and wages and still greater defense spending — to the amount to

$50 billion, more than four times the defense budget at the start of the the year. Charles E. Wilson, head of the General Electric Company, was put in charge of a new office of Defense Mobilization. He appointed General Eisenhower as Supreme Commander of NATO, and in a radio and television address on December 15 called on every citizen "to put aside their personal interests for the good of the country." While doing all he could to avoid a wider war, he was preparing for one.

Ridgway's progress distressed MacArthur. He needed to upstage Ridgway in a way that verged on the ridiculous. Once, MacArthur flew to the front and stood before a dozen correspondents, while Ridgway remained in the background. On March 7, 1951 MacArthur lamented the "savage slaughter" of Americans inevitable in a war of attrition. Truman, for his part, ordered preparation of a cease-fire proposal. On March 21, the draft was submitted for approval to the other seventeen UN Nations with troops in Korea. Meantime, MacArthur threatened to expand the War. He said an expansion of the military operations to the coastal areas and interior bases would doom Red China, this to avoid the risk of imminent military collapse. Many thought that MacArthur had lost his mind. MacArthur had cut the ground out from under President Truman. Acheson, among others, decided that MacArthur must be removed at once.

Already, Truman knew what he must do, if only he could bring himself to do it. He said as much in his *Memoirs*:

> This was a most extraordinary statement for a military commander of the United Nations to issue on his own responsibility. It was an act totally disregarding all directives to abstain from any declarations on foreign policy. It was an open defiance of my orders as President and as Commander in Chief. This was a challenge to the President under the Constitution. It also flaunted the policy of the United Nations
>
> By this act MacArthur left me no choice — I could no longer tolerate his insubordination....[6]

Yet, Truman did not fire MacArthur at that time.

---

[6]Truman, *Memoris, Volume 2, op. cit.*, pp. 441–442. McCullough has the date of these remarks as April 23, 1951. This cannot be the case because the *Washington Post* has MacArthur being fired prior to that date on April 11.

Somewhat later, Truman was thinking of the relationship between Abraham Lincoln and General George B. McClellan during the Civil War, in the autumn of 1862. Lincoln had wanted McClellan to attack and McClellan refused time and again. McClellan, like MacArthur, ignored the President's orders. Lincoln said it reminded him of the man who, when his horse kicked up and stuck a hoof through the stirrup, said to the horse, "If you are going to get on, I will get off."

Truman Fires MacArthur

With McClellan in mind, Truman fired MacArthur. The firing was the headline across the early edition of the *Washington Post*, April 11, 1951. The outcry from the American people was shattering. Truman knew what kind of storm he was to face. Republicans spoke of impeachment. Senator Richard Nixon demanded MacArthur's immediate reinstatement. The next day the *Tribune* called for immediate impeachment proceedings.

> President Truman must be impeached and convicted. His hasty and vindictive removal of Gen. MacArthur is the culmination of a series of acts which have shown that he is unfit, morally and mentally, for his high office.... The American nation has never been in greater danger. It is led by a fool who is surrounded by knaves.[7]

Other editorials were less kind. Republicans were dancing in the streets. Still there were endorsements from the *Washington Post, New York Times, New York Post, Baltimore Sun, Atlanta Journal, Miami Daily News, Boston Globe, Chicago Sun-Times, Milwaukee Journal, St. Louis Post-Dispatch,* Denver *Post, Seattle Times, Christian Science Monitor,* as well as many others. Still, to a great part of the country MacArthur was a real-life, proven American hero, the brilliant, handsome general who had led American forces to stunning triumphs in the greatest of all wars. He was a glorious figure, Romanesque. In a Gallup Poll, 59 percent of the populace backed General MacArthur.

Soon, MacArthur was invited to speak to a packed joint session of Congress. 30 times in 34 minutes resounding applause or cheers followed again and again during the speech. He was provocative and defiant. "You cannot appease or

---

[7] *Chicago Tribune* editorial, April 12, 1951.

otherwise surrender to Communism in Asia without simultaneously undermining our efforts to halt its advance in Europe," he asserted. Confining the war to Chinese aggression in Korea only was to follow a path of "prolonged indecision." A record 30 million people were watching the masterful performance on TV. The timing and the use of his rich voice surpassed that of most actors. A greater part of the huge audience was wholly enraptured. But the speech would be remembered for the famous last lines — the stirring, sentimental, ambiguous peroration:

> The hopes and dreams have long since vanished. But I still remember the refrain of one of their most popular barracks ballads of that day which proclaimed most proudly that, "Old soldiers never die. They just fade away." And like the old soldier of the ballad, I now close my military career and just fade away — an old soldier who tried to do his duty as God gave him the light to see that duty. Goodbye.[8]

It was MacArthur's finest hour. Next came a triumphal parade through Washington DC, and a thunderous ticker-tape parade in New York the next day. Some 7,500,000 people lined the streets of New York, more than had welcomed Eisenhower in 1945 or even Lindbergh in 1927.

In the spring of 1951, the Senate Foreign Relations and Armed Services committees held joint hearings to investigate MacArthur's dismissal. MacArthur, the first witness, argued that his way in Korea was the way to victory and an end to the slaughter. He would admit to no mistakes, no errors of judgment. Failure to anticipate the size of the Chinese invasion, for example, was the fault of the CIA. All this was refuted in testimony by Marshall, Bradley, and the Joint Chiefs. Bradley said that to step up and widen the war with China would "involve us in the wrong war at the wrong place, at the wrong time, and with the wrong enemy." Truman, for his part, insisted, "General MacArthur was insubordinate and I fired him. That was all there was to it."[9] Much was at stake namely, civilian control of the military.

Peace talks began in Korea, at Kaesong on July 8, but the war ground on with unabated savagery. The struggle had become increasingly like that of

---

[8] Quoted by William Manchester, *American Caesar: Douglas MacArthur, 1880–1964* (Boston: Little, Brown 1978), p. 661. Cited by MeCullough, *Truman, op. cit.*, p. 851.
[9] Quoted in Cabell Phillips, *The Truman Presidency, The History of a Triumphant Succession* (New York: Macmillan 1966), p. 350.

World War I. By summer's end total American casualties had passed 80,000. Losses among the Republic of Korea and other UN Forces were greater still. The war ended in a stalemate.

The 1952 Presidential Election

It was 1952 and time· for another presidential election. The Republicans, it was thought, would choose Senator Robert A. Taft, and the prospect of Taft as President was intolerable to Truman. He said there must not be an isolationist takeover. He favored Chief Justice Fred Vinson (1890–1953) for the Democratic nomination. Vinson declined. Eisenhower was a possibility as a national hero, but he insisted that he was a Republican. Ultimately, he accepted the Republican nomination and proceeded to prove that he indeed was a Republican. Adlai Stevenson II, the governor of Illinois, eventually won the Democratic nomination. Once Harry Truman took himself out of the running, he proceeded to name both the Democratic presidential and vice presidential nominees. Truman was unpopular everywhere except on the convention floor.

Stevenson had gained a reputation in Illinois as an intellectual and eloquent orator.[10] His Republican counterpart turned out indeed to be the popular General Dwight D. Eisenhower (1890–1969). Eisenhower, at 62, was the oldest man to become President since James Buchanan in 1856. Truman was 60 when he became President in April 1945, upon the death of Franklin D. Roosevelt, and 64 when elected President in 1948. This election was the first since 1928 in which the Republican presidential nominee was elected. It was also the last election until 2008 in which neither an incumbent President or an incumbent Vice President was on the ticket of one of the two major parties.

When the Republican National Convention opened in Chicago, most political experts rated Taft and Eisenhower as neck-and-neck in the delegate vote totals. In the end, Eisenhower narrowly defeated Taft on the first ballot. Following that nomination, the convention chose young Senator Richard Nixon of California as Eisenhower's running mate; it was felt that Nixon's credentials as fierce campaigner and strong anti-Communist would be valuable. Nixon also

---

[10] I had the pleasure of meeting Adlai Stevenson II when he was Governor of Illinois at the home of Delyte W. Morris, President of Southern Illinois University. He impressed me as a witty intellectual and orator.

had ties to both the Eastern moderates (led by Thomas Dewey) and the conservative Taft wing of the party.

At the Democratic Convention, Stevenson was asked to give the welcoming address to the delegates. He proceeded to give a witty and stirring address that led his supporters to begin a renewed round of efforts to nominate him, despite his protests. Stevenson finally agreed to enter his name as a candidate for the nomination. He was nominated on the third ballot. The convention turned to selecting a Vice President. The main candidates were Kefauver, Russell, Barkley, Senator John Sparkman, and Senator A. S. Mike Monroney. After narrowing it down to Senator Sparkman and Senator Monroney, President Truman and a small group of political insiders chose Sparkman, a conservative and segregationist from Alabama, for the nomination. Despite his unpopularity nationally, Truman carried the day at the Democratic convention.

The Eisenhower campaign was one of the first to make a major, concerted effort to win the female vote. Many of his radio and television commercials discussed topics such as education, inflation, ending the war in Korea, and other issues then thought to appeal to woman. And "I Like Ike" turned out to be the most effective slogan in campaign history. In a major speech, Eisenhower declared that if he won the election he would go to Korea and see if he could end the war. His great military prestige combined with the public's weariness with the conflict, gave Eisenhower the final boost he needed to win the election. On election day, Eisenhower won a decisive victory, winning over 55 percent of the popular vote and carrying 39 of the 48 states. He took three Southern states that the Republicans had won only once since Reconstruction — Virginia, Florida, and Texas. Thus began a new era in American life.

Chapter 10

Afterward

Harry Truman's decision not to run again in 1952 was not an easy one because at the time he did not find the alternatives appealing. Thus, it is hardly surprising to find that he did not really retire. Rather, he remained active in politics, speaking his mind on issues, attacking the Republicans, and feuding with his nemesis Eisenhower. Just shy of his 69th birthday, Truman remained vigorous. Even before leaving office he had began planning a presidential library. He had a lot to do with site selection and other matters, and proudly opened it five years later.

A sign of what was to come happened when Mayor Robert Weaherford asked him to describe the first thing he had done after getting settled in Independence. There was no pomposity in his answer, no grand thoughts or plans. He was just an ordinary man who had come back home after a long trip: "I took the grips up to the attic."[1]

Setting the Tone of an Ex-Presidency

Truman set the tone of his ex-presidency with a speech in Detroit on Labor Day, 1953. In it he accused the Republicans of practicing "trickle-down" economics, pandering to the private electrical utilities, and telling the farmers to "go it alone." Furthermore, Public housing had been "condemned to death." Still further, the

---

[1] Monte M. Poen (ed.), *Letters Home by Harry Truman* (New York: Putnam, 1984), p. 259.

transfer of offshore oil fields to individual states made "Teapot Dome look like petty larceny." Finally, ongoing defense cuts were jeopardizing national security. From the crowd came the familiar shout, "Give 'em hell, Harry!"

All of these issues had economic content. "Trickle-down" economics, named perhaps for the first time by Truman, was the favorite tool of the Republican party. It had been practiced by Calvin Cooledge and President Herbert Hoover and had resulted in the ultimate disaster of the Great Depression. It essentially says that the economy operates best with minimal government interference; the private sector automatically adjusts itself as if by an invisible hand. Franklin Roosevelt as President turned to "trickle-up" economics with his pragmatic Keynesian instincts. Though not an admirer of Keynes himself, Truman as President mostly practiced Keynesian economics when he (sometimes belatedly) recognized an economic downturn. "Trickle-up" economics is essentially Keynesian.

If anything, Truman was more confrontational out of office. In policy disputes, his cantankerous demeanor did not always serve him well. For example, as early as November 1953, he got into a brawl with the Eisenhower Administration. Herbert

Harry Dexter White and John Maynard Keynes at the inaugural International Monetary Fund (IMF) meeting, 8 March 1946.

Source: International Monetary Fund.

Brownell, the Attorney General, accused Truman of having appointed Treasury Department official Harry Dexter White to the board of directors of the International Monetary Fund (IMF) in 1947 despite evidence that he was a Soviet agent.[2] Instead of sticking to the facts, Truman wildly swung back, and inaccurately asserted that he had been given no prior FBI warning whatever about White and that he had discharged White when shown evidence of disloyalty. As we have come to note, J. Edgar Hoover was always warning Truman about Communists in the government, real and imagined. Truman was presented with a subpoena commanding his testimony before the infamous Un-American Activities Committee.[3]

Charles Murphy and William Hillman helped Truman write a speech, given in a nationally televised broadcast. He resorted to the cool medium of TV. In every respect, it was most unfortunate. He claimed wrongly that White had been appointed simply to facilitate a wide-ranging FBI investigation of subversion. Truman also labeled the Eisenhower Administration with "McCarthyism," "shameful demagoguery," and "cheap political trickery." This was fair enough because it was true, in this instance. By now, even Eisenhower was upset with his own attorney general. Ike and others were not willing to drag a former President into a political circus, and the brawl dwindled down to partisan talk. While Truman was relieved, his acrimonious feelings for Eisenhower became more and more personal. These feelings were only superseded by those he felt for Richard Nixon, who he had never liked.

Truman, Eisenhower, and Stevenson

Two old adversaries, Eisenhower and Adlai Stevenson, brought some tough times for the ex-President. As noted earlier, he and "Ike" seldom saw eye to eye. Truman imagined one slight after another — a failure to consult from the beginning, more or less partisan political attacks, and unreturned phone calls. Come to think of it, some of these "slights" were real. He attacked Eisenhower for using "political assassins," bypassing his by-partisanship in foreign affairs, and generally misrepresenting the facts.

What was a problem for Stevenson, his centrist position in a Democratic Party, was an asset for Ike, a centrist in a Republican Party. In contrast to Stevenson's Party disaffection, Eisenhower remained popular with Americans and with his Party. He

---

[2] See the *New York Times*, November 7, 1953. The case against White was never very solid.
[3] See the *New York Times*, November 7, 11, 1953.

also had a vast following among independents. The Hungarian and Suez crises of the fall of 1956, though propelled in part by his own foreign policy, helped Ike immensely. In the 1956 Election, the vote was overwhelmingly for the General and against Stevenson. Characteristically, Truman considered the results less a measure of Eisenhower's strength than of Stevenson's ineptness. Truman summed up his opinion of Eisenhower later: "... I wouldn't have *ever* supported Eisenhower under any circumstances for President even if I didn't ... hadn't known about his personal life"[4]

Truman's relationship with Adlai Stevenson was difficult but was a love affair compared with that of Eisenhower. Stevenson, unlike Ike, was solicitous of Truman and always hoping to co-opt his support. Still, Truman never forgave Stevenson for the distance he had put between them in the 1952 Election. They

Truman with Adlai Stevenson at the White House, 4 December 1952.
Source: Harry S. Truman Library (73–3941).

---

[4] Merle Miller, *Plain Speaking: An Oral Biography of Harry S. Truman, 1945–1948* (New York: Berkeley, 1974), p. 327. The unlikely reference to Ike's personal life has to do with his relations with Kay Summersby, who was his jeep driver. The reference by Eisenhower in a letter to George Marshall mentions only an "Englishwoman." Marshall reprimanded Eisenhower in reply. Truman claims that he destroyed the letters as one of his last acts as President (see pp. 327–328). The attack on Eisenhower goes on for several pages.

were different in personal style and by the tone of moderation so prominent in Stevenson's statements. To Truman, Stevenson was seldom a true Democrat. This reflected Truman's partisan bias.

Later, Harry Truman mentions an exchange that, he recalled, epitomized their essential differences. In July 1956, a month or so before the Democratic National Convention, he met with Stevenson at the Blackstone Hotel in Chicago. After discussing politics and prospects, Stevenson asked, " What am I doing wrong?" Truman recalls taking Adlai to a window, pointing down to a man-in-the-street, and saying, "The thing you have got to do is learn how to reach that man."[5] While Stevenson was graceful and affable, he, in Truman's view, lacked the common touch. In short, Stevenson was not a progressive populist.

Truman and John F. Kennedy's Economic Policies

Rarely did Truman find a politician liberal enough to satisfy him. As noted early on, he was often torn between liberalism and progressive populism. John F. Kennedy was a slightly left-of-center, Cold Warrior senator with good traditional Democratic credentials. Others liked the idea of a Harvard-educated president with a patrician background. Truman did not. Worse, he could not separate the son from the father, Joseph P. Kennedy. The father exhibited the worst tendencies of Irish-American Catholicism in his isolationism and his McCarthyism; this was the antithesis of Truman's internationalism and his view of Senator McCarthy. In 1960 before the election, Truman claims to have said, "It's not the Pope I'm afraid of; it's the pop."[6] While Truman would have resented being called an anti-Catholic bigot, He believed that American Catholics did not fully respect the separation of church and state. On the basis of principle, though it was *his* principle, he was not ready for a Catholic president. Still, and this is what people loved about the man. In what might seem a contradiction for anyone but a politician, Truman was pleased by Kennedy's narrow victory over Richard Nixon. Most of all, he did not want Nixon in the White House.

In what must be described as inadequate *Memoirs*, JFK does not appear in the index.[7] Still, when Kennedy was assassinated, Truman was very shaken. In

---

[5] Harry S. Truman, *Mr. Citizen* (New York: Geis, 1960), p. 74.

[6] Miller, *Plain Speaking*, p. 177.

[7] John F. Kennedy appears several times in Miller's *Plain Speaking* Index, but appears in the text only once! There are errors in all the indexes of the biographies, but Miller's are especially maddening.

part, the severity of these effects may have been worsened by bourbon (absent water) and age. Even as he aged, nonetheless, Truman's mind still performed well.

Actually, there was much to admire by Truman in the Kennedy Administration. JFK brought the Council of Economic Advisers (CEA) up-to-date. The CEA was headed by the charming and persuasive Walter W. Heller, who was aided, in turn, by the most talented staff and consultants in history.[8] Until sometime in 1962, James Tobin, later a Nobel Prize winner, served on a three-man Council that included Kermit Gordon. Most importantly, Heller was instrumental in crafting a Keynesian-style tax cut during an economic recession inherited by Kennedy from Eisenhower. The Tax Revenue Acts of 1962 and 1964 (the latter under Lyndon B. Johnson) made the Federal government for the first time an avowed instrument for facilitating a more rapid rate of economic growth, something Truman had aspired to. This was accompanied by a cooperative Federal Reserve and an adequately easy monetary policy. It was a perfect Keynesian blend. There was some poetic justice in the Fed's actions; the recession was primarily caused by the Federal Reserve raising of interest rates in 1959. (Truman surely must have noticed that.) When the economy emerged from this short recession (April 1960–February 1961), it began the second longest period of sustained growth in the history of the National Bureau of Economic Research (NBER). As predicted by the Keynesians, with economic growth came Federal budget surpluses so that the budget was balanced over the business cycle.[9]

Sophisticated economic tools were deployed by the Kennedy economists to explain the causes of economic growth. Kennedy himself "graduated" when he gave an address at Yale University explaining his economic policies. (Heller claimed to have little to do with drafting the speech.) The economists used the concept of the potential growth rate or the growth rate permitted by growth in the labor force and in industrial efficiency measured in terms of the advance in output per worker. They used the following example. During the half-century ending in 1950, the labor force grew 1.4 percent per year, and output per worker advanced some 1.6 percent per annum. These two increases yielded a potential

---

[8] For the complete story, see again E. Ray Canterbery, *Economics on a New Frontier* (Belmont, CA: Wadsworth Publishing Co., 1968).

[9] Economic growth is traditionally measured as the rate of growth in real GDP or (then) GNP.

growth rate of approximately 3 percent. The comparable potential growth rate estimated by the CEA for the postwar period to 1960 was 3.5 percent per year.[10]

Since the economy was growing at less than its potential (in real terms), the policy problem resolves to the causes of economic growth and how to stimulate it. To assure that the potential output is realized, investment in machines and plants is required; the growth in potential yields an estimated demand for capital goods. If enough capital is bought and utilized, the potential can be *realized*. How much plant and machinery investment is required depends on how productive the capital is. The ratio [change (capital)/change (output)] multiplied by the potential rate of growth determines capital requirements.[11] Suppose that an *extra* unit of output requires 3.3 *extra* units of capital (the *marginal* capital-output ratio). At a potential growth rate of 3 percent per year, an investment equal to 10 percent of real GNP in new capital each year would have enabled such a growth rate to have been *realized*. Growing at the higher 3.5 percent rate would require a savings-investment rate of over 11.5 percent.[12]

As with Edwin Nourse and Leon H. Keyserling under Truman, the Kennedy economists were not all of one mind. A competing growth theory was the neoclassical theory of Robert Solow, a CEA staff member and later, Nobel Prize winner. Solow once told me that no President ever paid him much attention. Still, Solow's was the other theory in play. Heller was quite aware of it. In contrast to Harrod-Domar, in neoclassical theory capital and labor are interchangeable. Thus, even if the labor force is not expanding, a greater quantity of capital will generate higher levels of yearly production. Machines do what workers would have had to do (if

---

[10] In a continuous theoretical function the growth rates are additive. In practice, however, each percent is converted to its relative and then multiplied because actual data are discontinuous. This calculation gives a relative growth rate of 3.53 percent, hence the estimated growth rate by the CEA.

[11] In detail, [Net New Investment/ Change (Output)]X(Rate of Potential Growth) = (Net New Investment/Output). The simplifying assumption, rather naively, is that technological progress embodied in the new tools and equipment and disembodied technological change do not alter the capital-to-output ratio.

[12] Let the ratio of capital to annual full employment output (Q) equal the constant B and the proportion of output saved be s, the Harrod-Domar equilibrium growth rate formula is $dQ/Q = s/B$. If savings *and* investment each comprise 11.5 percent of real GNP(Q), and the marginal capital-output ratio (B) is 3:1, the realized growth rate can be some 3.5 percent per year. The average capital-output ratio is used here. However, if the marginal capital-output ratio is different from the average ratio, its value must be substituted for B.

they were available). This greater capital per worker is called "capital deepening." Instead of output slowing abruptly against a slightly upward-slanted ceiling, the neoclassical economy functions more smoothly and continuously.

Truman should have favored what Kennedy favored. It is difficult to think of either one as neoclassical. Kennedy's inquisitiveness drove him to understand two rather complex sets of relations. On the one side are the components of spending (and its antithesis, saving), and on the other side are the instruments for satisfying these demands, the resource inputs of the economy. He could see the vague linking of the two sets of associations: Business investment spending yielding usually more efficient capacity and sometimes expanded capacity and government investment in people generating a more efficient and capable working force. He saw that the realized growth rate could be increased via tax cuts as long as total demand was below total efficient capacity. But to assure continued growth with price stability, it was necessary to plan early for adding to the economy's overall production capabilities. One can be confident that Harry S. Truman would not have disagreed with this summary of Kennedy economics.[13]

Much more could be said about Kennedy's economic policies and the theories behind them. But much more has been said elsewhere.[14] For example, more could be said about what transpired after the assassination. Kennedy and his economists had already drafted the legislation and introduced the bills, but Lyndon B. Johnson was responsible for completing the program and continuing with the War on Poverty which Kennedy had discussed with his Cabinet the day before leaving for Dallas.

Back Home in Independence

When Truman went back to Independence, it was without any Secret Service protection. He came home without any salary, and with only his Army pension of $112.56 a month. At the time, there was no Presidential pension, and most

---

[13] There is a new set of equations related to Solow's neoclassical theory. See Robert Solow, "Technical Change and the Aggregate Production Function," *The Review of Economics and Statistics*, Volume 39 (August 1957), and his "Technical Progress, Capital Formation, and Economic Growth, *American Economic Review*, Volume 52 (May 1962). Truman would not have been interested in these equations.

[14] Again, see Canterbery, *Economics on a New Frontier, op. cit.*

of the occupants of the White House had needed none, with the exception of Ulysses S. Grant. Like Grant, Truman decided to write his *Memoirs*. Meanwhile, the Trumans got by on small inheritances; later, Truman said that these netted them $37,000. During these times, Truman turned down offers from organizations willing to pay him $100,000 a year, a princely sum in those days. On February 12, 1953, the press reported that he had sold worldwide rights to *Life* magazine for an undisclosed amount, which turned out to be $600,000, a fantastic sum to be paid in installments over five years. Still, he put off writing his *Memoirs* because of his efforts to launch the Truman Library. It was not until July 4, 1955, that Truman turned in a 500,000-word manuscript, saying "I never really appreciated before what is involved in trying to write a book."[15]

Before turning to the *Memoirs*, he, Bess, and Margaret went on a vacation trip to Hawaii at the end of March, 1953. They traveled first to San Francisco as the guests of Averell Harriman in his private railroad car. Since Truman had attacked the railroads as a senator, there was some irony attached to this trip. Harriman, however, was a long time friend. They sailed on the *President Cleveland*, of the American Presidents Line, out under the Golden Gate Bridge. When they arrived off Oahu, Truman wrote: "Diamond Head and then Honolulu with the Pali in the background, rainbows, clouds, sunshine and a beautiful city all in one scene."[16] They stayed a month, as the guests of Ed Pauley at his estate on little Coconut Island, in Kaneohe Bay. The Trumans were engaging in some consumerism, with a little irony on the side.

They stayed a month in Hawaii. Since Truman had long been a champion of statehood for the islands, he was given a warm welcome when the ship landed. "[They] covered us with leis and smothered us with questions and flash bulbs."[17] They flew over the saddle between Mauna Kea and Mauna Loa, and on the return

---

[15] Robert T. Elston, *The World of Time Inc. The Intimate History of a Publishing Enterprise 1941–1960* (New York: Atheneum, 1973), p. 299.

[16] Quoted by David McCullough, *Truman* (New York, London: Simon & Schuster, 1992), p. 932. Some of the rest of this chapter relies on McCullough, Chapter 13–14, as well as Alonzo L. Hamby, *A Life of Harry S. Truman: Man of the People* (New York, Oxford: Oxford University Press, 1995), Chapter 34 and Epilogue. More recently, Dallek says that he relies on Chapter 13 of McCullough and Chapter 34 of Hamby; however, there is very little similarity between the balance of my chapter and his final chapter. See Robert Dallek, *Harry S. Truman* (New York: Henry Holt and Company, 2008), Chapter 9.

[17] Quoted by McCullough, *Truman*, p. 932.

flight spotted a school of whales off Maui. Besides this good luck omen, Truman was awarded an honorary degree at the University of Hawaii. He had at last a college degree. Ever restless, he swam, walked, loafed, read, and thoroughly enjoyed himself.

Truman had a love affair with cars (and railroads). After returning home to Independence, he bought another car, this one for himself, a two-tone green Dodge coupe, to drive to his office in Kansas City. On May 20th he wrote in his diary: "This morning at 7 A.M., I took off for my morning walk." He goes on the describe how he just had the car washed so it looked like new, then put it in the garage. He said Hawaii made him "lazy," but he knew he should get started on his *Memoirs*, something he obviously dreaded. Still more irony, a vigorous man reluctant to take on what would be a formidable task.

The Truman Library in Independence

Truman much more enjoyed the creation of a presidential library and museum in Independence than he did the writing of his *Memoirs*. The private fund-raising for the building and the transfer of papers and artifacts began in 1950. It took the toils of seven years. He followed the Franklin Roosevelt model in Hyde Park, New York. The library formally opened in 1957 with Eleanor Roosevelt, former President Herbert Hoover (who was building his own library in Iowa), Dean Acheson, and other dignitaries. We recall that Hoover and Truman had become close friends and that Hoover was instrumental in providing background material for the Marshall Plan (especially on Germany). Eventually, the Truman Library was put under the control of the National Archives, though Truman continued to dominate the proceedings. He had the final say on everything related to his beloved library.

Truman had an office in the library and watched closely various research projects that were being developed. While these projects relied on the library's resources, he held back the release of the most important documents related to his presidency. Some 30 years after the library had opened and several years after Truman passed away, the best of the materials were made available. To his credit, Truman's high regard for history ultimately gave scholars such as myself the opportunity to study him in detail. He succeeded in persuading Congress to appropriate funds to microfilm presidential papers that were scattered around the country. Today, scholars have access to a well-trained staff which provides access to library materials. Moreover, quite a few documents now are available online.

The *Memoirs*, At Last

Harry Truman reluctantly returned to the *Memoirs* project in 1953. They occupied the bulk of his time for the next two years. He relied on several ghostwriters and researchers.[18] He turned in a 500,000-word manuscript to Ed Thompson in Kansas City on July 4, 1955, with a bow to the ghostwriters and apologies to everyone else.[19] His first check was for $110,000, and the last installment was not paid until January 1960. The Trumans were never rich, but they managed to live a comfortable life in retirement.

The book was an unfortunate collaboration that produced less than satisfying results. Roughly half the *Memoirs* (Volume 1 in 1955) is devoted to Truman's first year as President. The second volume (1956) covers the remaining years of his presidency. They do provide a detailed account of his presidency, but lack the force of his formidable personality. Still, he was criticized for being "self-serving," and, appropriately, for some inaccurate depiction of some events. Stacked alongside other presidential memoirs, it still ranks as the best account of a presidency.

Aging Along With the Bourbon

As noted, the Kennedy assassination was devastating to Truman. Soon thereafter came Truman's 80th birthday and many celebrations. In May 1964, the birthday celebrations in Independence, Kansas City, and Washington, DC went on for more than a week. In the Senate a new rule was adopted the year before, whereby former presidents could be granted "the privilege of the floor" — a rule that left Truman scarcely able to speak.

---

[18] The best account of an almost humorous effort of ghostwriting (overtaken by Truman himself) is provided by McCullough, *Truman, op. cit.*, pp. 944–949.
[19] *Ibid.*

Thank you very much. I am so overcome that I cannot take advantage of this rule right now. It is one of the greatest things that has ever happened to me in my whole lifetime. It is unique. It is something that has never been done before. And between you, and me, and the gatepost, since I profit by it, I think it is a good rule.[20]

The senators crowded about him to shake his hand. But bourbon and age were taking their toll.

Only five months later, on October 13, 1964, Truman took a nasty fall in his home in Independence. He cracked his head against a washbasin, shattered his glasses and cut himself over the right eye. Then he fell against the bathtub, fracturing two ribs. He was taken to the hospital in a ambulance. Though he was soon home again and returning to his old routine, it is said that he never fully recovered from the fall.[21] He looked frail, but his voice remained firm and he talked of several projects he planned for the library. In 1967, in his 84th year, Truman stopped coming to his beloved library. Nothing much was said about it, but he was not around much any more.

The summer of 1972 Truman was hospitalized again. Once again, on Tuesday, December 5, he was taken to the hospital by ambulance, leaving the house on North Delaware for the last time. He seemed to rally for a few days, especially after being joined by Margaret and Bess. However, he was reported no longer able to talk on December 14. Suffering from lung congestion, heart irregularity, kidney blockages, and a failing digestive system, Truman died in Kansas City's Research Hospital and Medical Center the day after Christmas. He had lived 88 years and not quite eight months.[22] Much of the spirit of progressive populism went with him.

Three days later Mary McGrory wrote, in one of hundreds of published tributes:

He was not a hero or a magician or a chess player, or an obsession. He was a certifiable member of the human race, direct, fallible, and unexpectedly wise when it counted.

---

[20] "Remarks by Former President Harry S. Truman, Being the Occasion of Mr. Truman's 80th Birthday, May 8, 1964," 88th Congress, 2nd Session, Senate Document No. 88.

[21] McCullough, *Truman, op. cit.*, pp. 984–992.

[22] Bess Truman lived for another ten years, and was buried beside Mr Truman in the courtyard of the Truman Library.

He did not require to be loved. He did not expect to be followed blindly. Congressional opposition never struck him as subversive, nor did he regard his critics as traitors. He never whined.

He walked around Washington every morning — it was safe then. He met reporters frequently as a matter of course, and did not blame them for his failures. He did not use the office as a club or a shield, or a hiding place. He worked at it.... He said he lived by the Bible and history. So armed, he proved that the ordinary American is capable of grandeur. And that a President can be a human being.[23]

The members of the US Senate were more specific in a day devoted to eulogies. He was the President who faced the momentous decision to use the atomic bomb, who helped to create the United Nations, crafted the Truman Doctrine and the Marshall Plan, was responsible for the Berlin Airlift, known for the recognition of Israel and NATO, and for committing American forces in Korea, while upholding the principle of civilian control over the military. They also remember him as the first President to recommend Medicare, and for a courageous stand on civil rights at the risk of his political fortunes. Truman was also famous for his Whistle-Stop Campaign, one of the more affirming moments in the history of America. Except for the Truman Doctrine, the Marshall Plan, and Medicare, economics is once again slighted, something hopefully remedied herein. This nonetheless helps to position Truman among the greats of the American Presidents. Those who ignore much of what made him great (his progressive Populist economic policies) elevate his other achievements and his overall stature.

---

[23] Mary McGrory, *Washington Star*, December 29, 1972.

Index

Printed in the United States
By Bookmasters